COMMUNITY
AND MONEY

this book is dedicated
to the memory of a neighbour
Mrs. Bradwell

and to my father
Don Raddon
for the way he passes on her gift

COMMUNITY
AND MONEY

Men and Women Making Change

Mary-Beth Raddon

Montréal/New York/London

Black Rose Books No. FF315

National Library of Canada Cataloguing in Publication Data

Raddon, Mary-Beth

Community and money : men and women making change / Mary-Beth Raddon

Includes bibliographical references and index.

Hardcover ISBN: 1-55164-215-8 (bound) Paperback ISBN: 1-55164-214-X (pbk.)

1. Local exchange trading systems. 2. Women in community development.
3. Money--Social aspects. 4. Barter. 5. Consumption (Economics). I. Title.

HD3430.R33 2002   332'.5   C2002-903116-8

Every effort has been made to secure permission for materials reproduced herein.

Cover design: Associés libres

BLACK ROSE BOOKS

C.P. 1258	2250 Military Road	99 Wallis Road
Succ. Place du Parc	Tonawanda, NY	London, E9 5LN
Montréal, H2X 4A7	14150	England
Canada	USA	UK

To order books:

In Canada: (phone) 1-800-565-9523 (fax) 1-800-221-9985
email: utpbooks@utpress.utoronto.ca

In United States: (phone) 1-800-283-3572 (fax) 1-651-917-6406

In the UK & Europe: (phone) London 44 (0)20 8986-4854 (fax) 44 (0)20 8533-5821
email: order@centralbooks.com

Our Web Site address: http://www.web.net/blackrosebooks

A publication of the Institute of Policy Alternatives of Montréal (IPAM)

Printed in Canada

The Canada Council | Le Conseil des Arts
for the Arts | du Canada

Table of Contents

Acknowledgments   vi
Introduction   vii

Chapter One   1
Community Currencies: Barter, Money and Social
Experiments

Chapter Two   23
"What's Wrong with Regular Money?": Frameworks for a
Gender Analysis

Chapter Three   45
"Not a Perfect Leveller": Revaluation and Gender Equality

Chapter Four   68
"Currency of Friendship": Community Currencies as Gift
Economies

Chapter Five   99
"What my Freedom is all About": Women, Men and Money

Chapter Six   139
"A Very Social Thing": Consumer Politics and Community

Chapter Seven   169
"There's a Flow to it": Gender Balance and Balanced
Accounts

Bibliography   184
Index   195

Acknowledgments

IN 1997, LIZ BOSMA-DONOVAN AND I SPENT a few days as sojourning researchers at the E. F. Schumacher Society library. Liz was beginning work on her Masters and I on my doctoral thesis, both on community currencies. As we were saying our good-byes, Executive Director Susan Witt reached into her pocket and pulled out a large wad of imaginary dollars. Dividing them between us she said, "Take these and be sure to come back. You can always spend them here."

I have understood those Schumacher dollars as bundles of gratitude. As the work of my thesis, and later this book, proceeded, I was fortunate to have had them in large supply. I dip deeply into them for all the community currency practitioners who were willing to share their insights and experiences in interviews. When Liz completed her MA thesis, she passed on to me another six transcripts of interviews with women LETS members. I thank her for being such a strong collaborator, and I thank these women for permission to include their voices. In the text I have changed members' names and altered details of their work to help ensure their anonymity.

In the course of my research, I have had the privilege of meeting several community currency champions, creative geniuses and practical realizers, including Paul Glover and Margaret McCasland of Ithaca HOURS, Diana McCourt and Jane Wilson of WomanShare, Susan Witt and Robert Swann of the E. F. Schumacher Society, Joy Kogawa and David Walsh of the Toronto Dollar, Sat Khalsa, Michael Schreiner and David Burman of Toronto LETS, Thomas Greco and Brian Milani. I thank them for their dedicated and inspired leadership.

The doctoral dissertation stage of this work was assisted, with the usual kind of dollars, in the form of a fellowship from the Social Sciences and Humanities Research Council of Canada, for which, I am grateful.

A great number of colleagues, mentors, friends and family have supported and contributed to my work in many ways. It is not possible to mention all by name, instead, I will take the opportunity simply to air drop my many sheafs of Schumacher dollars with this message: *May you find them everywhere, spend them freely, and know that they never run out.*

Introduction

THIS BOOK IS BASED ON INTENSIVE interviews with thirty-seven men and women who are actively doing business using local money. They come from six different cities in Ontario and New York State, and are involved in two different types of community currencies, known as LETS and HOURS. The themes that emerged in the interviews were already part of my own experience as a member of LETS in Toronto. For four years, I advertised in the LETS directory, attended trading fairs as buyer and seller, and belonged to a women's skills-exchange circle in my east end Toronto neighbourhood. Finding items I wanted to buy in LETS was not difficult. My purchases included cards and gifts, earrings, voice lessons, organic vegetables, graphic design, assistance with a bibliographical database and car rentals. The greater challenge for me was in knowing what to offer in exchange. Unconvinced that there would be much demand in LETS for the skills of a sociology graduate student, I advertised a specialty product for gardeners that is something of a household hobby: vermi-compost, a high quality soil conditioner that is the product of composting with worms. Not surprisingly, I had only one regular customer for this item. With not enough income to balance my LETS account, I turned to my domestic skills, which I would not have considered marketing for dollars, even if they were marketable. As one member later said in an interview: "LETS certainly gives you a chance to use those skills that are a woman's skills anyhow." My jobs included child care, baking, deliveries, kitchen service at special events, and gardening. The work was occasional and came about though personal contacts. There were enough requests that I did not have to advertise my availability for casual labour, but on one occasion I extended a special offer to women's circle members. I had just done some spring cleaning and, with squeegee and bucket out of the closet, I offered a window-washing service to those in my immediate neighbourhood. These experiences in monetizing what is regularly, for me, unpaid domestic work raised issues of valuation and pricing, which later became key themes in my interviews with women.

A second experience that is reflected in the book occurred within the women's trading circle. One of the main purposes of the women's circle was to create opportunities for networking and marketing of our products, and generally to support each other in our self-employment within and beyond LETS, whether we were engaged in full time businesses, secondary income-generating strategies, or, in my case, casual and occasional work. We wanted to see what we could do as a group of women to counter the undervaluation of "women's" work in the conventional economy. By trading with each other through LETS, we had the chance to test our products and prices, and strengthen our own sense of fairness before selling more widely so that our network, in effect, served as an incubator for re-valuation.

The more we traded with each other, however, the more we encountered an unexpected pressure to lower our prices: the dynamics of our growing friendships. In some price negotiations I began to notice a pattern of *reverse* bargaining, when the buyer would suggest the seller raise the price, and the seller would protest or offer to lower it. For some of us, accustomed to signifying friendship and neighbourliness through an ongoing exchange of favours, the balanced reciprocity and record-keeping of LETS exchange seemed inadequate to express feelings between friends of gratitude and affection and the desire that the relationship continue, and even deepen, through increasing cycles of generosity. To hold the tension between the gift impulse and our commitment to revaluation, we had to re-think the local currency as compatible with our norms of friendship and standards of equality. One LETS group in the UK addressed the issue by naming its currency unit "favours." When the matter arose in my interviews it was closely tied to the particulars of the relationship. Ultimately, I came to see the ambiguity of LETS exchange as a creative resource for challenging limiting assumptions about whether something is a payment or a gift.

INTRODUCTION

A prominent set of themes in my interviews had to do with desires, especially desires for bettering one's quality of life and quality of relationships in community. Members spoke to me of their wish to create a world in which a range of personal desires—to be equal, to give and to enjoy others' gifts, to be recognized, to be self-sufficient and secure, to be fulfilled in one's work, to belong—could be realized on deeper levels. This book is loosely organized around themes of desire. After setting the context in the first two chapters, each latter chapter explores the complex ways desires are bound up with the social organization of gender, money and livelihood. Significantly, not all desires are shared or experienced the same way, but all members spoke of some personal and political desires in relation to community currency and how they tried to resolve felt contradictions among desires.

The theme of desire is apropos to a book on money. "Money becomes money only at the instant it incorporates a wish," writes James Buchan in his philosophical inquiry into the meaning of money (1997, p. 13). Another *Philosophy of Money*, the classic by Georg Simmel (1991), written at the turn of the previous century, also considers modern money as symbolic of desire. Because modern money has no inherent purposes, it represents pure potentiality:

> Since money is not related at all to a specific purpose, it acquires a relation to the totality of purposes...The mere possibility of unlimited uses that money has, or represents, on account of its lack of any content of its own, is manifested in a positive way by the restlessness of money, by its urge to be used, so to speak... In the last analysis, the whole vast range of commodities can only be exchanged for one value, namely money; but money can be exchanged for any one of the range of commodities. By contrast with labour, which can rarely change its application...capital in the form of money can almost always be transferred from one use to another (pp. 212-213).

Unlike modern money, community currencies cannot represent the "possibility of unlimited uses" because they are intentionally limited to a specific place or group of users. Community currency projects are attempts to moderate the social-psychological consequences of the modern money system: the situation of boundless material desires and scarce means.

As I set out to trace how narratives of desire are gendered, the psychological and symbolic came strongly to the fore—all the more so because the topic is money. I took the view that money is a "symbolic medium," (Dodd 1994, p. 154), but that its symbolism is not fixed. On the level of the individual, it is a commonplace among psychologists that money is one of the psyche's most effective carriers of projection, and so the whole range of human feelings, desires and defences can be connected with money (Guggenbuhl-Craig 1982). On the level of culture, anthropological studies affirm the variability of what money can symbolize: the same physical tokens can circulate within different economies and serve quite different political functions (Lambek 2001). Money's substance, properties and rules are indeterminate of its meanings, except insofar as these are co-constructed.

The variability and indeterminacy of money's meanings pertain also to my questions about gender associations. Sometimes money is associated with "masculine" attributes of virility, power, mastery and dominance (Vaughan 1997). Nigel Dodd, in *The Sociology of Money* (1994), argues that money represents "unfettered empowerment," a "masculine" ideal:

> The ideal of unfettered empowerment, of complete freedom to act and assimilate at will, is...at the heart of the conceptualization of money in general as a transparent symbolic medium. This is the basis of the desire to possess money, of the very concept of money which is essential to any decision to accept it as payment, to work for it, to save or hoard it, and to be both repelled and fascinated by what money seems to enable people and institutions to do. Other economic instruments are associated with these ideas and activities. But only money is synonymous with them, co-extensive with the very idea of economic empowerment itself (p. 154).

Other writers have begun to explore money's origins in, and associations with, the "feminine" (Crawford 1994). For Helen Luke, money represents the "feminine principle of relatedness." The values of exchange, practised in our everyday paying and earning, are a vital expression of human interconnectedness and interdependence (Luke 1995). Clearly money can have various associations linked to gender. As my examples would suggest, the "gender of money" is most likely related to the gender of the one ascribing gender. This is Valerie Wilson's theme in *The Secret Life of Money* (1999). Her own research findings and those of others "tend to show that for men, money is power whereas women relate to money in different ways, connected with personal and social relationships" (p. 152). These gender differences in the meanings of conventional money derive from the gendered structure of the economy. I became interested in how far community currencies can go towards reducing gender divisions by expanding the ways empowerment and relatedness can be experienced by women and men.

In the end, the importance of psychological and symbolic perspectives is not only that they show money's variability, but that whatever money does symbolize individually or collectively in a given context is highly significant to personal storylines and larger cultural narratives. James Hillman sums up my perspective on the symbolism of money when he argues that money represents no single idea: "exchange, energy, value, reality, evil, or whatever," but must be understood as plural: "moneys." He defines money as "that which possibilizes the imagination" (1982, p. 36). Its "possibilizing" effects are what suit money for utopian projects and why participants spoke of LETS and HOURS as potential means of self-fulfilment and as tools for achieving collective political aspirations. At the same time, however, individual and collective strategies with experimental money are shaped by psychological limits to how freely people can acknowledge desires, structural constraints on how far desires can be realized, and conflict over how best to realize them. Political desires and strategies, as well as sticking points, contradictions and points of strain are all of interest in the book because of the ways they reveal the larger structures of economy and gender relations and the current scope for change.

Chapter Overview

The first chapter introduces LETS and HOURS, how they work, their origins as a movement, their closest parallels and precedents. In Chapter Two, I present the rationale for community currencies through a critique of the conventional monetary system. Earmarking the national currency for local spending does not go far enough towards renewing the local economy, I argue, because dollars easily leak from local circulation, whereas community currencies are earned in the community where they are spent. In Chapter Two I also introduce the main theoretical positions I take up concerning the gendered economy. "Gendering" in this study refers to the processes through which the male/female dichotomy becomes an ordering principle within the major social institutions, including the processes by which we create gendered identities and make ourselves accountable as women or men within a given context. Economic innovations such as community currencies potentially challenge gendered structures. Not only do they provide opportunities for individuals to "do gender" somewhat differently, their viability as an economic alternative depends on shifts in gender patterns, such as divisions of labour. Effective implementation of community currencies is constrained by the degree that specialization in wage earning is considered "masculine" and "productive," and is differentiated from "feminine" specializations in reproductive activity, including caring work, the gift work of maintaining group ties, and the extensive consumption work of converting the wage into the means of life.

In Chapter Three I discuss the potentials of community currencies to revalue such "women's" work that is undervalued in the market or unpaid in the household. Focusing in particular on HOURS, I show that the attempt to equalize wages by encouraging valuation with the "labour hour" standard is limited by the perception that many men would not agree to cooperate with a programme to promote gender equality by levelling wages. Some all-women exchange networks set out to equalize payment for all types of labour as a principle, but in HOURS and LETS, which aim to create broad-based networks with men's involvement, hour-for-hour equivalences are less strongly encouraged.

In the fourth chapter I focus on LETS and consider the idea of the community currency network as a gift economy. I argue that, although the principles of reciprocity and cooperation underlying gift exchange are considered "feminine" in western culture, enlarging and formalizing those principles through LETS is not necessarily advantageous to women so long as women continue to be held to a higher standard of giving.

Next, in Chapter Five, I examine related issues that arise for some women LETS members in negotiating prices and setting monetary values on their work. Contrary to appearances that women in LETS simply "undervalue" their labour, I argue that price negotiations are also negotiations of the meanings of paid and unpaid work that define women's place in class and gender hierarchies. I identify examples of women attempting to redefine relationships by changing the way they would usually approach price negotiations, and discuss where these negotiations meet their limits.

In Chapter Six, I consider the extent to which LETS and HOURS can be characterized as a consumption-based movement. I argue that gendered divisions of consumption and production create imbalances that limit trading, particularly as the work of shopping in the local money network falls primarily to women.

I conclude the book with stories of those practitioners who are most successfully engaged in the movement. A slogan of Paul Glover's captures their central endeavour: HOURS are a strategy for "making community while making a living." Community currencies "make community" by reconnecting producers and consumers in more personal, visible and balanced relationships of earning and paying. For these members, new livelihood strategies become possible partly because of how they achieve a balance of gender attributes in their approach to work and exchange. Their experience provides evidence for community currencies' potential to reduce gender divisions, and support meaningful work and secure livelihoods embedded in place-based communities.

National Equitable Exchange, Grays Inn Road, London

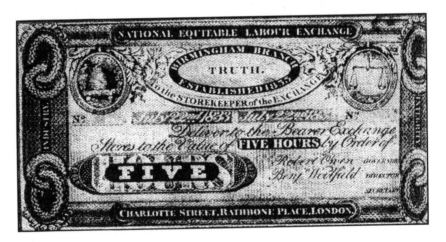

Five Hour Labour Note

Reproduced from Harrison 1969, plates 25, 26.

Chapter One

Community Currencies
Barter, Money and Social Experiments

LEAFING THROUGH A DIRECTORY, Sonya notices an ad for a used computer. She calls Ray; they settle on a price. Some time later, Ray gets a chiropractic treatment from Lynne using the money from Sonya. When Lynne goes away for the weekend, she pays her young neighbour, Derek, to feed and walk her dog with part of the payment from Ray. Derek's earnings from Lynne allow him to get math tutoring from Sonya. Now, with her new computer, Sonya is about to offer a resumé service, available to Ray, Derek, Lynne and others.

Sonya, Ray, Lynne and Derek illustrate the workings of a community currency. They have established a miniature exchange circuit, and none of them requires dollars to acquire the items they want. Nor do they have to rely on a small number of family and friends to barter and swap favours—people who might not have what they need or need what they can offer. A community currency network could comprise tens or hundreds of people, including members offering labour, homemade and second hand goods, professional service providers, micro enterprises, storefront businesses and community agencies, all of whom list their wants and offers in a directory or on an electronic noticeboard. Through their buying and selling, working for others and receiving services, a market of face to face transactions and interpersonal negotiation takes shape, also known as a "community."

Community currency users do not aspire to replace the national currency, but see their activities as a vital complement to the dollar economy. They have dozens of motives for getting involved. Some are drawn by the conviction that community currencies are harbingers of a more sensitive and sensible monetary and financial system, one that could ameliorate poverty, reduce ecological harms and inspire more cooperation. Some want to save money and do more with less. Some want to disengage from business-as-usual and find opportunities to connect more personally with others in their locality. Some want to showcase their talents among people who are equally passionate about finding and rewarding meaningful work. Some want to help their neighbours with everyday needs, and to receive help in turn. Many want all of the above.

This book is about their experience, including the pitfalls and promises of community commerce. What can we learn from the community currency experience through the women and men who are actively doing it—not the fictitious foursome above who lead off discussions of how such schemes work? Specifically, what is their experience *as* women and men? What obstacles do they encounter as they seek out face to face transactions with each other as neighbours? What larger patterns of money, work and relationship limit their initiatives? What circumstances make for their success? The two best-known models of community currency in North America, LETS and HOURS, provide the context for these questions. This chapter puts these initiatives in the broader context of economic life and gender relations.

All manner of local money projects have been implemented the world over at various times. They range from the relatively simple and elegant, grassroots skills-exchange to more institutionalized systems of currency, credit and banking. Various schemes could be differentiated in several ways: according to how the currency is issued into circulation, its standard of value, who accepts and spends it, what it can buy, whether it is convertible, and so on. In the set of projects known as "community currencies," such design differences do not obscure their overarching commonalities; the social goals of community currencies all constellate in the concept of community. These are money projects for which, to paraphrase E. F. Schumacher, "local is beautiful" and "people matter."

A central theme of the book is that community currencies straddle a shifting boundary between two routinely polarized ways of organizing economic life: according to principles of the gift and the market. The first evi-

2

dence that LETS and HOURS may have the potential for bridging conventional divisions appears in contrasting accounts of their parallels and precedents. They are understood both as an improvement on informal barter and as successors of depression-era currencies, particularly municipally issued scrip. Each of these associations is based in a contrast between reciprocity and money exchange, which can be linked to gendered conceptions of economic life. A lesser known historical model, which fits less easily into a polarized view, provides an alternative comparison. A nineteenth century forerunner of community currencies, Robert Owen's Equitable Labour Notes, clarifies how these projects can be both social innovations for extending the circle of gift relations and monetary innovations for expanding local commerce.

The double perception of community currencies can be taken, not as a sign of a split movement, but as a promising indicator. The coexistence of these perspectives affirms the potential of LETS and HOURS to encompass conventional divisions. In so doing they would loosen the subtle gender associations that organize and legitimize male/female hierarchies. Participation for individuals would, therefore, be a process of loosening constricted desires and opening up potentials to pursue less gender-polarized ways of being in relation to their work and relationships.

The Community Currency Movement

The recent history of LETS and HOURS reveals a grassroots movement aiming to provide a viable complement to national currencies, but also striving just to sustain its contribution to life in the community. Recognizing that community currencies face administrative challenges common to all community-based organizations, this book is less concerned with assessing their status as projects than it is with examining the processes and relationships they catalyse. A brief description of the movement and each of the models of interest will be helpful to understanding the experiences of members, including the interpersonal dynamics of exchange, which are the main subject of later chapters.

A community currency project typically starts when a few enthusiasts set out to generate a trading network, or to issue and manage a local paper currency within a town, city or neighbourhood. Sometimes the organizing group affiliates itself with an established agency. Just as often it is led by the few who champion the idea and do the work of gathering support around it. Since the late 1980s, more than a thousand community currencies have been started in North America, Europe, Australia and New Zealand. Cases also exist in several non-western and less industrial countries, some of which are funded projects of western development organizations.

Although the movement burgeoned in the mid-1990s, it is impossible to project the growth of the movement based on a tally of the groups in existence. Nascent groups can be quite small, and some do not fledge past the planning stages. In some of the larger systems, with memberships numbering in the hundreds, trading has gradually stagnated, while other groups that once went into dormancy have since been revived. Groups tend to form and grow in response to recession, then dwindle as employment levels improve. Supportive state policies towards community development initiatives in general account for the larger numbers of LETS in countries such as Australia, New Zealand and the UK where community leaders have been able to apply to local councils for small grants and other forms of support. Even if their magnitude fluctuates, the current manifestation of community currencies is still remarkable for how widely the experimentation has been taken up. Among the various models, LETS and HOURS have been replicated most extensively.

LETS

Michael Linton, inventor of LETS, founded the first system in the Comox Valley, British Columbia, in 1983. His action was spurred by the high levels of unemployment in a region whose major industries, forestry and fishing, suddenly had gone into decline. Linton, who holds an MBA and has a background in electrical engineering, was working at that time as an alternative health care provider, specializing in back therapy. As his clients became less able to afford his services, he concluded that the cause of economic recession (for which job loss is only a symptom) is a flawed monetary system that results in the loss of liquidity to communities.

Linton argued that money shortage would no longer be a problem if we reconceptualized money as a system of symbols for registering transfers of value. An accounting currency, which is purely information, can never be in short supply. As he explained,

> Money is really just an immaterial measure, like an inch, or a gallon, a pound, or degree. While there is certainly a limit on real resources—only so many hours in the day—there need never be a shortage of measure...Yet this is precisely the situation in which we persist regarding money. Money is, for the most part, merely a symbol, accepted to be valuable generally throughout the society that uses it. Why should we ever be short of symbols to keep account of how we serve one another? (cited in Meeker-Lowry 1996, p. 449)

Linton named his solution "LETS" as a call to cooperate, invite, engage, enable and allow. It is also a handy acronym, he suggests, for several possible titles: "Local Employment and Trading System," "Local Energy Transfer System," "Local Exchange Trading System," or "Let's Eat Together Soon." LETS invites people to engage in exchange unhindered by the insufficiency of conventional currency to match needs with skills and resources. The availability of the national currency in local communities fluctuates with extra-local factors, including wider market conditions, interest rate policies, and the prerogative of large companies to move production to where it is more profitable. In contrast, local economic capacities—levels of skill, availability of tools and resources, people's willingness and readiness to work—remain quite steady. In LETS, the availability of money is always sufficient to meet the requirements of exchange. When dollars flee the community, LETS can provide an indefinitely expandable source of credit and means of exchange to harness local capacities.

The LETS idea spread quickly in the late 1980s. Within its first twenty months, the system Linton founded had traded a quarter of a million dollars worth of goods and services (Nozick 1992, p. 54). Linton was invited to travel and promote LETS in other parts of Canada, the UK and Australia. Initially, "The Other Economic Summit," TOES, held in parallel with the G7 Economic Summit, was a key forum for disseminating the LETS model.

5

LETS works as follows. Members agree that the currency unit, usually called the "greendollar" but sometimes given a local name, is nominally equivalent in value to the federal dollar. Each new member receives an account with a balance of zero. In any transaction, buyer and seller negotiate the price, which may have a federal dollar component or consist fully in greendollars. The buyer then reports the exchange by leaving a telephone voice message or writing a cheque. In doing so, the buyer authorizes the LETS administrator to debit his or her account and credit the seller's for the greendollar price of the item. Greendollars come into being at this point—the buyer issues them directly into the seller's amount. No interest charges apply to account balances. With active trading, individual accounts fluctuate between the positive and negative. Provided there are no accounting errors, the sum of balances on all accounts in the system should be zero.

The money supply in LETS is self-regulating, but there remain a few policy decisions for the LETS association. Some systems set limits on positive and negative balances. Most charge a membership fee in federal dollars and service fees in greendollars, either monthly or per transaction, to support the administration of the system. An open book policy, whereby any member can request to see another's balance and turnover, is in place to prevent abuses. Apart from moral pressures, there is no clear way to ensure that members restore their balances to zero when they leave LETS. Larger commercial barter networks operate similarly, but charge much higher entry and transaction fees, use more brokerage to generate exchange, and take advantage of legal contracts. The unenforceability of the LETS agreement may be one reason LETS has had difficulty recruiting formal businesses into membership. Bad debts and, equally, unspent positive balances do not affect members as individuals, but they cause confidence to weaken and trading to slow. Low business involvement limits the attractiveness of LETS to prospective members who want more basic items such as food and clothing to become available for greendollars. Current strategies for LETS development focus on strengthening member agreements and appealing to business members. Some LETS are experimenting with projects such as using smart cards to simplify transactions at the point of sale; networking regional LETS to create possibilities for trading between communities without jeopardizing the integrity of each accounting system; and schemes for creating circuits of donations and patronage between businesses, charitable organizations and consumers, known as "Community Way."

HOURS

The HOURS model, based on the example of Ithaca, New York, is the brainchild of regional planner and community activist, Paul Glover. Michael Linton, knowing of Glover's talent for clear writing about community alternatives, first approached him to write about LETS. Glover then worked with a group of Ithacans to start a LETS in Ithaca in the late 1980s. Meanwhile he continued researching formal and community economics. The first Ithaca HOURS paper notes were printed and issued in 1991. Since that time approximately fifty communities in the U.S. and Canada have replicated or adapted the Ithaca HOURS model.

One Ithaca HOUR represents the value of one hour of labour or its negotiated equivalent in goods or services. Ten dollars, the average hourly wage in the Ithaca region, is the accepted U.S. dollar equivalent. The notes are denominated in eighth hour ($1.25), quarter hour ($2.50), half hour ($5), one hour ($10) and two hour ($20) units.[1] Each note commemorates a special feature of Ithaca, such as a calendar clock invented in Ithaca, and a rare salamander species found only in the region. One denomination is made from hemp paper, another from a locally made watermarked cattail paper. The face side reads: "This note is useful tender for many local needs." The reverse explains:

> Ithaca HOURS stimulate local business by recycling our wealth locally, and they help fund new job creation. Ithaca HOURS are backed by real capital: our skills, our time, our tools, forests, fields and rivers.

Ithaca HOURS are issued into circulation in three ways. New subscribers receive one to two HOURS (depending on the demand for their specialty) for "backing" the currency by placing their names in a newspaper listing saying that they agree to accept it as payment. The majority of the $95,000

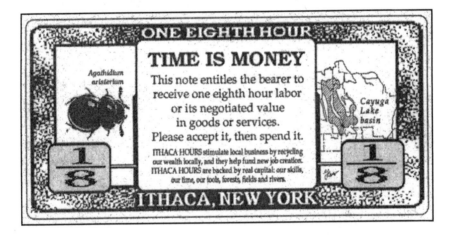

Ithaca HOURS, Eighth-HOUR Note, face side and reverse.

worth of Ithaca HOURS have gone into circulation in this way, as bonuses for first time sign-ups and renewals. Approximately ten percent of HOURS have been issued as grants to community organizations. The rest have gone into circulation as interest-free, productive loans. An advisory board determines the quantity of HOURS to print, how to issue them into circulation and how to allocate them between loan and grant applicants. An HOURS directory, like an alternative yellow pages, has 1500 listings for goods and services on offer for full or partial payment in HOURS. Among the listings are approximately 350 businesses. The directory appears in the quarterly "HOUR Town" newspaper, which also carries advertisements, HOURS "success stories," and feature articles about community economics.

Since one does not have to be a subscriber to accept and spend the HOURS that are in circulation, thousands of individuals have participated in local commerce with HOURS and generated millions of dollars worth of transactions (Beesten 1997). Figures on the amount of trading in HOURS and LETS underestimate their actual economic impact. Some transactions, especially for food and retail merchandise, are priced in a combination of community currency and dollars. HOURS further stimulate cash transactions because people who do not have HOURS in hand still use the directory as a labour market for special skills, small jobs and casual labour.

Ithaca HOURS has continued to thrive, but many of the first LETS and HOURS groups have faced administrative crises and loss of member confidence. The work of developing and maintaining the community currency network, which is mostly unrecompensed, is more extensive than many founding members had anticipated. Workload pressures, particularly at the point when the networks were expanding, tempted some administrators to pay greendollars or HOURS to operate the currency system itself. Inflationary situations have arisen in some LETS when the administrative account was debited in excess of what the system was receiving in transaction fees, or in some HOURS, when local money was issued to pay for organizing the directory and bazaars. Administrative demands are heavy, experience has shown, because trading does not happen automatically. Members need opportunities to meet face to face at trading fairs and social get-togethers. LETS and HOURS also work best when there is active brokering by an administrator, who stays in contact with the membership, knows each person's talents and needs and how much local currency they are earning and spending. Without this work, known as "massaging the system," eventually LETS and HOURS tend to fall into disuse. In recognition of these institutional needs, second genera-tion and mature systems have been setting up more formal structures of ad-ministration.

HOURS and LETS, and the continuing experimentation that has built on these models, amount to a relatively recent movement, but discus-sion often turns to the question of whether they are really new. The search for precedents and antecedents commonly nets two comparisons. Accord-ing to the first, community currencies represent an extension of "old-fash-ioned" barter. The comparison to barter calls up idealized images of a more communal, close knit, perhaps moneyless, society. According to the sec-ond, LETS and HOURS represent the re-emergence of a monetary re-sponse to economic crisis, such as that which sprang up during the depression and was subsequently repressed or sidelined. The second com-parison raises the spectre of a large scale monetary collapse and presents community currencies as a source of security and means of community control over basic conditions of livelihood.

These parallel accounts of barter and crisis response measures repre-sent a double emphasis in the movement: the view that community curren-cies promote a culture of reciprocity and that they are a monetary innovation that could restructure the local economy. These are not con-tradictory positions—indeed, much of the promotional literature on com-munity currencies takes up both—but there are different implications of each way of framing what community currencies are about. Notably for the analysis that is to follow, these two frames correspond with perspec-tives on economic life commonly designated "male" and "female."

Community Currencies as Barter

When people are asked what drew them to LETS or HOURS, many explain that they have always bartered, or they speak of a rural past when barter was a way of life. Familiarity with barter, they say, makes community currencies easy to grasp, and gives them an advantage over people less skilled at striking up deals. Community currencies also offer advantages over barter. As LETS member Ron explained, "[In] any small community, barter is part and parcel of how you live your life. This [LETS] just helps you expand it out a little more. Gives us a wider circle."

Not only do LETS and HOURS provide a larger circle in terms of the number of people who are potential exchange partners, it allows for multilateral barter, which, according to classical economic theory, is the primary function of money. Beverly, a wood carver, explained the advantages of LETS in exactly these terms:

> Beverly: *There's not always that chance, you know, that you want a carving and I want whatever you do. That's the beauty of the LETS. You can't spend all your life going around finding someone that wants what you have that has what you want. In a system this size where you have hundreds of people to choose from, it's perfect for finding what you need and getting a much broader base too for what you have.*

Why do people persist in associating community currencies with barter when, strictly speaking, barter refers to moneyless exchange? Certainly opportunities for barter abound in community currency circles. A vegetable farmer, Dan, for example, says that even when he does not have HOURS on hand, he uses the HOURS listings as a way to identify who in the community is "barterable." Even so, community currency listings just as readily result in new cash transactions as they do unrecorded barter. People may designate community currencies into the barter category to differentiate them from "real" money—federal cash and credit cards. Yet, HOURS and greendollars are money-like enough that transactions are frequently priced in a combination of both "local" and "federal."

The barter associations do not have to follow from the negative definition of barter—exchange in the absence of money. It is just as likely that people invoke the notion of barter to conjure up positive associations, particularly with notions of reciprocity. This connection provides a wider frame for capturing unspoken patterns within LETS and HOURS trading relationships. The positive notion of barter conveys the personal, face-to-face and relational nature of community currency activity. When you barter you get something of another person's, and they get something of yours. Unlike the typical retail situation, barter always requires a conversation. Community currency exchange can be similarly personal and intimate, as stories to come will show.

Reciprocity in a barter arrangement does not have to be immediate. There may be a time lag between the two halves of the transaction. A skilled tradesman, Tom, explained that he often barters his labour on building projects—working on a friend's roof, for example, and later having that friend help him pour cement for his drive. Nor does barter have to involve bilateral reciprocity. HOURS and LETS members described how they at times have engaged in elaborate three-way barter arrangements. This potential complexity of barter within a small circle requires some effort to "keep track," as Vince noted when he explained that barter was the basis of his attraction to HOURS:

> Vince: I think I've always...traded things with people. Favours, you know, "I'll do this for you; you do that for me"...You know, you don't write it down, you just kind of keep track.

Unlike money exchange, the goal of keeping track of barter is not necessarily to establish equivalence. In fact, barter exchanges are often asymmetrical. The purpose of keeping track in barter, rather, is to keep abreast of expectations of the relationship. Various expectations may apply, as the following examples illustrate.

Consider, first, the baby-sitting cooperative, which uses tokens for keeping track of obligations. Equal numbers of playing cards or Popsicle sticks are distributed to each member. Babysitters receive tokens according to each hour spent caring for a child in their home. The tokens make it transparent whether fairness has been achieved—after some time, one person should not be left holding all the cards.

Dan and Ellen's vegetable farm provides a contrasting example of the norms of "keeping track." Ellen described a barter relationship between her family and their farm neighbours. The neighbour family receives all the vegetables they can eat; in return, Ellen, Dan and children receive all the eggs they need. When I asked if the exchange of vegetables for eggs was equitable, Ellen replied emphatically that the equitability was not the goal.

Ellen: *Early on we were keeping track and then we decided this really doesn't matter...It's not going to make or break us either way if it's not equitable. If we're giving them a little more...what difference does it make? It's sort of a feeling of—it's sort of like family...You give a little more of something to your brother, what difference does it make? You don't keep an account.*

The goal of their barter was to maintain a mutually beneficial relationship in which positive feelings matter above an individual calculus of benefits and losses.

These two attitudes towards keeping track come together in HOURS member Cheryl's description of her upbringing:

Cheryl: *I grew up...first in a small fishing village and then in a small farming community, and people just did things for each other. [There] everybody's a little uptight, so you kept track of "Do I owe them more than they owe me? Have I done as many favours for them as they did for me lately." And people obsessed over it. As soon as somebody did a favour for you, your family did the first favour that you could do back. There were just huge amounts of favours going around. If somebody was really in trouble there was absolutely no accounting of favours. Everything was suspended if there was a serious illness or a death or anything. Everybody just pitched in. It was wonderful.*

In Cheryl's place of origin, barter was the route to securing one's belonging in the gift community. Having established membership through concerted generosity and goodwill, one could be assured of help in the event of a crisis, and help one must if one expected to depend on others in the future.

So the notion of barter, more than the moneyless exchange of equivalents, suggests a continuum of relationships, from the balanced reciprocity of the baby-sitting circle, to the exchange of favours in which temporary imbalances perpetuate a cycle of giving, to the community-wide barn-raising or potlatch. When people invoke the concept of barter to describe community currencies, they are referring to the broader social pattern, such as Cheryl described, of the gift community. This meaning is captured by the phrase Finn Bowring (1998) applied to LETS—a system for "serial reciprocity."

As upcoming chapters will show, the gift community is not always experienced as "wonderful," as Cheryl remembers it. Caitlin is one who came to LETS hoping to improve on her negative experiences with barter. "On the LETS," she explained, "it seems that people know, 'That person did this for me and I'm doing this for them.' That's an equal trade." She most appreciates that the moneyness of LETS can reinforce her expectations of equivalence.

Community Currencies as Money: Depression-era Scrip

The second common parallel drawn with the community currency movement is the proliferation of local scrip during the depression of the 1930s (Greco 1994; Meeker-Lowry 1996; Savdie and Cohen-Mitchell 1997). The most famous of these local currencies, stamp scrip, was invented by the German economist, Silvio Gesell, and implemented, first, in the German village of Schwanenkirchen, and then in the town of Voergl, Austria, in the early 1930s. Here it was reported to have been remarkably successful in financing public works and reducing unemployment. Receipts of taxes in arrears increased eightfold, and there were even reports of people paying taxes before they were due (Cole 1933, p. 400). Before long, however, the banking system, threatened by how well received these innovations were, began to lobby the national governments to legislate them to an end (Fisher 1933).

In the case of Schwanenkirchen, stamp scrip was issued by a consortium of businesses and banks, but in Voergl, it was the municipality that paid public employees half in scrip and half in state schillings. Each note had fifty-two squares on the back, to which a stamp had to be affixed every week in order to renew the value of the note. The cost of the stamp, two percent of the face value of the note, provided a revenue of the equivalent of $1.04 for every dollar per year, which went into a fund for poor relief. To avoid paying the demurrage, or negative interest charge, people spent the scrip quickly, creating an effective stimulus to the local economies.

The Yale economist, Irving Fisher, introduced the municipal stamp scrip idea to the U.S. Already commercial scrip issued by manufacturing firms or banks was in circulation in hundreds of towns as a response to the depression (Mitchell and Shafer 1984). New plans for approximately 200 municipalities to start issuing stamp scrip suddenly were cancelled, however, when Roosevelt passed the New Deal legislation.[2]

Unlike community currencies of today, most depression scrip was considered an emergency measure not a permanent feature for re-localizing work and consumption. In spite of this difference, the examples of the 1930s are important to today's community currency advocates because they provide a historical instance of local money receiving strong backing of businesses and municipal governments. Such innovations, once necessitated by crisis, could be reimplemented in a more intentional way. Even though the scrip projects were aborted early, their short record recommends local money as a way to address unemployment and the fiscal problems of local government.

The depression cases also encourage people to think of community currencies as money projects, which, in contrast to barter schemes, are manifestly political—focusing their attempts at change on the institutional rather than the interpersonal. As money projects, their criteria for success are those tangible indicators that the money is making its mark: volume of transactions, rates of circulation, the range of goods available, the number who accept the currency, its proportion of their income, and so on. The goal of organizers is to build the legitimacy and visibility of the money so that all manner of local institutions—businesses, co-ops, farmer's markets, banks, credit unions, non-profit and municipal agencies—can endorse and partake in its agenda.

These two portraits of community currency, as akin to "old-fashioned" barter and to currency reform movements, therefore, correspond with different perspectives on social change. The one presents LETS and HOURS as a way of working for change through the familiar and ordinary, and the other as an attempt to organize a new alternative to existing institutions. Whenever such contrasting orientations appear, it becomes easy to ascribe gender to either side. Sometimes the basis for doing so is observable differences between actual women and men. For example, Mark Jackson, a graduate student researching New Zealand LETS, noted that men and women have different objectives for advancing LETS.

> Overwhelmingly it was women who comprised a majority on committees. The commitment of women was strong at the genesis of exchanges and seemed to increase as they matured. From my own observations many men seem to be more involved at the outset because of a perception that LETS is either part of a radical transformation about to happen to the economy, or that it will be a profitable business proposal. The current structures of LETS do not seem to sustain such plans, and they inevitably become more of a domestic skills trading system, which requires a lot of unrecompensed and time consuming work. Perhaps it is upon such a realization that many men become disenchanted and leave administrative positions. I would argue that it is the women, benefiting from exchanging their normally unrecompensed labours, who are more committed to maintaining the structure which allows them to give value to the 'economically valueless.' (Jackson 1995)

This study supports Jackson's analysis of the New Zealand women's motivations. In my own observation, however, men and women in LETS and HOURS do not clearly differentiate themselves according to the two conceptions of what community currencies are about. Nor did I anticipate that gendered meanings would correspond neatly to individuals' social behaviours or philosophical commitments. Some men are strongly committed to fostering a gift community. Some women are attracted to the potentials within the movement for institutional change. While it is true that many women seek to give value to domestic skills, they are just as likely to describe their participation in terms of business opportunities as barter. The attribution of gender to community currencies, then, does not necessarily reflect the attributes of real men and women. The lack of correspondence of individuals to the dual framework for understanding community currencies, however, does not preclude the meaningful ascription of "male" and "female" to each part of this framework.

LETS theorist, advocate and organizer, Ross Dobson, is deliberate in his use of gender attribution to make a case for LETS as a gift economy. Dobson examines LETS through an analysis of a dual economy. The "hunt" and the "hearth," he argues, are prototypes of what we characterize as "male" and "female." "Our general 'market-money'-based, capital-driven 'world-class' economy of competition" typifies the "male" pattern. The contrasting "female" pattern is "the internal economy of the hearth, planting and gathering, in which the sustaining, sacral flow of the gift can function day by day." For Dobson, "the two distinct economies still comprise very different and distinct behaviour patterns and substance, and foster and require diametrically different ethics, morality and values" (1993, p. 59).

Dobson affirms that it is not necessary to differentiate these two patterns according to gender. The very postulation of a dichotomous pattern, however, lends itself to gender ascription. There follows, also, the tendency to elevate one side of the dichotomy. For example, Paul Glover is reported once to have said: "Local currency activists generally seek to fundamentally transform society, rather than merely make it endurable" (Meeker-Lowry 1996. p. 458). The statement suggests an opposition between transforming society and accommodating to it as a survival strategy. It favours the conception of community currencies as new monetary institutions rather than as creative extensions of those everyday efforts to stretch the household budget and, in other ways, enrich one's life. For his part, Dobson is concerned at how the cooperative, life-affirming economy of the gift is subordinated to the competitive, risk-taking money economy. The highest potential he sees in LETS is to revalue the economy of the "hearth." To this end, he advances LETS as a system of "Barter Credit," and downplays associations of LETS with money.

To see the possibility for community currencies to fulfill multiple goals, and to hold out potential for both interpersonal and community-wide transformation, it would be important to avoid an analysis that reinforces polarities. Recognizing that the "male" and "female" economies are out of balance, a better response would be to attempt to reduce their opposition, that is, to harmonize them. I have presented the two most common associations with community currencies—barter and 1930s scrip—which are really ways of describing what community currencies are in the present. To enlarge that description and go beyond a dualistic framework, a third parallel is called for. Robert Owen's Equitable Labour Hours are seldom acknowledged as an antecedent to community currencies. Yet Owen's story brings together the view of community currencies both as catalysts for relationships of reciprocity and as tools for structural change. Fittingly, Owen initially chose as his theme the concept of "harmony." The Owenite experience provides such a strong parallel, I will introduce the story here, and continue it throughout the book.

Community Currencies and Owen's Equitable Labour Hours

The story begins in 1824, when Owen set sail to the United States, bringing with him a small fortune and a grand vision. He had sold his share in the renowned and profitable New Lanark textile mills to embark on the more ambitious project of creating working models of egalitarian communities. He bought a large tract of land in Indiana and founded New Harmony, the first of sixteen Owenite communities to be settled between 1825 and 1829. In New Harmony, Owen wanted to create conditions under which manual labour would be recognized as "the source of all wealth and of national prosperity" (cited in Claeys 1987, p. 44). He sought a community in which exchanges would be equitable and all persons would enjoy the full product of their labours.

The circulation of labour-hour notes was one of the first practical expressions of Owen's ideals in New Harmony. Like HOURS, this was a currency denominated in hours to promote the equal exchange of labour time. Within a few years, however, ill-planning, fraud and dissension about communal property split New Harmony into factions. Even after a disharmonious community was reorganized into three villages, the labour notes continued to be exchanged between them. By then the idea of basing a currency on labour hours had reached wider circles and continued to inspire experimentation, as Owenites joined with other American currency reformers to implement various labour money schemes (Harrison 1969).[3]

18

Owen himself became convinced that labour currency held out greater promise for instituting a moral economy then did communal living. He returned to England in 1929 to establish "Equitable Labour Exchanges" using labour notes and time-based accounting in conjunction with consumer cooperatives and artisan bazaars to promote self-employment, mutual aid and equal remuneration.

Although seldom mentioned in relation to present day community currencies, the Owenite experience has had at least some influence in Paul Glover's story of inventing Ithaca HOURS. He recalls, in 1991, sketching his first "cartoon Ithaca Money note" for a child. Then, as he tells it, "a few weeks later I saw a sample 'Hour' note issued by British industrialist Robert Owen in 1847" (Glover 1995). Shortly afterward he conceived of plans for Ithaca HOURS, and began to organize.

Perhaps this small event in the story of HOURS is the only direct influence of Owen's labour hours on today's community currency projects, but further parallels can be found. I have explained how present day projects recreate the barter experience of more personal, less mediated exchange. At the same time, they share with their Depression precursors a focus on the exigency of protecting jobs and purchasing power in response to economic downturns. They also share with Owenism a unifying vision that Karl Polanyi best described when writing of Owen. Foregrounded in the vision is the desire to enhance the security and material well-being of communities by connecting producers and consumers in local networks. On this immediate goal of enhancing self-reliance through re-localizing exchange, community currency pioneers and Owenites are in unity. In the following passages we can hear Michael Linton and Thomas Greco seeming to echo Polanyi as he, in turn, trumpeted Owen:

> Conventional money will generally drain out of the community to the cheapest available source of labor or goods. A community with its own currency has the capacity to adopt and maintain coherent and relevant directions of development with minimal dislocation by external events (Linton and Greco 1987).

> At the heart of the [Owenite] Exchange or Bazaar there was reliance on the complementary nature of the crafts; by providing for

one another's needs, artisans would emancipate themselves, it was thought, from the ups and downs of the market (Polanyi 1957, p. 168).

Both the Owenite and contemporary visions are more broadly grounded in the conviction that new money must serve to renew community. Whereas formal economics considers money in the service of markets, functioning in the efficient allocation of scarce means, community currencies connect people in multiple ways—not just through markets—for ends that are politically defined (Polanyi 1968). For Polanyi, Owen's genius as a money reformer was that "he grasped the fact that what appeared primarily as an economic problem was essentially a social one" (Polanyi 1957, p. 129). Owen understood that economic disparity and immiseration were, at the root, problems of social dislocation, which could be reversed only by creating conditions for closer relationships of people to land and communities. Owen's insistence on the social approach spoke to Polanyi of an "inner vision" (pp. 129). The failure of Owenism to take hold was, therefore, for Polanyi, cause for lament:

> Owenism in England showed all the characteristics of spiritual inspiration. That its impetus was lost...was the greatest single defeat of spiritual forces in the history of industrial England (pp. 169).

The resemblances between Owen's labour notes and the contemporary community currency movement go beyond form. Owen's work may be considered a fitting precedent because of the centrality of moral sensibilities to present day projects. Although there is little evidence for considering LETS and HOURS a direct legacy of Owen's efforts, they would appear to be commonly inspired.

Polanyi's analysis of Owenism suggests another parallel: both the nineteenth century and contemporary movements are similarly utopian and experimental. Of course, the utopianism of Owenite projects does not begin to match, in scale or design, what Polanyi called the "stark utopia" involved in organizing an economic system around the idea of self-regulating markets. Nor does the experimentalism of such projects approximate the far-reaching experimentation involved in central banking and high finance. What distinguishes community currency from conventional money projects is not that they are utopian and experimental, but the style in which they are: that their quest for "new harmony" consciously aims to embed money exchange in a social ground of cooperation, conviviality and equality. In so doing it would harmonize those aspects of economic life designated "masculine" and "feminine," which are often deemed incommensurable.

Returning again to Owen's story: the labour exchanges in England achieved spectacular success,[4] but, like other of his large scale endeavours, only in the short term. As reasons for their breakdown, historians have pointed to lack of confidence in the money, problems achieving a range of products on offer to match what people wanted to buy, and difficulties setting prices in labour notes to cover the cost of inputs. Shortcomings in Owen's leadership are also thought to have played a role (Claeys 1987, p. 56), but as one historian concluded, the demise of the labour exchange mainly served to highlight "the baffling problem of how to operate socialist institutions in the midst of a still competitive society" (Harrison 1969, p. 207).

This book addresses that same "baffling problem" for today's community currency movement. The challenge is not simply to introduce a cooperative form of money into a competitive money economy, but to come to understand how the opposition between competition and cooperation already organizes economic relations, ideologically and institutionally. Cultural oppositions—competition and cooperation, currency and barter, exchange and reciprocity, hunt and hearth—have subtle and complex gender associations. The association of binary oppositions with gender categories is a key process through which practices and institutions deemed "feminine" are culturally subordinated.

It follows that inventing new monies and new norms of exchange can disrupt the ideological underpinnings of a gendered economy, in addition to creating sought-after outcomes such as enlivening community, enhancing the material lives of members and re-localizing the economy. The effects of such innovations will be felt first in interpersonal relationships, where strategies for material well-being and for "doing gender" are closely intertwined. It is on this interpersonal level that the potential of community currencies for changing the balance of gender relations will be, in various ways, embraced or resisted. By closely observing gender dimensions of community currency exchange, this study aims to reduce the bafflement at why such economic innovations encounter limits in practice, even among their ardent supporters.

Notes

1. Some HOURS cities, including those in Canada, take $12 as the average wage and HOUR equivalent. It follows that a Half HOUR = $6, Quarter HOUR = $3, Eighth HOUR = $1.50.

2. Canada had one short-lived stamp scrip experiment. The Province of Alberta under the Social Credit government of William Aberhart introduced the Alberta Prosperity Certificate in 1936. These were issued to civil servants in partial payment of their salaries. As in Europe, the Bank of Canada pressured the province to cancel the scheme, and it lasted only one year. Public complaints that the scrip did not have enough government backing (it was not accepted for corporate taxes, school and university fees, provincial licences and amusement taxes) also contributed to its demise.

3. Former New Harmonist, Josiah Warren, was prominent among the experimenters. He operated a "time store" in Cincinnati, Ohio, where he priced goods, first according to cost and rent, and then according to his own labour time in ordering and selling them.

4. In the highest week of trading in the London labour exchange, the week of 15th December 1832, accounts show a total of 38,772 hours deposited, representing labour product given in exchange. A slightly lower figure would have been withdrawn, or received in exchange. In the four month period from September to December of that year, approximately 400,000 labour hours were exchanged (Harrison, 1969, p. 205).

Chapter Two

"What's Wrong with Regular Money?" Frameworks for a Gender Analysis

COMMUNITY CURRENCIES ARE UNMISTAKABLY a critique of the conventional monetary system. Promotional materials for LETS and HOURS and a small body of literature by the movement's intellectual leaders advance community currencies, foremost, as a solution to local social problems deriving from the organization of national currencies within a global monetary system (Linton and Greco 1987; Dobson 1993; Greco 1994; Douthwaite 1996; Solomon 1996; Savdie and Cohen-Mitchell 1997). A LETS brochure, for example, announces in its front page headline that LETS is about "Employing your Skills. Building your Community." The overleaf describes "The Problem with Money," and the facing page explains how "LETS is a Solution." Yet this focus on "what's wrong with money" does not fully describe the ambition of local money experiments. While no one suggests that schemes like LETS and HOURS, in themselves, are panaceas for the social ills of corporate globalism, the project of inventing new monies has political scope and depth beyond what are commonly taken to be monetary, and even "economic," issues.

First, in terms of their scope, community currencies belong together with a cluster of movements, local in organization and cosmopolitan in outlook (Sachs 1995), each of which tries to implement a practical reorganization of a particular set of globalized structures. This movement of local movements does not set out to overturn monolithic institutions only to see them replaced with new monoliths, but aims instead to create, from below, a myriad of alternative institutional forms. Community land trusts, co-housing and eco-villages, community shared agriculture, alternative credit and financing arrangements, worker-owned enterprises, energy and transportation alternatives are being invented concurrently with commu-

23

nity currencies, and often in conjunction (Benello, Swann et al. 1989; Nozick 1992; Roberts and Brandum 1995; Milani 2000). Each initiative addresses itself to a particular systemic issue: land speculation, lack of affordable housing and credit, the agro-industrial system, dependence on footloose corporations, use of non-renewable fossil fuels. This collection of singularly focused movements, all promoting local self-reliance, community economic revitalization and ecological sustainability, all sharing the strategy of creating parallel institutions, and complementary in their design for re-localization, together amount to a wide-ranging program for self-protection of communities and systemic change.

Second, the objects of these movements for local alternatives—money, food, land, home, work, energy—are basic to human life, infused with multiple meanings and deeply embedded in social relations on all levels, from intimate relations to international relations. While a number of studies have already begun to examine the scope of diverse local movements—to identify unifying ideologies, linkages or potentials to become a broad-based political alternative (Mander and Goldsmith 1996; McMichael 1996), it is this second dimension, the "depth" of these politics, that this book takes up.

Among the many small-scale re-localization initiatives, community currencies provide unique opportunities for exploring gender relations because they call for renegotiation of everyday practices. The points of tension that arise can be revealing of what Joan Acker (1992) calls the "gendered understructure" of economic institutions. A close examination of gender dynamics within LETS and HOURS demonstrates the importance of gender analysis, not only to community currencies, but also to allied political movements. It underscores how all political-economic change has specific implications for gender relations. For supporters and organizers of the movement who consider gender equity at least an abstract goal and an assumed outcome of other goals, the analysis to follow is an encouragement to create organizing strategies that are intentional about gender issues. It calls on progressive movements to be attentive to the ways change is resisted or limited on account of gendered patterns.

Much of the research into how economic institutions are gendered investigates the disruption, change and reconstitution of gender relations in response to abrupt changes or upheavals in the economy. Whereas I am interested in the effects of intentional local innovations, these works primarily examine local innovations necessitated by crises such as recession, unemployment and loss of industry (Wheelock 1990), occupational restructuring (Cockburn 1983; Bradley 1999), the contraction of public sector employment (Lomnitz and Melnick 1994), and disasters such as drought and famine (Agarwal 1992). Such works show how economic crises precipitate gender crises and give rise to the extensive "work" of redefining gender identities, meanings, practices and relationships within family and wider social networks (Beneria and Feldman 1992). Their findings consistently emphasize that economic activity is eminently social, and that economic relations are at the same time relations of gender, class, race and nation (Lustinger-Thaler and Salee 1994).

In this study I take the main findings of this body of work as my first premise: that gender is an organizing principle of social life, and that all major institutions—economy, politics, law, state, education, religion, family—are gendered (Acker 1992). I assume that a "deep" challenge to the monetary system would also disrupt its gendered underpinnings. However, the intentionality of introducing community currencies, however, means that engagement in gender struggles is more voluntary than it would be under circumstances of economic crises. Therefore, rather than take gender struggles as an effect of some more widespread change, I take the gender politics of the community currency movement as an indicator of its effectiveness in changing local exchange relations in desired ways. In other words, I assume that if introducing a parallel currency is to expose and buffer problems with the conventional monetary system, it will necessarily come up against the framework of socially constructed male/female differences, inequalities and relations of dominance and "subordinance" that the monetary system supports and on which it depends. How the movement is able to confront and transform the resulting tensions will partially determine its limits as a practical solution to "the problem with money."

Three tasks are in order before I begin to describe the movement's critique of money. First, I want to acknowledge the strength of support for feminist ideals that runs through the movement, particularly the theorizing of how community currencies can advance gender equity. Second, I want to comment on how, in spite of the feminism of the movement, gender asymmetries are de-politicized and become difficult to observe. Third, before any further discussion of how social relations are gendered, I want to present what I mean by "gender" and the "gendering" process, and describe how these concepts inform my analysis throughout the book.

Observing "Gender" in LETS and HOURS

Observers of the community currency movement have characterized its political values as green and communitarian (Lee 1996, p. 1387; Bowring 1998; Helleiner 2000), but the currents of feminism within the movement tend to receive less attention. The symbolism of publicity materials, the arguments of the supportive literature, and the commitments of leaders often suggest that community currencies uphold various feminist ideals. The HOURS system in Boulder, Colorado, for example, visibly promotes ecological feminism. The highest denomination HOUR note, worth two hours of labour or the equivalent of twenty dollars, carries a picture of a woman's face and the saying "honor the goddess in all women." Similar slogans appear on the four corners of the opposite side: "honor the maiden, honor the mother, honor all women and honor the wise woman." Beyond such positive messages, community currencies are thought to support gender equity just by structuring opportunities for advancement of women and the "feminine." First, they are thought to revalorize "feminine" principles, such as the principles of reciprocity that underlie gift economies (Lietaer 1997). Second, they are considered to provide opportunities for "women's" work, especially unpaid domestic work, to be recognized, renegotiated and revalued (Brandt 1995). Third, because they create opportunities for expanding social networks—forming new types of relationships, receiving new services and performing new types of work, even incubating new businesses (Lang 1994)—they are thought to establish a social space that allows women and men to test, transgress and transcend customary boundaries of class and gender.

Ideas about how community currencies bring about balance and equity in gender relations may be partly self-fulfilling through the power of assertion, but there is no reason to assume that feminist outcomes are automatic. Survey research in the UK, in fact, shows that patterns of gender inequity in the mainstream economy appear also in UK LETS.

> A gender division of labour between "men's" and "women's" work is apparent... with men tending to offer household maintenance and repair and to offer equipment and tools for hire, and women offering time in the form of mundane domestic services. Gendered wage inequalities are also reproduced from the wider economy, with men not only demanding more than twice the rate per offer than women but being more prepared than women to negotiate a price (Lee 1996, p. 1383).

My research findings confirm the continuity of conventional patterns of gender relations within LETS and HOURS, as might be expected, given that community currency activities actually account for a small part of most people's daily lives. However, my findings also demonstrate that considerable creative negotiation of gender relations goes on in LETS and HOURS. Consequently, I share the conviction that community currencies present opportunities for transformation, but place the emphasis of the research on how regular gender inequalities compromise the structure of the money schemes and limit their effectiveness as economic alternatives. Community currencies are egalitarian in potential only, and more effort is needed towards observing, problematizing and politicizing the areas where they fall short.

Even when ideological commitments to gender equity are widespread in the group, as they are among most community currency practitioners, gender divisions are often normalized and not seen, perhaps partly because of a limited vision of what egalitarian gender relationships within the community would look like. Too often energy is focused merely on cultivating non-sexist attitudes, putting up (with) defensive postures, smoothing out awkwardness and avoiding intense feelings, when the larger challenge is to identify and transform the systemic processes that give rise to gender imbalances.

Joan Acker argues that the assumption that institutions, such as money, banking, labour markets and so on, are gender neutral contributes further to the imperceptibility of systemic issues:

[G]endered reality is obscured... in the ways that institutions, other than the family, are conceptualized and theorized in gender-neutral terms. Understanding how the appearance of gender neutrality is maintained in the face of overwhelming evidence of gendered structures is an important part of analysing gendered institutions (Acker 1992, p. 568).

Feminist economists have observed that one way "the appearance of gender neutrality is maintained" is through the pervasive assumption that we all behave like "rational economic man" (Ferber and Nelson 1993). This construct supposes that we are all free agents whose choices are based on rational, individual preferences and interests. Going beyond the ideology of "economic man" in the community currency movement would require identifying how individual members' choices and desires are shaped by the concrete conditions of their lives, as women and men specifically located within a complex gender order. I will give a few examples of the kind of analysis that would make visible the ways LETS and HOURS are gendered.

Take, first, the finding of another survey of UK LETS, that the majority of coordinators are women (Thorne 1996, p. 1366). On first glance it would appear that LETS advances women and welcomes them into leadership. LETS' attractiveness to women leaders, however, must be understood in light of women's differential access to full time paid employment, and the organization of the household economy such that women are more likely to seek flexible work, varied income sources, support of community networks, and opportunities to substitute household production for marketed goods, all of which LETS can offer.

The demographics of support for community currencies provide a second example of the specific class and gender interests in the movement. In a discussion of community currencies among a group of friends, a former pollster and adviser to a leftist political party put the usual question to me: "What's wrong with money? From a political perspective, I just don't see what problem it solves." He listened as I summarized the main arguments that I will put forward later in this chapter and then commented: "It is an interesting idea, but it will never catch on in the suburbs." I agreed. Community currencies have flourished in small towns, city centres and rural areas, but none, to my knowledge, has been started in a suburb. A LETS member, Kevin, said in an interview: "If it was my goal to make lots of money and live out in the suburbs with two cars, I probably wouldn't be in [LETS] because I might see it as a waste of time." The conventional monetary system is integral to the organization of the major features of suburban culture: the wage relation, personal mortgages and car loans, the spacial and ideological separation of public and domestic spheres, the devaluation of domestic work, the gender and racial divisions of domestic labour, and the tradeoffs between money and time, all of which are organized through gender divisions. The observation that community currencies would not attract suburban "votes" underscores that their politics advance specific class and gender interests.

One last story illustrates the difficulty of acknowledging the gender politics of community currencies. A supporter of HOURS, Emily, told me about an encounter with a skeptical friend who challenged her to justify the movement's political goals. Emily is an artist who sells her work at the farmer's market. The story came up when she was explaining to me that most of her fellow vendors at the market also accept HOURS. I was interested in the exceptions:

MB: Is there anybody in the farmer's market who doesn't take HOURS?

Emily: *Actually, one person...[friend's name]. He doesn't take HOURS. I just talked to him this morning.* (Relaying their conversation) *"Do you take HOURS?"*

He said, "No." He said, (mimicking him with a loud, low pitched, gruff voice) *"What's wrong with regular money?"*

Like, "Oh goodness," (mimicking herself with a soft, high pitched, sing-song voice) *"Ah, I just wanted to know if you did. You don't. Thank you."*

The exaggerated performance of gender difference in this short scene is meaningful.[1] Apparently, Emily did not pursue her friend's questioning of HOURS at the time. When she re-enacted the conversation with me, however, she caricatured the tone of his retort and her follow-up to convey that, in this instance, their political difference is gendered. Her dramatization of the conversation may well be taken as her commentary on "what's wrong with money." Rather than give a direct answer, she gave a show of deference. In the interview, by amplifying how their performances were gendered, she gave an answer of sorts by conveying the difficulty of speaking openly of the gendered politics of HOURS.

In each of these three examples of the challenges of observing gender in the community currency movement, I have been referring to different ways gender is manifested: in statistical patterns of difference between women and men (gender patterns), in the way institutions reproduce relations of difference and hierarchy (the gender order), and in the language and practices people use to invoke ideas of difference and identity ("doing" gender).

At this point a definition of "gender" is due. I am now using quotation marks to emphasize that "gender" does not refer to observable items, such as persons or even attributes of persons. "Gender" is the process of assigning persons and attributes to categories according to socially constructed rules and definitions. These rules are usually thought to relate to persons' biological sex—to their having certain genitals or chromosomes. This is the common understanding of the relation between "sex" and "gender": the biologically-determined sex of bodies destines the lives of persons to be imbued with socially-constructed gender attributes. However, as Michel Foucault and others began to point out in the 1980s, the ongoing practice of defining binary sex categories and assigning all bodies to either "male" or "female" is as much a discursive process as is gender attribution (Foucault 1984; Connell 1987; Moore 1994). Moreover, except in the few moments upon a person's birth, in most actual social circumstances persons are designated to one or the other gender category, while the corresponding sex category is merely assumed. In other words, the apparent determination of "gender" by "sex" typically works in reverse. Some scholars use the notation "sex/gender" to connote that these discursive practices of designating bodies and attributes to categories are better understood as a single process (Davies 1990).

Collective social arrangements are gendered, as Acker explains, in the way that "advantage and disadvantage, exploitation and control, action and emotion, and meaning and identity are patterned through and in terms of a distinction between male and female" (1990, p. 146). The binary categories of sex and gender—male/female, man/woman, masculine/feminine—take their meaning in relation to one another. Feminist post-structuralist theory emphasizes that in the modern West, the terms of the binary are phallocentric and hierarchical. "Female" is the negative term: "that which is not-male" (Hewitson 1999). The "female" is the excluded "other" in relation to the self-present "male" term. The post-structuralist influence in feminist thought has been to underscore that gender is an ordering principle, not only of human bodies and social characteristics of persons, but more fundamentally of language, social thought and institutions. Dominant gender discourse is asymmetrical; that which is associated with "femaleness" is devalued in relation to the opposite category, whose "maleness" is masked behind its non-gendered, neutral, self-evident appearance: "that which is."

Let me use the three examples I have reported above to clarify the analytical implications of understanding "gender" as a relational process. In the first example, the report that most leaders of LETS are women, "gender" is evident in the observable patterns of difference between women and men. The act of counting women and men is itself a gendering process. Counting and measuring fixes people to gender categories and reveals nothing of the historical and discursive processes through which the patterns came about and the categories themselves took shape. Statistical practices of identifying male/female difference reify gender. Statistics are meaningful and politically valuable, nevertheless, because they indicate that other systemic practices of gendering are occurring within institutions, as I began to point out in the example of suburban political culture.

The second observation, that there is less support for community currencies in the suburbs, could be elaborated to show the variability of gendering processes across different social contexts. This level of analysis would emphasize historical change in the content of gender ideologies and concrete institutional practices. It would show the contingency of the gender order, including the interrelation of gender processes to the processes that produce "race," class and other social identities. It would focus on the ways institutions exercise social control through gendered practices, ranging from overt gender-based violence to the mostly symbolic or conceptual practices that use gender categories to exclude, segregate, devalue and marginalize.

The third example, Emily's story, illustrates the main type of gender analysis I undertake in this book. By describing Emily's response to her friend's lack of support for HOURS as "gendered," I am not making a statistical inference that women are more likely than men to hold positive attitudes towards HOURS. I am using the story to illustrate the subtlety and significance of gendering processes in everyday life. In this level of analysis, "gender" is not a role or a categorical identity. The "gender" of individuals is an ongoing performance whereby we try to make ourselves accountable to other people while situated in an institutional context and a context of relationship. In this understanding, "gender" is a "practical accomplishment" (West and Zimmerman 1987), that is integral to the other ends we try to achieve as we continuously recreate ourselves in interaction with others. Gendering involves associating persons, bodies, aspects or attributes with the culturally constructed categories of "masculine" and "feminine." For the most part, we "do" gender by displaying the attributes and behaviours we expect others to recognize as appropriately "masculine" or "feminine" for that context, such that our performances are completely unremarkable. However, gender is not necessarily performed in conformity with stereotypes, but can also be in some other kind of creative relation to the norm, including gender bending and uses of hyper-masculinity or femininity. Whether performances are destabilizing of gender norms or well in conformity with them, of most importance is that they are recognizable because of shared understandings of the cultural content of, and relations between, the categories, especially the understanding that "masculine" categories are culturally deemed superior. To return to the example, by Emily's tone of voice and show of deference she conveyed that support for HOURS is associated with the "feminine" and is devalued. At the same time as drawing attention to the devaluation of the "feminine," her exaggerated performance mocked these associations and evaluations.

Robert Connell's (1995) study of "masculinities" emphasizes the interplay of multiple gender constructs. A hierarchy of masculinities is produced relative to "hegemonic masculinity" associated with elite, white men. Subordination, complicity and marginalization describe some of the relationships of men to the dominant group that shape the construction of masculinities. Connell's work is valuable to this study because it helps account for the tremendous variation in the ways individual men and women "do" gender. It maintains that gender constructs are historical products of collective projects to achieve (or resist) a particular kind of social order. It also helps explain why, despite the broad range of gender discourse in the culture, individuals' social location within these larger projects constrains discursive and practical resources available for "doing" gender.

Connell considers the various masculinities he describes to be "configurations of practice" rather than types (p. 81). Another non-categorical approach to the complexity of gender practices is given in *A Male/Female Continuum: Paths to Colleagueship* (Pierce, Wagner et al. 1998). With the focus more on the constraints of individual life histories than of large scale processes, this book charts the "stages of our gender journeys" (p. viii). It was written primarily to promote gender equity within organizations through awareness of the gender dynamics of interpersonal relationships, and how these are complicated by the dynamics of race, class and sexuality. In the early part of the continuum, male/female relationships are patterned by men's assumed entitlement to control women with violence and sexual exploitation through to sexual harassment, discrimination, courtesy and paternalism. Women's survival behaviour in such relationships also involves forms of control such as explosive or self-destructive violence, psychological punishment, manipulation, deference and maternalism. In relationships further along the continuum, women have stopped colluding with men in the role stereotyping that sustains the relationship of dominance and subordinance.[2] Women at this stage have begun to enjoy their own power and to identify positively with other women. In response to women's changes, men begin their own developmental journeys, which, among other challenges, involve addressing homophobia and dealing with other men who act as dominants. Colleagueship between women and men is the end stage, the state of equity and mutual empowerment. Even though the tasks required of men and women on their "gender journeys" differ, the goal is the same: "becoming balanced human beings each responsible for their own development as connective, loving, and caring people, *and* independent and differentiated, living in context with each other" (Pierce, Wagner et al. 1998, p. 62).

The idea that women and men move forwards or backwards across a spectrum of relationships within a culture that predominantly supports a collusion of dominance and subordinance is useful in understanding the diversity of gender performances. The male/female continuum provides a conceptual framework for observing gender performances without assigning people to static categories. In this study I avoid typologies of gender ideologies, and masculinities and femininities, such as those that would divide men and women into "traditional," "transitional" and "egalitarian" groups, to take the example of Arlie Hochschild's (1989) ethnography of dual career couples. The continuum idea places the research focus on the goals each person is trying to achieve in a particular relationship. So when considering stories of exchanges with community currencies, the question is not, "what kind of person is he or she?" but, "where do gender tensions or contradictions arise in his or her dealings? What shifts in his or her customary gender practices are now required in the situation he or she describes? How does the community currency system structure the interpersonal dynamics he or she is experiencing?" The perspective of a continuum prevents the framing of questions that require a dichotomous answer, such as whether community currencies are "feminist." They allow for more open ended questions, such as, "in what ways do LETS and HOURS reproduce conventional arrangements?" And, "in what ways do they enlarge the freedom of women and men to pursue meaningful work and relationships based on wholeness, balance and equity?"

These are the questions I take up in the following chapters. In the remainder of this chapter I will review the critique of money advanced by supporters of community currencies that has been developing in tandem with the practical experimentation. Here I am focusing on the movement's theoretical grounds, whereas in the main part of the book I observe the gendered economy more from the perspective of practice, as people attempt to introduce LETS and HOURS into their own lives and communities, with all the negotiation of meaning this entails. As I will show, the obstacles members encounter most immediately concern the wage gap between "men's" and "women's" work; gender differences in the implications of monetizing "gift" labour; other non-pecuniary interests that sometimes enter women's price negotiations and give the appearance that women "undervalue" themselves; and finally, the gendered division of production and consumption. The thrust of the book, therefore, is to demonstrate how these gender divisions broadly relate to the social and political organization of the money economy, which rests on socially constructed divisions between money and gift, formal and informal, domestic and public, and so on. The following section, in which I introduce the critique of the conventional monetary system that spurs LETS and HOURS, presents arguments that are more specific to the institutional forms of money, their political regulation and direct effects. However, the gender perspective, that I work towards in the book as a whole enlarges the focus to show how gender divisions are often constituted through divisions between the "monetary" and "non-monetary": which are really, to use the cliché, two sides of a coin.

The "Problem with Money" and the Call for Parallel Currencies

If the argument for community currencies can be summarized in a single idea, it is that the present system of national currencies merges several monetary functions in an all-purpose money form that would be better separated into any number of complementary currencies. Textbooks in economics often define money by way of listing these functions: medium of exchange, means of payment, store of abstract value, standard of value and unit of account. Accounts of the origin of money carry on a tradition from the classical economists of explaining how the properties of modern money overcome the limitations of simple, bilateral barter (Jennings 1994; Ingham 2000). Typically, there is a list of the stuff of primitive money—wampum, cows, tobacco, slaves, and so on—followed by an argument about the superiority of modern money in fulfilling the exchange function. A medium of exchange that is portable, divisible, generally accepted and likely to hold its value in the future, is, in contrast to simple barter, vastly advantageous. As a recurrent theme in modern economic thought, this contrast between modern money and barter is so often cast in evolutionary terms "many economists are apt to view our modern type of general purpose money as some final pinnacle of progress" (Rotstein and Duncan 1991, p. 417).

The evidence of cultural anthropology refutes modernist conceptions of money's origins in simple barter (Ingham 2000). Karl Polanyi's economic history reveals the range of distinct money forms used in non-modern societies. Monies for exchange, payment, accountancy, hoarding and storage all have unique institutional histories (Polanyi 1968, p. 185). The earliest purpose for which money originated is, most likely, for payment to discharge specific religious and political obligations, not for payment-in-exchange. Non-market payments included temple offerings, *wergild* or blood money, bridewealth, fines, taxes and rents. In societies that relied on the storage and distribution of staples, accounting monies arose separately from these early payment monies and, again, independently of markets. Furthermore, separate circuits of long distance trade, internal trade and subsistence markets in pre-modern societies relied on different currencies.

Contrary to the tendency of economic theory to feature the development of markets as the central culminating process of economic history, Polanyi emphasizes that money, trade and markets have distinct origins and social functions. Moreover, he gives prominence to the sociological aspects of the various forms of money. Money's role is broader than providing a technical solution to the problems of exchange, allocation, equivalency, and so on, because the entire organization of the economy, including money, is embedded in the larger cultural system. The evidence of economic anthropology affirms there is nothing necessary about having all of money's functions rolled up in a single form. And so, from a Polanyian perspective it is conceivable to (re)create complementary systems of local money for purposes that extend beyond the "economic" in its formal sense as "a set of rules referring to choice between alternative uses of insufficient means" (Polanyi 1968, p. 140). What is wrong with "general purpose" money that would call for "special purpose" local monies is the important question.

WHAT'S WRONG WITH REGULAR MONEY?

Taking up this theme of money's social embeddedness, Viviana Zelizer (1994) examines the special purposes to which modern "general purpose" money is even now put. She argues that we moderns, even though we may use a single currency, continue to distinguish between "monies" according to their various uses for gifts, payment-in-exchange and non-market payment, state transfers, tips, tithes, bribes, and so on. Through the examples of wives' allowances, gifts, and poor relief in the U.S. from the late nineteenth to early twentieth centuries, she explores how, even with an undifferentiated money form, people, in effect, persist in creating special pseudo-currencies. The purpose of this "constant, vigorous, and pervasive differentiation of modern monies" is to mark the status of social relations, indicating relations of intimacy, dependence, entitlement, formal equality, hierarchy or rank (p. 214). Pseudo-monies, therefore, mediate "delicate and difficult" social interactions between people of different gender, age, family, ethnic, class and organizational statuses (p. 25).

Like Polanyi's anthropology of multi-currency societies, Zelizer's observations on the differentiation of modern money further a reconceptualization of (plural) monies as culturally produced symbols of multifaceted social relations, against the view that (singular) money is merely a neutral facilitator of rational, means-ends relationships, and the perfect technical instrument of price-setting markets. From the point of view of creating local monies, Zelizer's exposition of the multiple social meanings of money supports the basic premise of this study:

> Multiple monies matter as powerful, visible symbols of particular types of social relations and meanings. But they are more than that; they directly affect social practices. People not only think or feel differently about their various monies, but they spend them, save them, or give them for different purposes and to different people (Zelizer 1994, p. 211).

Upcoming chapters explore how community currencies "directly affect social practices" in the area of gender relations, but before going on, Zelizer's findings return us to the question of what's wrong with money? If modern money relations are already sociologically complex and differentiable, why is a new kind of money necessary? Can we not simply earmark the national currency for local spending and, thereby, renew the local economy and foster closer local ties with dollars?

Zelizer stresses the cultural embeddedness of modern money, in contrast to Polanyi's arguments that the market system disembeds economic relationships from social and cultural life. She also takes issue with Georg Simmel (1991 [1900]), who was concerned that modern money relations imbue social life with the character of market exchange: homogeneity, objectivity, abstractness, impersonality. Our predisposition for earmarking modern money, for Zelizer, "provides the most powerful evidence *against* a homogenized, instrumental model of social life," and demonstrates that, "the vision of society fully transformed into a commodity market is no more than a mirage" (p. 215).

As I have been explaining, Zelizer and Polanyi share a similar conception that "money is a system of symbols similar to language, writing, or weights and measures" (Polanyi 1968, p. 175), but they have divergent interpretations of the impact of modern money as a social institution, owing to different points of reference and levels of analysis. Zelizer's purpose is to demonstrate how market money is given new meanings as it is transferred into non-market settings such as the household. She succeeds in showing that not all modern money is market money, not all transfers are payment-in-exchange, and not all relationships are about individual gain. Simmel and Polanyi, taking such observations as given, were instead concerned to emphasize the permeation of market relations into ever more aspects of modern culture. In other words, Zelizer contrasts modern money with Simmel's negative "vision of society fully transformed into a commodity market," and finds that such fears have not been realized. Simmel's and Polanyi's point of reference, which gave rise to such a disturbing vision, was the historical transformation of non-modern cultures as they were monetized and integrated into world markets.

Polanyi's work provides an answer to the question of why create new monies when general purpose money may be earmarked for specific ends. He emphasizes the institutional power of social groups to control the "system of symbols" so that one meaning of money prevails over the many possible meanings and functions. Monetary integration of all levels of economy, from the household to world trade, is facilitated by singular, general purpose, internationally convertible, national currencies. For Polanyi, cultural "disembedding" refers to these processes by which the market functions of money come to dominate and people live more of their lives by the fiction that money is a commodity. He and Zelizer would agree that "multiple monies matter" politically, but he calls more attention to the way political struggles to control monies' rules and definitions on the highest levels of the state system and world economy affect the kinds of political struggles Zelizer describes further down between sub-national classes, household members, and so on. The political power of elite social groups to set the terms of credit, savings and investment, to regulate supply of money and determine its basis of issuance, is backed up with force and with the supporting ideology that monetary rules are natural, necessary and immutable. Although the ability to personalize money for household relations, and earmark it for support of local enterprise and community works remains, how we do this in practice can be severely limited by the apparent eventuality of recession and unemployment. These limitations apply not only to households and communities; Polanyi argues that the "market mentality" is so firmly entrenched that the disruption and displacement of cultures and the despoiling of ecosystems are held to be the inevitable results of impersonal, abstract forces, rather than a particular system of political economy (Polanyi 1957).

Many examples could be given of the dominance of market money and the suppression of the ability to create new monies or to earmark. For every state there is a story of how defining the boundaries of state sovereignty through the establishment of the national currency entailed the often violent suppression of competing citizen loyalties along with the elimination of local currencies used to mark these loyalties (Gilbert and Helleiner 1999). Other illustrations of how the introduction of one regulatory mechanism for money required the suppression of alternatives are to be found in the histories of financial institutions: central banking (Davies 1994), the Bretton Woods system (Strange 1994), offshore markets (Roberts 1994; Hudson 1999), pension funds (Clark 1999), and so on. I will give one historical example to illustrate a key political dimension of general purpose money which the local currency movement addresses—the problem of monetary scarcity.

This example refers to one of the rare moments when money's political organization was widely called into question, illustrating how general purpose money requires a balance between competing interests in money's functions. Bruce Carruthers and Sarah Babb (1996) analyze a debate as it was conducted through popular literature over the proper form of national currency in the U.S. in the 1870s, just prior to the period Zelizer wrote about. The debate arose following the Civil War, when monetary crisis had forced the U.S. off the gold standard. It ended with a triumph of "bullionists" over "greenbackers" when the U.S. switched again from paper fiat money back to commodity money based on fixed gold values. Carruthers and Babb show how the technical issues that seemed to drive the gold standard debate were really political ones, and the two sides in the debate were pulled by different political and economic interests. The supporters of "hard currency" tended to be Republicans, and included bondholders, bankers, financiers, and importers who wanted a non-inflationary, internationally-convertible currency. Support for the "soft currency" option tended to come from farmers and labour in the south and west who wanted more democratic control over measures to regulate the supply of money, which is of critical importance to levels of industry and employment.

The particulars of this short chapter in the history of the gold standard in the U.S. are not as important as what was at stake in the debate. Other significant events, such as the adoption of central banking in the U.S. through the 1913 Federal Reserve Act (Galbraith 1975), or Nixon's decision in 1971 to unpeg the dollar from gold and, by "closing the gold window," move the international monetary system to a system of floating exchange rates (Block 1978), would illustrate similar themes of political compromise. Landmark events in the history of money, especially where there is significant public debate, more readily expose the political interests underlying monetary policy than periods of relative stability. The 1870s debate revealed the ideological basis for acceptance of the gold standard

—the belief that gold has intrinsic value. When the "greenbackers" questioned the "naturalness" of gold as the foundation of the money system, they openly challenged the legitimacy of monetary authority. The debate also revealed that the monetary system has definite distributive consequences:

> For domestic economic activity, an increase in the money supply was a good thing. For the holders of financial assets, the opposite was true. So the battle between the means of exchange and the store of value function took place in the arena of banking policy with regard to the setting of the gold value of the currency (Rotstein and Duncan 1991, p. 421).

The shape of the compromise between "bullionists" and "greenbackers" would reflect what each saw as the right balance between inflation and unemployment.

Today's monetary system is based on the legal authority of banks, primarily commercial banks, to issue money as credit. The money form no longer has reference to a commodity (gold) that is conceived as the general equivalent in the determination of the exchange ratios of other commodities. In one respect, this makes little difference, as credit money is still thought of both as representing the abstract value of other commodities and as a store of abstract value. In orthodox economic analysis money remains "*essentially* a commodity" (Ingham 2000, p. 17). Competing interests in the store of abstract value and the means of exchange functions are still a core political problem. Whatever compromise is reached between the monetary requirements of trade, finance and investment, on the one hand, and circulation on the other, scarcity of the means of exchange is endemic to general purpose money.

There is a major difference, however, when the financial system is based in credit money. In addition to the tension between the means of exchange and store of value functions, the means of payment function assumes greater importance and places additional demands on money (Rowbotham 1998). Money comes into existence in parallel with consumer, commercial and national debt, but in the aggregate there is never enough money for payment of debt with interest. Intense competition arises as not only individuals but regions, classes and nation states risk being left without sufficient means of exchange to conduct the regular business of manufacture, retail, provision of services and of infrastructure (Kennedy 1995). The price of money will always be out of reach for some, with bankruptcies and foreclosures occurring as a direct consequence of a debt-based financial system. The pressure not to be the "losers" in the scramble for scarce money drives economic growth.

> An economy based almost entirely upon bank-credit and debt experiences an intense drive for growth, regardless of need or demand. Bank credit engenders financial dependence, injects instability and fosters growth-distortions, both within an economy and throughout the international arena (Rowbotham 1998, p. 8).

The situation of monetary scarcity is problematic from the perspective of local economies. Money is removed from circulation through debt repayment, investment or spending on imported goods. It is reinvested anywhere it can get the highest rate of return, which means it will eventually flow to financial centres, leaving pockets of disadvantage. Communities facing money shortages compete to attract investment by agreeing to lower wages or extract "resources." They also become dependent on continued import of lower priced goods, even though cheap prices only benefit consumers in the short run and do not indicate the eventual loss of purchasing power as liquidity flows out of the local economy (Rowbotham 1998).

Richard Gregg (1963) was one of the first to propose local money as a remedy for the problems of the "mingling of functions" of money.[3] Gregg emphasized how the incongruity between money's functions as a store of value and means of exchange contributes to a confusion between money and wealth.

> In no other instance do we store up a great quantity of symbols to gain a great amount of the intangible reality which the symbol is supposed to represent; nor do we accumulate many measuring instruments to get a great quantity of the thing to be measured (Gregg 1963, p. 27).

WHAT'S WRONG WITH REGULAR MONEY?

Recall the similar argument LETS founder Michael Linton makes for the primacy of the exchange function in LETS. Mutual exchanges need not stop, he argues, just for want of a symbol, yet this is what happens when we define the symbol as scarce. We persist in regarding general purpose money as scarce because it also symbolizes stored value and the potential to make money from money. The multiple demands on money are so organized that local economies experience constant leakage of liquidity. Because of the centralizing effects of the monetary system, efforts to bring about local economic autonomy and community-building through the conventional "earmarking" strategies of community economic development are limited (Dobson 1993). A changed monetary structure is needed that would more fully disentangle the symbolism so that various "special purpose" monies could become political tools to serve specific needs.

Community currencies, as "special purpose" monies, are designed specifically to fill the circulation needs of local economies. They are not interest-bearing and not a store of wealth. They only circulate locally. In their restricted function as means of exchange, they are intended to increase exchange activity at the local level and support all of the positive cultural and social outcomes of greater local employment, mutual self-help and cooperation. As explained in Chapter One, the "money supply" in LETS networks is never scarce, nor is there risk of inflation, except through mismanagement, because credits are created automatically in the ledger books or computer accounts at the time of transaction. Credits are created and retired as a direct reflection of the level of trading: money comes into existence in response to need.

In the HOURS networks, managing the supply of paper money to avoid inflation is more of a concern. In the most successful systems, decisions about issuance tend to be democratic and conservative, and managers are accountable to the community of users. The level of HOURS trading is monitored so that the supply can be gradually increased in response to growing activity. Continuous re-circulation of HOURS, which never leave the community (except a small percentage as souvenirs), means that a small amount of money works hard to facilitate exchange. In principle, then, LETS and HOURS currencies are available in sufficient supply to match local needs with capacities to the fullest extent of people's willingness and imagination, or at any rate, so that mutual exchange is not limited by scarcity of money. Limitations on exchange arise from the sociological, not the design, aspects of community currencies.

Here I have sketched the broadest dimensions of the "problem with money" from the perspective of local economies and money scarcity. In the chapters to come I enlarge the critique from a gender perspective, but not by approaching the analysis in the problem/solution manner of some of the promotional literature. Instead, I treat community currencies as ongoing experiments, where the gender dimensions of "the problem with money" are discovered as members pursue overlapping sets of desires, for equity, community, freedom, security and meaningful work. Seen this way, community currencies are not a technical fix, but are complex approaches to the multitude of desires and lacks associated with the situation of monetary scarcity, which is a multilayered problem, at once systemic and personal and, as I will show, patterned through gender divisions. These gendered patterns appear when obstacles arise in the implementation of community currency projects.

Notes

1. In the course of our interview, Emily described other conversations and told stories of barter, dollar and HOURS transactions with women and men, including this same friend. In none of these descriptions did she put on a falsetto or baritone voice to convey differences in viewpoint.

2. Pierce, *et al.* use the term "subordinance" rather than "subordination" to insist that women maintain some form of agency, even in relationships of dependence on controlling men and in situations when they may be unable to leave abusive partners without support and intervention.

3. Gregg's book is significant because of its influence on some community currency leaders, most notably Robert Swann, who had a large hand in the origins of the current wave of local money experimentation in the U.S. Swann first worked on a scheme started by economist Ralph Borsodi in 1977 to issue commodity-backed money that was not pegged to the U.S. dollar (Borsodi 1989). He continued to promote community currencies, along with Susan Witt, through the E.F. Schumacher Society in Massachusetts.

Chapter Three

"Not a Perfect Leveller"
Revaluation and Gender Equality

COMMUNITY CURRENCY PROJECTS ATTEMPT to mitigate some of the systemic inequities of the conventional money system. Just by virtue of their scale, their restrictedness to the local, and their resistance to being used or accumulated as capital, community currencies are thought to prevent large differences in how much individuals may profit through participation in the schemes. Specific design features, such as using time as the unit of value, also promote equality. This chapter examines general desires for economic equality among LETS and HOURS members, as well as specific desires for gender equality. Of particular interest is how community currencies address the systemic undervaluation of "women's" work in the wider economy. To what extent does the design of community currencies advance standards and norms that support revaluation? To what extent do members support these politics as a step towards reducing wage gaps between "women's" and "men's" work?

Most community currency members that I interviewed hold egalitarian ideals, some more strongly than others. Not all seek gender equality. Women and men's attitudes in this regard show noticeable differences, as one would expect. This study, with its small sample, is not designed for carrying out systematic comparison of the beliefs of women and men in community currencies, but I will begin by briefly presenting the major observable differences in perspective. In the main part of the chapter I look closely at conflicts and dilemmas that arise for certain individuals as they attempt to put their egalitarian ideals into practice. A comparison of individual women and men matched by their advocacy of labour hour valuation will allow me to ask how tensions around egalitarianism relate to gender identities and ideologies.

As mentioned, my purpose in interviewing small numbers was not to describe gender differences, but to closely observe how individuals negotiate the constraints of gender as they create new monies. Nevertheless, certain patterns of gender difference emerged so consistently among my participants that I present them as qualified generalizations. The most readily observable of these gender patterns support the detailed analysis that follows in the last part of the chapter.

The first notable difference was that the women I interviewed were more likely than the men to express outrage at the gross inequities in wealth and power in mainstream society:

Leanne (HOURS member): *It's just so ridiculous that we're fighting [through HOURS] to get a minimum wage for people of talent to get twelve dollars an hour when some people are making twelve hundred dollars an hour. I mean, it's just crazy.*

Judith (LETS member): *I'd really like to get up on the soap box and get everyone's attention and say: [Stop buying] all those little things: chocolate bars, coffee, you know, newspapers and stuff like that. That's who's getting rich. And even your vehicles. Stop bitching about the person beside you who gets $500 welfare. Bitch about the General Motors executives who are making a million dollars a year salary, which works out to 400-and-something an hour and could put a lot of people to work.*

Indignation at such huge gaps in income was part of what motivated these women's involvement in community currency. Overall, the women tended to favour revaluation of "women's" work as part of a broad vision of equality, mutuality and interdependence. When making assessments of value, the women were more likely to compare "male" and "female" occupations. In addition, they tended to be sensitive to imbalances in exchange relationships so that when they were sellers, they appeared to be more willing to negotiate and to work out alternative arrangements, rather than stick to a fixed rate. For example, Judith, a horseback riding instructor, was occasionally sought out by promising young riders whose parents were unable to pay. In such situations she worked out a labour exchange in lieu of payment. The importance of the child's labour to her was not that it relieved her of work, but that it indicated the child's appreciation of the value of the lessons, her time, and the "horse's time."

For the men, comparisons used to determine relative values were more likely to be comparisons between themselves and their male peers within the network, or between the market value of different "masculine" activities in which they themselves engage. Differential valuation of "masculine" activities raised problems for some men about how to allocate their time and what services to offer for local currency. For example, Kevin offers manual labour (yard work, repairs, indoor painting, cleaning, sanding) in LETS for $10/hour. He enjoys the feelings he gets from manual labour, that he has "done a good day's work and [he's] learned something." Yet, the discrepancy between his "handyman" rate and what he could receive for computer services ($35/hour) leads him to question whether the work he actually prefers is "worth my time."

I present these general observations tentatively and note also the wide range of views presented by women and men that resist easy differentiation, as well as the considerable overlap in men's and women's perspectives. As I have explained, more important than marking gender distinctions among the members of community currencies is to examine tensions felt by women and men as they seek to realize diverse and conflicting desires for more equitable relationships and rewarding livelihoods. Especially important is to reveal the pressures on those who break with the conventionally-gendered patterns of desire and who try to implement alternatives.

The design of the community currency is one factor that shapes the politics of revaluation within the group. In LETS, the membership agreement requires members to value the greendollar as equivalent to the federal dollar. Members negotiate prices of goods and labour in dollar values, and rely on comparisons with federal dollar prices. In interviews with LETS members I asked if they support the idea of pricing on the basis of equal labour hours, as other community currency models promote. Keith's response represents the negative end of the range of attitudes towards revaluation in LETS. Keith is single, in his early thirties, works as a lab technician and prepares income tax returns for people in LETS. He initially rejected the idea of hour-for-hour payment, arguing that lesser skilled people would receive a higher wage than better skilled people within the same line of work because they would take more time to perform the same work. He suggested the example of a professional painter who could do the same job more quickly than an amateur but would earn fewer labour hours. I softened the proposition by suggesting that some negotiability could be involved to take into account skill differences, and asked him again about the principle of equality of labour time.

> Keith: *Well, it's a good idea because we're all—you only have so many hours in a day, right. Yeah, I guess it would be okay. If what you're offering was of equal value.*

Keith is hesitant, but willing to accept the principle of equal time—so long as it is balanced by the principle of "equal value." But "equal value" in his example of the professional versus unskilled painter is predicated on skill, competence and quality of work. The standard of performance is worked out through comparisons between workers in a predominantly male field. He does not appear sensitive to potential difficulties in determining what is of "equal value" when comparing different types of gendered work.

When asked outright, Keith could see no disparity in LETS in the value of what women and men offer, or in men and women's potential to earn. Yet, earlier in the interview I asked him how the prices in LETS compared with the wider economy. He responded, "From what I've seen from the food, it tends to be about the same or a little bit higher." He had just mentioned buying a container of home-cooked food that he thought was "kind of expensive for the size," although, "it was good, it was good." Pricing of food remained his theme as I asked further questions about prices.

> MB: I'm asking people whether they've ever experienced a time when arriving at the price of something was uncomfortable or difficult or problematic in any way.
>
> Keith: *I've never really had that.*
>
> MB: Looking forward, in what kinds of situations do you think there might be problems with coming up with a price?

Keith: *For someone trying to purchase my services, I think I've priced it so that if they can't afford it, then—Well, (pause) I think my price is fair and if they don't, then I won't work with them. That's all.*

I might haggle with some of the members over their prices. The food. I think some of it's kinda high. Like I could go to the store and buy stuff that's as good or better. There's other ways around town for getting discounts on things. There's, like for example, at bakeries and that, you can get day old stuff for half price. And in any supermarket you can get dented tins and that for cheap and stuff that is less than fresh. Pies and that, that are marked down. Go to the fresh fruit [section] and you can get stuff that's, you know, not quite fresh for a bargain. If I wanted something and I thought it was too high, I'd probably remind people, you know, that it's a bit too high.

The prepared food offered in Keith's LETS is only provided by women. Keith uses the price of stale or damaged, discounted, mass produced, mass marketed food as his yardstick for judging the price of food freshly prepared in the home by women LETS members. He does not compare women's labour to his own. On the contrary, he is unwilling to negotiate his rate of pay, but plans to "haggle" with women to lower their food prices. Time, skill or quality are not matters of consideration when it comes to food, a "woman's" product, as they are in the comparison of prices for men's painting. Keith's approach is consistent in that he uses market criteria to assess the price of food and his own prices as well. This use of LETS, however, replicates the bias in the wider economy that places a low value on "women's" time, skills and domestic labour. LETS does not appear to challenge Keith to revalue his own labour or the labour of the women from whom he buys. He feels entitled to set his own price or withdraw his service, as well as to "haggle" with women over the price of their offerings.

I do not present Keith's views as typical of the men in LETS, but use them to illustrate that the organization of LETS in itself does not necessarily promote revaluation. LETS provides a political space for revaluation that can be activated in potential, but revaluation is not automatic. In contrast to Keith, Kevin, mentioned earlier, expressed the clearest desire for gender equality among the men I interviewed in LETS. He offers two types of work: "household stuff" (yard work and other manual work) and "specialized work" (servicing computers), with two corresponding price standards. He mainly offers lower paid manual labour even though he has enough requests for the more highly paid work to do only that, if he so chooses. He makes conscious attempts to hire women for "specialized work" and pay them at least what he charges or what they ask, whichever is the higher.

In HOURS the labour hour is valued at ten dollars. This higher-than-minimum wage equivalent, as well as the promotional writings that accompany the directory, convey to people newly introduced to HOURS that revaluation is a strong collective ideal. Ithaca HOURS advisory board member Margaret McCasland explains:

> Margaret McCasland: *HOURS have that effect [of revaluation] because they are saying, 'Hey, this [HOUR] is an hour of your time.' And you start saying, 'What is the value of my time? What is the value of your time?'*

In practice, the value of products and services in HOURS is usually negotiated in dollars. Formal businesses, in particular, typically determine prices in HOURS through direct conversion into dollars. Many people treat HOURS as though they were dollar notes rather than denominate the money in units of time, especially when selling a product that already has a dollar price. Take Michael, for example:

> MB: How do you use HOURS in your prices? Do you use it as ten dollars?
>
> Michael: *Yeah, I do. I've thought a lot about that in terms of the scaling of it. Ultimately I've ended up being confused. It sort of seems like the initial intention is that an HOUR is ten bucks and your hour is an HOUR, my hour is an HOUR. But I don't know anybody who actually uses it as such...My feeling is that probably people re-scale it to whatever they charge...You always end up at the cash register sort of totalling the numbers. And then when you have these minimums..."Okay, I need to do a ten dollar purchase and I've purchased thirteen-fifty worth of stuff, so ten dollars out of 13.50 is 3.50 and I'm going to spend a quarter of an HOUR,*

which is 2.50. That means an extra dollar. That means I have to give eleven dollars cash"—and it's just that confusing.

When HOURS are paid as wages, rates are sometimes determined through conversion into dollar values. For example, employees at a food co-op receive HOURS as a percentage of their pay where the value of the HOUR is first represented in dollars and then added to the pay envelope. But often, wages are paid according to the HOUR-for-hour ideal, which results in a higher wage in most cases. Margaret McCasland tells the story of an early breakthrough in starting the circulation of HOURS in Ithaca that illustrates the potential of HOURS for wage revaluation. A projectionist working in a locally-owned movie theatre agreed to accept his wage in HOURS. This allowed the theatre to accept HOURS, which brought in additional business. The projectionist, by taking HOURS, raised his wage rate from six dollars an hour to the equivalent of ten dollars an hour.

In general, HOURS members were more likely than LETS to favour equal time exchanges and to perceive the local currency as promoting egalitarianism. For example, Lenore supports HOURS even though the demands of her paid and domestic work do not leave her time to participate fully, and the language lessons she offers have not been requested. She supports HOURS by purchasing the notes with federal dollars and re-spending them with local merchants. Part of what motivates this participation is her Bahai faith, which "unequivocally supports the end of all economic oppression and the end of extremes of wealth and poverty, and the like." In her observation, HOURS activities such as child care, which in the conventional economy would receive less than $10, receive an HOUR for an hour. When Lenore compares HOURS to the wage differentials in the wider economy, she is satisfied that HOURS advances her principles of egalitarianism.

Lenore: *It's not a perfect leveller, but I'm sure that it is levelling...It is conceivable that, for example, doctors could charge more than an HOUR for an hour, and they do...[Even so,] it's an enormous leveller. Like I doubt the best paid gets more than three times, possibly four times [more than] the worst paid. As opposed to, what?—300 times—you know, CEOs.*

Even if not all HOURS members share the same ideal of revaluation or interpret it in the same ways, those I interviewed were likely to have thought about the value of time and work in new ways as a result of HOURS.

Comparison of HOURS Artisans Seeking "New Harmony"

In Chapter One, I drew a parallel between Robert Own's Equitable Labour Exchange and present day community currencies. The common feature of the Owenite labour note and HOURS is their encouragement of valuation in time units rather than the national currency unit. This ideal, however, was incompletely realized in Owen's scheme, as it is in HOURS.

> The labour notes in fact remained tied to current market values...Theoretically the labour note was a device for exchanging goods with reference to the amount of labour in each, expressed in labour hours. But the definition of a labour hour was taken to be an hour's work at the standard rate of sixpence an hour, and adjustment was made for workers whose standard rate was higher. This in effect meant that the labour notes were not an independent currency but only a translation into labour time of values determined by that competitive economy which the Owenites rejected (Harrison 1969, p. 206).

To examine more closely the tensions that arise for the "new harmonists" in HOURS, and how these may be gendered, I now compare two sets of HOURS members: three women, interviewed as a group, and one man. These were among the most ardent advocates of egalitarianism that I interviewed. I have selected these members for comparison because of the basic similarities in their perspectives towards their work and towards the question of revaluation. The points at which their views diverge suggest that gender difference may be at play to some extent, but the finding of subtle difference is not necessary to demonstrate the salience of gender in the context of community currency use for these members. I note how gendered meanings are invoked at the point when members begin to express tension, ambivalence or contradiction around their own beliefs and actions towards the local money. Identifying gendered meanings reveals that

52

struggles to revalue work are also struggles to reorganize gender relations and, simultaneously, that gender relations structure and limit revaluation efforts.

Gil, Leanne and Sara all happen to be craftspeople who do various types of painting. Leanne and Sara live together and have a joint business making picture frames and designing greeting cards. They sell their work mainly in local craft markets. They supplement their earnings with part time wage work for small, independent restaurants and retail businesses. I interviewed the two women along with a friend, Helen, a graduate student. Gil is a fine artist and also a professional landscaper. Like Leanne and Sara, he is in a non-traditional family arrangement in that his wife is the primary income earner; Gil stayed at home to care for their two preschool children while his wife continued a professional career. After the children reached school age, Gil devoted more time to painting and to marketing his work through a craft cooperative. He also began to accept more part-time work in landscaping, trying to take jobs that are most challenging or aesthetically satisfying and in line with his environmental ideals.

Of all the HOURS users I interviewed, none stated unequivocally that HOURS should apply the principle of payment by labour hour for all categories of work performed and all categories of workers, but Gil, Sara and Leanne were among the firmest supporters of the idea. Gil and Leanne each told stories of how transactions with HOURS expressed their commitment to revaluation. In Leanne's case, she and another woman arranged a direct barter of an ornate frame for a woven blanket. She asked the weaver to estimate the number of hours it would take to make the blanket. Rather than simply agree to make a frame that would involve the same amount of labour, Leanne assigned a value of $20 to their labour hours and calculated the dollar price of both items—a wholly symbolic gesture, as both were equal. By doing so she wanted to reinforce that in the relationship of the two women, not only was the value of their time equal, but their work was undervalued by conventional market pricing.

Leanne: *I said something about, "How would $20 an hour feel? Would that feel okay for you?"...I was saying, "I would like to be paid $20 an hour if I could and I certainly want you to be paid the same." I was trying to do that philosophy.*

For his part, Gil was arranging to contract a woodworker friend to build him a specially designed easel and work bench in his studio. He would pay his friend, Dennis, in HOURS earned through his landscaping work. Like Leanne, the first step in his thinking was to convert the HOURS payment into its dollar value. Initially, he proposed to pay Dennis $350 in HOURS for the job:

> Gil: ...then I got home and I started thinking about it and I thought $450 would be better...He didn't say what his rate was going to be for this. But his time's valuable. He's trying to make a living but there's times when he doesn't have anything coming in and this would fit into his schedule too. So I think it will work out great. And we can collaborate on the project. And we like each other, so it's good.

In describing these same-sex exchanges, Gil and Leanne conveyed enormous respect for their co-transactor's time and skill. They emphasized the friendliness and equality of the relationship, and they attempted to encourage their fellow artisan to accept a higher rate of pay than either of them would have received in conventional market situations.

Although they were able to act on their desire for artisanal equality, both Gil and the women expressed dissatisfaction at the degree to which HOURS accomplishes revaluation of different kinds of labour. As they did, subtle differences in perspective became evident. I will present the women's discussion first.

Helen, Leanne and Sara

In the group interview, Helen, Leanne and Sara shared their frustration at the gap between their vision of egalitarianism and the ability of HOURS to realize it more fully among the members. Helen took the more moderate and pragmatic position, defending HOURS' official policy of not requiring high wage earners to lower their rates to a common scale. She explained that some professionals, such as lawyers, must charge high hourly rates to cover office expenses, employees' salaries and overhead costs. She explained that the goal of HOURS is to move towards equality by increasing employment and purchasing power, and raising the accepted minimum wage. HOURS will not necessarily "make stuff less expensive," but "what it does is make things more accessible because it gives people another source of income" and it raises the minimum wage to a "decent standard."

Sara and Leanne listened to Helen's explanation of the strategy, "in the early stages" of HOURS development, of suggesting that people "put a dollar value to it [the HOUR] so that people can convert it" and pay people as they would with dollars so long as they observe the agreed-upon minimum. "It's okay to inflate it. So, if you want to value somebody's hour of labour at more than $10 then we encourage that," Helen argued. For Sara, the goal of raising the minimum without trying to eliminate wage differentials altogether is too limited. She softened her disagreement by talking about it in the past tense while trying to accept Helen's explanation.

> Sara: *I think I was confused about—I think I thought that the goal was trying to equalize everybody, so everybody should accept one HOUR for one hour of work. And so I think I thought it changed the way we pay people...And then I think I thought it was kind of frustrating that some people are paid three HOURS for some line of work whereas some people just take one HOUR...Maybe I'm wrong or don't have enough information, but it seems to me that the HOURS are not doing what they are supposed to be doing if they are not evening things out. But maybe I have a misunderstanding of the whole concept.*

Sara asserted her desire for equality and her frustration with HOURS for not making a stronger attempt to "change the way we pay people" according to their equal worth as persons. She simultaneously retreated from this assertion, disclaiming her ability to understand the "whole concept," claiming to be confused, suggesting that her desire may be wrong, distancing herself from what she "thinks she thought." The failure of HOURS to fulfill her desire for symbolic equality she attributed to a failure of her own thinking. By saying she thought she was confused, she implied that her desire for equality may be confused or irrational.

Leanne responded immediately to Sara's admission of discouragement with HOURS. She explained her vision that HOURS would foster a sense of cooperation, egalitarianism and close-knit village life: Owen's "new harmony."

Leanne: *My utopian idea was that, you know, when you live in a village you need the people who chop the wood that goes into the wood stove to stay warm, and you need the person who's going to take care of your children, and the person who's going to bake and the person who's going to be a lawyer, or whatever, to represent your community's best interest in dealing with the outside communities. And in that sort of idea, I love the idea that everybody should be paid the same. It's a community all working together and you need everybody's piece. And so...that's what I was really hoping for in it [HOURS].*

Leanne hoped that HOURS would support a simple division of labour in which "male" and "female" skills are complementary, equally valued and rewarded. She went further than Sara in advancing the idea she "loves"—that each member makes an equally necessary contribution to the quality of life in community. Equal payment in HOURS would symbolically recognize and practically realize the inherent worth and equality of all members. Like Sara, however, Leanne distanced herself from her desire for a "community all working together" by speaking of it in the past tense and calling it "utopian."

Helen stated her sympathy with Leanne and Sara's feminist, egalitarian ideals, but argued that paying everyone on the basis of equal labour hours would not in itself realize them. She described a situation in which a predominantly male profession would still be better compensated than a predominantly female caring profession:

Helen: *It gets tricky because if I am a massage therapist and I rely on my body to do my work, then I can only physically work a certain number of hours whereas somebody who, for example, if I worked in the academy, I'm just using my brain and so I can physically work more hours than a masseuse.*

In this speech, like those of Sara and Leanne, the importance of gender to Helen's thinking is understated, but the implication of her message is that professionals and "knowledge workers" would benefit more from labour hour valuation than would manual workers, people in the trades and "helping professions" because they can work longer hours for pay. Because of occupational segregation, the disparity would be gendered. She contrasts two examples of gendered work: the academic (thinker, expert, works with brain) and the massage therapist or "masseuse" (care-giver, healer, works with body). She seems to identify more readily with the "feminine" side of her dualism (the first hypothetical "I" in her speech) than with the "masculine" side: the "somebody who" does "masculine" work (the second "I").[1] Her argument suggests that labour hour payment is not in itself a solution to the undervaluation of "women's" work. The revaluation project must go further than merely instituting policies of equal pay.

Helen's concern draws attention to a series of interrelated problems with the organization of work, gender and payment systems. The first issue is the sex-typing of work and sex segregation of the labour force. Sex segregated employment, not overt discrimination, provides the core explanation for wage inequality. A body of sociological literature shows how the designation of jobs as "women's" and "men's" and the recruitment of "suitable" bodies into work categories takes place through complex processes that are inseparable from processes of radicalization, class and family formation and the life course (Siltanen 1994). Segregated work categories are constructed so as to be difficult to compare, and so it becomes possible to undervalue some jobs relative to others. Not only are women and men concentrated within different occupations, but when they do work in the same census occupation, there remains near complete sex segregation at the organizational level, as women are channelled into "women's" organizations or given "female" job titles within mixed organizations (Bielby and Baron 1986). "Women's" work is typically associated with "caring," and its undervaluation is justified by considering it an extension of women's "natural" reproductive roles. The construction of work as "feminine" or "masculine" has less to do with the characteristics of the work or the workers than with institutionalized personnel practices and job hierarchies that reflect gendered power interests. When women move into occupations previously held by men, often the same work is re-characterized as appropriate to women while the occupation is hierarchically restructured and the feminized positions are paid at lower rates (Milkman 1987; Armstrong 1996).[2]

57

In principle, labour hours should eliminate the wage gap, but, as Helen's statement suggests, so long as work is sex typed, the gender gap is about more than wages; it is about privileged access to certain kinds of work. The inequalities between pink and white collar occupations include gaps in the intrinsic rewards of work (prestige, autonomy, opportunities for advancement, workplace safety, etc.), gaps in employee benefits and gaps in paid labour time. Many local currency participants are self-employed or hobbyists, people who are excluded from, or seeking alternatives to, corporate and bureaucratic hierarchies. For this labour force category, issues of employer practices are not directly in force, but occupational sex segregation affects the self-employed through gender bias in access to financing and markets, and in their relationships with other players in the industry. So, Helen's reminder that there are serious disparities in the privileges of work life, in addition to wage disparities, applies also among the self-employed.

The second issue Helen flags in her speech has to do with occupational identities. She assumes that she can be either a massage therapist using her body, or work in the academy using her brain, but not both. "It gets tricky," she says, and it is unfair. At the root of the unfairness is the expectation that everyone must identify with a single occupation. Utopian socialists and kindred movements, like the community currency movement, have decried rigid divisions of labour. To do only one kind of work is stultifying and a waste of human potential, especially if the work is unfulfilling and exploited.

The "trickiness" of narrow occupational identities, however, lies in the way such human loss is gendered. First, occupational identities mask the many work roles most people actually perform. Second, they easily tie into the dichotomized familial roles of homemaker and breadwinner. Women as wives and mothers, especially, perform multiple jobs without title or pay in carrying out responsibilities for childcare and domestic work. The prominence given to occupational identity obscures the unpaid work and longer average working day of women. Men appear to work longer hours when work for pay at one's main occupation is the work that counts. Family studies show that not only are wives' longer work-hours hidden as a result of the narrowing of "work" to mean paid occupation, but so is the extent of their contribution to husbands' occupational success and bread winning ability (Luxton 1980). Wives' unpaid work supports husbands' capacity to work long hours for pay. So, the difference in earning power of the massage therapist and academic in Helen's example may be based more in the way these gendered professions are tied to family and occupational structures than in the physical limitations imposed by the work. Helen's main point was that revaluation through labour hours would not bring about equality if the local money system did not also challenge underlying gender issues. Even if all members received equal pay rates, those who could work at better jobs and work longer hours for pay would be in a better position; and statistically, such circumstances are more likely to hold for men than women.

Community currencies do attempt to alter conventional labour force patterns in ways that address Helen's concerns. Women members often discover they have opportunities for practising skills of value to other members of the network, but of little demand in regular labour markets. HOURS and LETS listings carry all manner of offerings, including "wifely" services such as cooking, cleaning, laundry and ironing, babysitting and pet care, sewing and tailoring, gardening, aesthetic services (cosmetics, hair-cutting, home decorating), offering knowledge and advice (consulting), emotional support services (coaching, counselling), teaching, organizing homes and offices, organizing special events, shopping, driving, and so on. Women whose multiple skills have been subsumed under "caring" are often surprised to find that they have a range of ways to participate. As Edith, an actively involved woman LETS member in her 60s noted, "All the things I do...are part of the skills of a housewife...[LETS] is an outlet for your talents. It certainly gives you a chance to use those skills which are a woman's skills anyhow." Another member in her 50s, noting that her unmarketable "life skills" were just as much in demand among women as were her "professional skills," reflected, "You know how they say: women need a wife."

A women's only skills exchange circle in New York City, WomanShare, combines the accounting functions of LETS with the practice of labour hour valuation of HOURS. This community currency model goes further than LETS or HOURS in promoting the larger conditions for gender equity beyond the simple goal of equal payment. As founding member, Jane Wilson, explained:

> Jane Wilson: [WomanShare] *fosters a sense of being able to see people in a number of capacities. Like, she's a professor and she's also doing clean up at the pot luck. And so by using all the aspects of yourself and having them called forth and honouring them equally, you have the sense of a whole person. And as a result having a sense of community of mind, community of spirit.*

WomanShare promotes equity between "male" and "female" work within a community of women. Members do a variety of work that is equally paid by the hour, disrupts traditional sex-typing, and may have no labour market equivalent. The major difference between WomanShare and HOURS is that WomanShare is designed to be an enclave of one hundred women with a capped membership. The aim of HOURS is to become integrated into the wider economy as a complementary currency. Even though the majority of transactions in HOURS and LETS are of casual services, these systems actively seek the involvement of formal businesses. Given this goal of gaining broad-based participation, Helen sees limitations to implementing feminist-egalitarianism within HOURS:

> Helen: *I think what happens with HOURS is that we have this as a philosophical idea, but then it's operating within a certain economic system and so the two always clash. If somebody has to pay "x" amount of dollars in order to go to school to get a degree, it's not fair. Culture is factoring out and valuing one thing over another. That person doesn't have to [accept conventional values], but when you try to get people to take HOURS like that, a lot of people just wouldn't do it...When you use HOURS you come face to face with those contradictions.*

To transform the local economy with community currency requires making the widest possible range of goods and services available for purchase. Ithaca HOURS, for example, offers a bonus of two HOURS for anyone who signs up with a "priority offer," which includes:

...accounting, advertisements, appliances, architects, car repair, churches, day care programmes, dentists, doctors, electricians, engineers, firewood, glaziers, physical therapists, piano tuners, plumbers, refrigeration, snow plowing, veterinarians (HOUR Town, Feb-Mar, 1999)

According to this list, "male" skills and domains of work are most highly in demand. HOURS' success as an economic alternative depends on involvement by community-minded men, but as Helen admits, not all such men will be sympathetic to the goals of feminist revaluation. So, the goal of recruiting men places limits on the vision of egalitarianism HOURS organizers can aspire to. Women like Sara and Leanne who are aware of these limitations but continue to hold out a larger vision can only then see themselves as utopian and, even, irrational. As Helen put it, "HOURS [brings them] face to face with those contradictions."

Gil

For comparison, I will now present a man's perspective on revaluation, although this man is no more meant to be representative of all men in local currencies, than are Leanne, Sara and Helen meant to be representative of women. As stated earlier, I chose Gil because he shares Leanne and Sara's desire that HOURS standardize rates of pay across different types of work. Although Gil's and the women's positions with respect to labour hours are broadly consistent, I will argue that his is also a gendered perspective and, like the women, his participation in HOURS is constrained. To reiterate, the comparison of women and men in this and the following chapters is not concerned with delineating specific facets of gender difference. My main purpose is to underscore the significance of gender to political change projects, as women and men try to create alternative money practices from their own social location within a gendered economy.

Gil's initial assertion of egalitarianism is unambiguous. As with all members of my study, however, there are times when these same desires became tentative, contradictory or, even, are retracted at a certain edge where political ideals meet social obstacles. In the following passage, like Sara and Leanne, he states clearly his disappointment in the inconsistent practice of hour-for-hour payment in HOURS.

Gil: One of my initial concerns about joining was that people were not us-
ing it as "an hour of my time is equal to an hour of yours." You know, peo-
ple with the professional degrees were not treating it that way. Car
mechanics, da-da-da. And different work is valued differently. Agricul-
tural work is valued at, maybe, $5 an hour. I've worked in agriculture
over the years. I think [a local orchard] is paying an HOUR for an hour of
work, which is very honourable of them. But there are other people who
would use it as even a cheaper way to do business. And I have trouble with
that. I would like to see an hour of time is worth an HOUR. Just because
you spent two years in law school doesn't mean you should get $75 an
hour, or $150 an hour, or whatever they're getting in New York City.

Here Gil compares work by "people with the professional degrees," particularly urban lawyers, with people who do manual work, particularly rural
agricultural workers. Note how these comparisons are between categories
of "men's" work—women lawyers, car mechanics and farm workers not-
withstanding. On this aspect, his statement contrasts with Leanne's "village" speech in which she included examples of a wide range of gendered
work: wood chopping, childcare, baking and law.

Most important to Gil's thinking about HOURS is that it provides a
way to resist the narrow profit-seeking that he sees in conventional money
relations. He does not want HOURS to become another means of exploit-
ing labour and "a cheaper way to do business." When he says the orchard is
"honourable" for paying with labour hours, he is appealing to principles of
a moral economy, by which profit should not be the only aim of business.
He practices these principles in his own work life, and especially in
HOURS. For example, he refused a landscaping job for a real estate broker
who wanted to make only superficial improvements on the property for
profit on resale.

Gil's ethics seem compatible with Leanne's "village" ideals of cooperation between closely interdependent artisans, except that whereas Leanne
clearly envisions a feminist harmony of women and men, Gil's statements
make no overt reference to gender. The following statement, however, in
which he comments on the adequacy of the ten dollar-HOUR wage rate,
reveals masculinist assumptions cloaked within universalist discourse:

Gil: *I mentioned to [a member of the HOURS board] that we should in-crease the HOUR value. Because even ten dollars an hour I feel isn't a very good wage. If you're running a business...As a landscaper, as an inde-pendent person, I should be getting $20 an hour as a return on investment and all these things that go into it. Ten dollars an hour is an okay wage. It certainly beats $6 an hour.*

Here his reference to himself as an "independent person" as the basis for his entitlement to a higher wage is resonant with a discourse of individuality and independent personhood by which historically men have claimed rights of citizenship from which women were excluded. Feminist historians and philosophers have shown that the two core concepts of western en-lightenment thought, which run through humanism, liberalism and Marx-ism—individual moral autonomy and universal human nature—are masculinist concepts that originated as a particular class-based ideology (Brittan 1989). Carole Pateman (1988) argues that the concept of "the indi-vidual" in western thought, beginning with seventeenth century social contract theory, did not originally apply to women, and the language of "the individual" in contract law today continues to imply social character-istics associated with men. Such historical analyses make the case that ap-parently gender-neutral concepts such as "independence" and "honour" may be relevant to a particular version of masculinity.

That masculinist references appear in Gil's speech, and feminist refer-ences do not, suggests that his egalitarianism in relation to HOURS is more of a fraternal than a feminist ideal. Gil may well be in sympathy with the feminist politics, though with me he does not make such indications. Instead, he conveys how values such as honour and independence find ex-pression in HOURS. For example, he describes how, in HOURS, other craftsmen, such as his woodworker friend, Dennis, share his values:

Gil: *I have a friend, Dennis, who is doing HOURS. We were talking about a barter a few years ago. He gave me a photograph and said, "I want a painting of this."*

So just last Friday he said, "So what's your hourly rate for painting?" I said, "I have to keep it at twelve. You know 10 to 15 an hour. Just for the actual painting." He said, "You should be getting twice that." I said, "I know. But the market here won't bear it." He said, "When you finish the painting I'll give you the equivalent hourly rate for the amount of time that I put in my woodcarving." So it was kind of nice to say, "Oh, I respect the amount of work that you put into this." And I think that should be the understanding in economy.

Gil advocates an "understanding in economy" that respects the time and skill requirements for artisans to practice their craft. Even though the craft is not practiced to get maximal returns on time, in this account of a barter arrangement the hourly rate was important as a way for the men to indicate their equality, just as Leanne arranged an equal barter with the weaver. Dennis' question about his usual hourly rate also seems to remind Gil of his dependence on what the market can bear in his particular location, and of his desire for a better economic status. In the end, he and Dennis agree that market standards would not govern their dealings. The competitive market economy undermines the conditions for quality craftsmanship and artisanal independence, but craftsmen can support each other, at least, to sustain the values that undergird their work.

Gil's economic status as an artist can be associated with a longstanding counter-cultural tradition of masculinity. Michael Kimmel relates the history of masculinities to the history of major structural changes in gender, race and class relations. He describes the position of the "Heroic Artisan" as a masculine image through two periods in American history. First, in the post-Independence, pre-civil war period, the ascendancy of the figure of the "Self-Made Man" as the "dominant American conception of manhood" corresponded with the gradual economic and political dominance of the industrial capitalist class over farmers, shop-keepers and small producers (Kimmel 1996, p. 42). In the late nineteenth century, a second "crisis of masculinity" manifested when independent producers, already in decline, rapidly lost ground in the struggle against industrialization, urbanization and the system of wage labour (Kimmel 1987). Kimmel's historical perspective is valuable because under present day circumstances of structural change and contested identities, marginal and oppositional masculinities can be a resource in personal and political struggles. Gil seems to draw on the masculine image of the Heroic Artisan not because his views

64

or livelihood strategies are a throwback to an earlier time period, but as a creative response to his current situation.

As I mentioned earlier in the chapter, Gil is a rare example of an involved father who devoted himself full time to preschool childcare while his wife worked full time. Kathleen Gerson's (1993) study of the "changing contours of American manhood" argues that the economic conditions that have drawn women away from domesticity have not opened up the option for men, except under unusual circumstances. The obstacles to involved fatherhood she describes are "varied, widespread, and deeply embedded in how work, the economy, and domestic life are organized," but among them are social disapproval and ideological pressures. In her interviews she found that "involved fathers were keenly aware that others frowned on the choice *not* to pursue a career" (p. 245), and this awareness of a culture of disrespect for "nurturing" men was confirmed in interviews with "autonomous" and "breadwinning" men presented in her book.

In our interview, Gil discussed HOURS less in relation to his parenting than in relation to his occupation, which for many men is central to achieving a masculine identity, even if the occupation is counter-cultural. In both parenting and work choices, Gil renounces the "breadwinner" model of masculinity based on the male wage and the separation of work and household. He can instead claim an oppositional masculinity based on economic autonomy, ownership of his shop and tools, control over the organization of work, solidarity with peers and integration of work, family and community. Participation in HOURS not only furthers his opportunity to practice his craft, but politically furthers key aspects of a positive masculine self-image, such as independence, understood as non-subordination to the market economy and the conventional money system. I asked if he thinks of HOURS as money, and he replied:

> Gil: *Yeah, but it's different money. It's definitely different money. In some ways I look on it as our money. And we can do with it—we can create this system the way we want it.*

As a community money system, HOURS can be politically empowering for men as well as women. For those men like Gil who seek economic autonomy as part of how they achieve manhood, it would not be possible to

separate the ways that HOURS is a community-based money project from
the ways it is also a gender project. As a gender project, however, HOURS
is not without its tensions.

After asking Gil about HOURS as money, I asked how he found it
differed from using federal dollars.

> Gil: *I think it slows down the transaction. I don't know how to say...
> There's more value in the transaction. It slows it down. There's something
> about it. There's more value to it. And, you know, there's a lot of belit-
> tling of, like, "Oh, it's funny money." Not a lot, but you hear people say
> that sometimes. As kind of a joke, and you know, I've joked about it some-
> times too, but...I think it does...And I can't get more of a thing on it.*

Ambivalence emerges when Gil starts talking about the social value of
HOURS. On the one hand, there's value to the slowing down of transactions so that the exchange relationship receives more attention. Gil sees in
the ordinary human values of exchange within HOURS a quality of the in-
effable: "There's something about it. There's more value to it...I can't get
more of a thing on it." On the other hand, he is sensitive to others' belittle-
ment of HOURS, to which he responds by joining in the joking himself at
times. Much is at stake in this joking. Even though he is empowered to create a system of money that furthers his independence, use of HOURS simultaneously marks and maintains his marginality in relation to the
dominant money system, which, as I have been arguing, is also a system of
gender.

My question to Gil about the difference between HOURS and conventional money prompted his remark about the belittling. It is significant
that the view of HOURS as "funny money" triggers defensive joking, considering that, as Gerson's study attests, he could be vulnerable to belittle-
ment on account of his involved fathering on an even deeper level.
Considering that prowess with money is so key a feature of the "hegemonic
masculinity" of the Self-Made Man, movement towards community
self-reliance and egalitarianism with HOURS, another form of prowess
with money, could be a symbolically powerful assertion of counter-hege-
monic masculinity. The "funny money" joke drives home the contrast and
cultural imbalance between these rival visions of manhood. On one hand,

the Heroic Artisan is a valiant figure. On the other hand, mockery of HOURS exposes his subaltern status within a hierarchical system of masculinities.

In sum, visions of egalitarianism of Gil, Leanne, Sara and Helen reflect gendered conceptions of money and work. Though all advocated labour hours, the women were particularly aware of gender relations as a constraint on the present ability of HOURS to create equality. Their desire for gender equality in particular was sometimes isolating and frustrating because it brought them up against their limitations in gaining men's cooperation for a feminist agenda of revaluation. For Gil, use of HOURS to build a moral economy in which he, as a craftsman, would enjoy greater autonomy within a community of equals seemed to be in tension with a sense of being belittled. HOURS presented a potential for empowerment in terms of his class position, but involvement in HOURS was also a source of backlash that had to be neutralized by joking. The larger context of Gil's emotional relationship to HOURS is his commitment to shared parenting at a time when changing career patterns of women and men in families heightens conflict between dominant and marginal masculinities. Therefore, the women and Gil all experienced how the political culture of HOURS, which promotes revaluation, is in conflict with the dominant culture and conventional gender arrangements.

In the next chapter, I will consider the theory of the gift as I continue to describe how the contradictions between personal desires and social visions on the one hand, and the gendered structures of opportunity and constraint on the other, create tensions for community currency members, as well as openings for creative responses.

Notes
1. This is not to imply that she does not also identify with the "masculine" side. As a graduate student, she also relies on her mind.
2. Pharmacy and school bus driving are examples of occupations that were restructured with lower wages as they were feminized.

Chapter Four

"Currency of Friendship"
Community Currencies as Gift Economies

LIKE ROBERT OWEN AND HIS GENERATION of utopian socialist experimenters, leaders of the present day community currency movement seek to demonstrate political alternatives to market society. For past and present money reformers, thriving models of community currency would confirm that social life need not be dominated by scarcity, market-dependence and individualized competition. This was the reason Karl Polanyi celebrated Owen. Movements like Owenism could counter the prevailing economic creed that would subordinate human purposes to the imperative of market expansion. Polanyi wanted to show that new patterns of social organization are practical possibilities, and that economic alternatives, like the New Lanark and labour hours experiments, need not be honed off from the market system, but may be fostered in its interstices. "The characteristic trait in Owenism," Polanyi wrote, "was that it insisted on the social approach: it refused to accept the division of society into an economic and political sphere" (1957, p. 170). So Owenism provided for Polanyi an example of a movement that sought to enlarge the scope of political choice for economic life. It sought to restore the social fabric, and it refused to fetter human communities to unregulated markets.

Another source of argument for alternative social arrangements on which Polanyi also drew and which, likewise, inspires the practical work of community currency organizing is the concept of the gift economy. In the first part of the chapter I will examine how economic anthropologists, including Polanyi, advance the idea of the gift as a critique of market society, and how that critique is taken up by local currency practitioners as they attempt to institute a "parallel economy" (Offe and Heinze 1992, p. viii). As I turn to interviews with members in the second part of the chapter, I will show that the gendered construction of the gift has surprising implications for community currency organizing. It would be expected, given the "femininity" of the gift in western culture, that the more community money groups promote exchange in the spirit of the gift, the more women's position would be enhanced. Instead, I find many of the women in my study either resistant, or less able than the men, to define their community currency transactions as gifts. Consequently, men who invoke discourses of the gift are better able to achieve "big man" status. A straightforward reason for the difference may be structural: men generally have greater resources to mobilize for giving, but a fuller explanation, I suggest, has to do with the gendered opposition of the gift and money.

To briefly state the argument: in the wider culture, it is often appropriate for men to use money in gift relations, whereas women's gifts are more appropriately gifts of labour or gifts in kind. Women's status in gift circles depends more than men's on the personal content of their gift, the "purity" and altruism of their motives and the directness of the gift relationship, all of which have traditionally been achieved by keeping money and payment separate from gift and caring. The ambiguity of community currency as payment or gift, therefore, can be a source of conflict for women, as well as an opportunity for redefinition. For some women in my study, the gender of the gift provides a partial explanation for their pricing dilemmas and the "undervaluation" of their labour. The men in my study who desire to enter gift relations do not appear to experience these issues in quite the same way as the women. These findings help reveal how the gift economy is presently instituted within the market system, and point to the kinds of changes required for a thoroughgoing revaluation of the "feminine," as well as for achieving a better balance between market and gift.

"The Gift" in Social Anthropology and Feminist Theory

Community currencies draw on a tradition of western social theorists who advance the idea of the "gift economy" as a critique of market society. Enlarging the gift economy has been held out as a way to moderate the market system, protecting communities from excessive individualism, rationalism, instability and dislocation. There are two strands of research on the gift economy that are relevant to community currency activity: economic anthropology of the gift, and feminist analysis of women's caring and the household economy.

Early in the century two major works in anthropology—Bronislaw Malinowski's 1922 ethnography, *Argonauts of the Western Pacific*, and Marcel Mauss's 1925 essay, "The Gift"—attempted to derive the general principles of the gift economy from comparison with characteristics of western economies and western assumptions about the nature of "economic man." Malinowski's contribution to a "general science of culture" was a detailed study of the kula gift cycle of the Trobriand Islanders. An implicit objective of describing Trobriand Islander gift practices was to refute western assumptions about universal economic behaviour. Malinowski wanted to expose errors in the "rationalistic conceptions of primitive mankind," such as "the very incorrect habit of calling all objects of value 'money' or 'currency'" (p. 516). He presented the study, largely,

> ...in order to criticise the view about the economic nature of primitive man, as it survives in our mental habits as well as in some text books—the conception of a rational being who wants nothing but to satisfy his simplest needs and does it according to the economic principle of least effort. This economic man always knows exactly where his material interests lie, and makes for them in a straight line...In everything he devises and pursues, [economic man] has nothing but his material advantage of a purely utilitarian type at heart (p. 516).

For his part, Mauss carried out a similar agenda when he undertook comparisons of the Pacific coast potlatch, Melanesian and Polynesian gift institutions and descriptions of the gift in classic Hindu texts. He also concluded his essay with a moral argument for resurrecting the gift motif in western society to temper the rationalism and individualism of "economic man."

Polanyi carried forward the goal of broadening the western conceptions of economy beyond the "market mentality" as he developed comparative economic anthropology into a recognized field of study, its research programme captured in his well-known statement: "The market cannot be superseded as a general frame of reference unless the social sciences succeed in developing a wider frame of reference to which the market itself is referable" (1968, p. 174). Polanyi argued that a source of confusion and ethnocentric bias in anthropology lies in the double meaning of "economic." According to the "formal" definition, the problem of how to rationally allocate scarce means is the basis of all economic organization. Research through the lens of formal economics interprets material life in non-market cultures according to expectations of rational, self-interest maximizing behaviour. However, when such assumptions are held in check, and inquiry is framed according to the "substantive" definition of economy—the question of how people interact with their social and natural environments to create patterns of livelihood—researchers discover a great variety of forms of economic organization. Polanyi compared four general principles that may coexist in different degrees in any cultural context: exchange, redistribution, reciprocity and householding.

Where reciprocity predominates, it is impossible to speak of an economy as distinct from social institutions of kinship, religion, law and politics. This integration is what Mauss meant when he called the gift a "total social institution," and what Polanyians mean when they refer to cultures of reciprocity as "embedded" economies. Although gift cultures are diverse and the rules of the gift vary widely, it is possible to delineate the main features. According to Mary Douglas,

> The system is quite simple; just the rule that every gift has to be returned in some specified way sets up a perpetual cycle of exchanges within and between generations. In some cases the specified return is of equal value, producing a stable system of statuses; in others it must exceed the value of the earlier gift, producing an escalating contest for honour (1990, pp. viii-ix).

Giving a gift obligates the recipient to make a counter-gift, though not necessarily to the original giver. Reciprocity may be direct, intergenerational or generalized to the group; it may be balanced or asymmetrical. What matters is that the return gift, in its turn, must be passed along so that the circulation of the gift creates a web of obligations. Shared ethics of generosity and sacrifice maintain a continuous flow of goods and labour through the community. Since obligations and opportunities for giving extend over time, the gift requires and establishes stable, close-knit, long-term relationships of mutual aid. The gift is at once a system for circulating goods to meet the material needs of members, and a means of enhancing, celebrating and solidifying community. And it has a third, spiritual dimension, of which Lewis Hyde writes:

> Wherever property circulates as a gift, the increase that accompanies that circulation is simultaneously material, social and spiritual; where wealth moves as a gift, any increase in material wealth is automatically accompanied by the increased conviviality of the group and the strengthening of the *hau*, the spirit of the gift (1983, p. 111).

Individual status in the gift circle depends on timely and generous gifts that deepen others' commitments to the group, but this potential for status and belonging has a dark side. In some gift communities, material and psychological rewards of the gift reproduce social hierarchies. In such contexts, obliging others, and thereby becoming a "big person," is achieved through public performances of giving. Intense rivalry in giving, as well as conflict over acceptable acknowledgement of gifts, may be part of the competition for honour. Conversely, some gift communities may use levelling practices to prevent members from accumulating wealth, converting gifts to capital and acquiring the means to leave the gift circle. In contexts that discourage hierarchy, conspicuous giving must be avoided, and so must be demonstrations of individual "giftedness." Members must claim of their gifts, "It is nothing." Calls to conduct more of western economic relations as gift relations, therefore, must not romanticize the gift. Although cooperation and generosity may counter the negative effects of excessive marketization of culture, gift ethics can be used to reinforce systems of status, coerce behaviour or deny individual freedom.

Nevertheless, appeals for mitigation of the market by the gift, such as those issued by Mauss and Polanyi, continue to be repeated—here in a passage by Pierre Bourdieu:

> At a time when, to make it easier to blame the victims, there is a greater tendency than ever to pose political problems in moral terms, the cult of individual success, preferably economic, which

has accompanied the expansion of neoliberalism...masks the need for collective investment in institutions that produce the economic and social conditions for virtue, or, to put it another way, that cause the civic virtues of disinterestedness and devotion—a gift to the group—to be rewarded by the group. The purely speculative and typically scholastic question of whether generosity and disinterestedness are possible should give way to the political question of the means that have to be implemented in order to create universes in which, as in gift economies, people have an interest in disinterestedness and generosity. (Bourdieu 1997, p. 240)

Such calls as this by Bourdieu tend to construct the gift and market as opposed principles that require balancing. Gift economies are studied as "other" to market economies. Overlooked is how the gift economy is already present in market society, and how these contrasting spheres are actually interwoven and mutually dependent. Here is where the social anthropology of the gift must meet feminist analysis of domestic work. In the statement above, Bourdieu identifies the "cult of individual success" as the key cultural obstacle to collective investment in gift institutions. As I will show in the case of community currencies, paradoxically, the "feminine" ethic of care, which is a gift ethic, may be as much an obstacle to introducing complementary gift institutions as is "masculine" competitiveness. The cult of individual success cannot be moderated without also affecting the cult of familism, since these constitute the two sides of a dualism. In the end it is the antagonism between market and gift—their construction as a hierarchical dualism—which needs to be transformed. Any movement towards reforming economic structures and re-embedding economy, therefore, must also be a process of loosening the boundaries of gendered spheres of gift and market.

In the most urbanized, industrialized contexts there is a deep familiarity with the gift, which is often attributed to cultural memory of a less market-oriented rural past. Familiarity with gift relations just as likely derives from direct experience, since the gift is still the major basis of the family economy and the feeling-bonds between extended family and friends. Unpaid caring work in families and neighbourhoods is gift labour, and is especially the responsibility of women (Baines, Evans et al. 1991). Invisible to conventional economic measures, it is the foundation of material life, including all market activity (Henderson 1991). If gift labour within households was monetized, its value would many times surpass the largest sector of the money economy (Waring 1999, p. xxix). An estimate using Australian data shows the value of household production as approximately equal to the entire value of production for markets (Ironmonger 1996). And so political questions such as Bourdieu's of how to institute the gift as a larger part of civic culture, which is what community currencies endeavour to do, must consider that the gift economy is already present as the hidden, subordinated and undervalued root economy of market society.

As an integral aspect of household labour, it falls largely to women to support gift networks of kin, friends, neighbours and acquaintances, including friendly relationships with key service providers. Such relationships are maintained through gift practices that range from swapping goods and favours between households to giving emotional support and advice, and performing symbolic gift acts such as exchanging cards and remembering birthdays (Stack 1974; Di Leonardo 1987; Cheal 1988). These gift acts, in addition to their economic and social value in reproducing extended families and communities, are also ways that women affirm their gender. As Lewis Hyde observed, in western culture: "To deal with gifts—to receive them, to express the gratitude, to intuit and act upon their spirit—is a mark of the female gender" (Hyde 1983, p. 103).

To a greater degree than the men, the women I interviewed in LETS and HOURS discussed their sense of involvement in a gift economy beyond their participation in community currency activity. Women's statements of belief in gift relations reflected the theories of social anthropology, especially on its major point: that gift exchange is integrated with all aspects of relationship, and is not primarily economic in the formal sense. Compare an observation of anthropologist Claude Lévi-Strauss with the following remarks of LETS members. Lévi-Strauss writes of the gift: "Goods are not only economic commodities, but vehicles and instruments for realities of another order, such as power, influence, sympathy, status and emotion" (cited in Stack 1974, p. 42). LETS member, Rhoda, describes how she first came to feel connected with members of her church. She went to the kitchen after the service and helped put out coffee for other people:

> Rhoda: *The job is like a vehicle that helps transport your social interaction. The vehicle was there to give you the opportunity to connect. You didn't connect because the [task] was important. You connected because people were important, but you needed a way to do it. So the object of putting out the coffee...provides the means to connect, not the other way around.*

Another LETS member, Marion, reflected:

> Marion: *I always think if I help somebody they may help my children...Whatever we do, our children will get back. We don't believe in accumulating wealth illegally or at the expense of others. You not only feed your body, but your soul too. Material wealth is not the only important kind of wealth.*

The association of the gift with femininity, as I will show, is achieved by its disassociation with "masculine" market money. Consequently, attempts to introduce a gift currency are disruptive to a polarized gender order.

LETS as a Gift Economy

Leaders of the community currency movement promote their initiatives, foremost, as local solutions to unemployment and under used capacity, but also, increasingly, as a way to create a parallel economy with a gift currency. Michael Linton, for example, argues that monetization in the manner of LETS is appropriate to a modern form of the gift economy:

> LETSystems support a modern, individuated and familiarly monetized means to recreate tribal or village, communitarian economics. They create patterns of trading comparable to gift exchange networks, within our present communities, within our present urban realities, and alongside our present economic structure (Linton 1999).

Another champion of community currencies as gift economies is Bernard Lietaer. Formerly of the Central Bank of Belgium, one-time currency trader and general manager of a large offshore currency fund, Lietaer is

now one of the most prominent advocates of local currencies. In a published interview widely acclaimed in internet discussions, he explained
how community currencies can extend the gift community.

> Bernard Lietaer: I define my community as a group of people who
> welcome and honor my gifts, and from whom I can reasonably ex-
> pect to receive gifts in return.
> Sarah van Gelder: And local currencies can facilitate that exchange
> of gifts,
> Lietaer: The majority of local currencies I know about have been
> started for the purpose of creating employment, but there is a grow-
> ing group of people who are starting local currencies specifically to
> create community.
>
> For example, I would feel funny calling my neighbor in the valley
> and saying, 'I notice you have a lot of pears on your tree. Can I have
> them?' I would feel I needed to offer something in return. But if I'm
> going to offer scarce dollars, I might just as well go to the supermar-
> ket, so we end up not using the pears. If I have local currency,
> there's no scarcity in the medium of exchange, so buying the pears
> becomes an excuse to interact. (Lietaer 1997, p.36)

That Lietaer first speaks of how the exchange of gifts defines community
and follows with the example of community currency payment for pears illustrates how local currencies blur the gift/payment distinction.

Part of the problem in writing about such exchanges is that there is no
English word for a general category that could refer to either gift or payment. Translators of Mauss's essay retain the French word, "prestation" to
refer to "any thing or series of things given freely or obligatorily as a gift or
in exchange" (Mauss 1966). Malinowski also imported the word
"prestation" to make up for this "unaccountable and intolerable gap" in the
English language (Malinowski 1935, p. 204). In describing community currency situations, the generality of the concept of "prestation" is helpful for
avoiding the too-sharp distinction between gift and payment as found in
the social construction of market situations. Taking the example Lietaer
provided, consider how the same act, a "prestation" of local currency for
pears, can have different social meanings. Suppose Lietaer was already

lending his neighbour garden tools from time to time, and their relationship was established through other, perhaps unspoken, gift arrangements. If Lietaer were then to propose an exchange of community currency for the pears, the local money might feel awkwardly like payment. If, on the other hand, he was approaching the neighbour for the first time, the local money proposition might instead establish a new sense of reciprocity and of being connected within a larger gift circle.

In the analysis of interviews with LETS members that follows, the important question is not whether the community currency is a money payment, a money gift or a symbolic gift of another kind, for these are not absolute categories. Rather, I am interested in how community currency members construct their exchange relations with reference to gendered categories of "gift" and "money," how they use the ambiguity of the currency, and in what situations they attempt to reify its gift or money properties. These are the type of observation that can help answer Bourdieu's question of what is required to establish structural conditions for generosity in the pattern of a gift economy.

Observations about how community currencies interact with the gift economy are available within both LETS and HOURS, but the prominence of the issues and how they are framed differ because most casual work in HOURS is paid by the hour standard, whereas in LETS rates of pay are negotiated in each instance. As a result, LETS members more regularly and directly undertake the exercise of setting dollar values on work that would not otherwise be monetized. In these types of situations they must work through the implications of accounting for the meaning of the exchange. Because these questions of meaning are most important to this chapter, and for the sake of consistency, I will draw most of my examples from the LETS interviews.

In his writings and community organizing, Ross Dobson has promoted LETS as a gift economy and reflected on the cultural constraints of doing so. Here he refers to LETS "greendollar" accounting units as "Barter Credit" as he explains the main obstacle to expanding and generalizing the gift economy through LETS.

Our habit of not accounting for the gifts of time and service that we do give to and receive from friends and neighbours—the gifts which

LETS seeks to expand and generalize—results in some embarrassment when members are asked to acknowledge even such gifts with Barter Credit. It seems wrong to *pay for* such things (emphasis in original) (Dobson 1993, p. 126).

Dobson argues that "people are correct in resisting *monetizing* such exchanges," and so he seeks to de-emphasize the monetary aspects of LETS. He advocates a particular notation to distinguish greendollars from conventional money and, thereby, indicate that LETS is a gift community, not an alternative monetary system. Conventional money ethics teach that savings are desired and debts must be avoided, but Dobson urges that in LETS a positive account balance be referred to as "acknowledgement" of value received, and a negative account balance be referred to as "commitment" to return value to the community. The logic of the gift suggests that it is just as important to receive gifts as it is to give them because, in receiving a gift (and incurring a negative balance), one becomes "committed" to passing it on in the future. Dobson reports having had limited success, however, in conveying to critics of LETS the message that LETS credits are unlike conventional money: "This is an argument that, to date, has usually fallen on unreceptive ears. People value gifting, in our society, as an ethical expression that counters the dollar-values of the marketplace" (p. 126). So Dobson, and those like him who seek to promote LETS as a gift economy, actually share with critics of LETS the desire to "[counter] the dollar-values of the marketplace" through the practice of gifting. They are divided on whether LETS is an appropriate vehicle for the gift.

In the interviews for this study, women and men seem to hold the full range of attitudes towards LETS as a gift culture that Dobson has encountered. Women expressed the strongest opinions on these questions, however, and so I will draw from women's interviews to illustrate the range. First, there are those who would agree with Dobson that LETS is an opportunity to extend gift relations.

Louise: *There's a sort of a spirit of some people in LETS of trying to help people out...and there is some karmic law that if you help someone out it comes back in some way, and LETS is a refined system that keeps that. And people who join know that. They've experienced that in their life and that's why they've kept to LETS because they've seen it. I like helping people out too, when I hear someone needs something and I've got that extra something lying around.*

For Louise, LETS retains the spirit of the gift even though it "refines" and systematizes it. The formality of LETS only makes the rules of the gift transparent and defines the boundaries of the community, which is necessary to the establishment of trust and to bringing strangers into an extended gift circle.

Others view LETS as intermediate to gift and money exchange. This intermediacy creates the most uncertainty in relationships where gift exchange would be the norm.

Erin: *When some of my friends started joining LETS it became a little bit uncomfortable to decide if we would put a dollar value on a trade, something you might have just done, particularly with child care. You know, I would watch my friend's child and she would watch mine, and we sort of kept track of the hours so that we were even, but once we were both members of LETS we'd always pay each other in green [dollars]. But there was a change that happened once a currency got attached to it that made it feel a bit different, sort of more formalized and less a currency of friendship. And it became like a monetary value kind of thing. So for me sometimes that's a bit awkward with people—is it a favour? is it a friend doing something for a friend? or do we put a green dollar value on it? So there's times when that's a little bit awkward.*

When friendship, for Erin, is enacted and affirmed through exchanges of favours, she is unsure whether LETS credits can still be a "currency of friendship." Using greendollars seems to place the transaction in an awkward nexus between gift and money exchange that introduces ambiguity into the relationship.

Finally, some regard LETS as threatening to the gift culture because it is too money-like. Rhoda, for example, is a strong believer in the gift economy and the general precept that, "what is given comes back to you somehow along the line." At the time of the interview she was leaving LETS, in part because it did not fulfill her wish to live in accordance with gift principles as she sees them. For her, LETS approaches the gift model, but it is too formal and abstract. More serious, the pricing and accounting aspects of LETS exchange undermine the gift elements. Rhoda prefers "informal reciprocity," even though it is "a lot more messy." In gift transactions, she argues, "there are strings attached. But as soon as you affix a dollar amount and payment is made the string is broken." Significantly, those like Rhoda, who differentiate most sharply between gift and money, are also those who associate the gift most strongly with the feminine:

> Rhoda: *The crux of the matter is LETS is an artificial way of organizing something that we have done, especially women, since time immemorial. Women traditionally have organized the communities in the schools, churches, farming communities. If the barn burned down, do you think those men could have got together for a barn raising if the women hadn't organized bringing the families together, organizing the food, supporting the men? If the women hadn't been there, trust me, the men wouldn't have been there either. The men couldn't have done it without the women organizing the whole community. We have always done that.*

In the remainder of the chapter I will focus on comparing only those women and men who wish to use the community currency to extend the gift circle. Participating in LETS, as I will show, can make men appear more giving and enhance their status in the group, especially as it indicates their dissension with "hegemonic masculinity" (Connell 1995). But for women, becoming a "big giver" through LETS is more difficult. Some kinds of LETS trading actually makes them appear as less giving and disaffirms their gender.

The different structural locations of women and men in the wider economy may partly account for their differing capacities for making big gifts in LETS. For example, Sandra, who is unemployed, turned to LETS as an alternative to volunteering because she found that her contributions seemed insignificant in comparison to men she worked alongside. She gave the example of a man friend whose "capacity for volunteerism is astounding." She explained, "If I were working at a $30,000 a year job, I might just do it [continue to volunteer] for free." Men who were devoted to the same causes seemed to receive greater psychic and status rewards because they were able, as Sandra described it, to "put hours and hours and *hours* into it.

It's incredible." Sandra could not muster the same resources for giving to the causes and communities in which she wanted a larger role. To the extent that women are relatively disadvantaged compared to men in terms of money and time, they will have less opportunity to use giving to increase their status. Where giving is a contest, men as a group are more likely to come out ahead because of their ability to transfer higher earnings and resources into gifts to the group.

Another explanation of the difference in ways women and men create gift relations through LETS has to do with gender associations with money and the gift. Hanne Heen (1995) presents a complex analysis of the gender asymmetries in the meaning of money, which provides explanation for, among other things: why it is more commonplace for men than women to make gifts of their money in intimate relationships; the difference in cultural attitudes towards men and women philanthropists; why traditional courtship is a gift relation involving a man spending money on a woman; and why contributions and personal sacrifices to work organizations, in which men predominate, are thought to require monetary compensation whereas contributions and personal sacrifices to caring work, in which women predominate, are uncompensated or poorly paid. Her main argument is that men experience greater ease in transferring money between the market and the gift "spheres." The explanation draws on the western association of money with a particular concept of independence that arose historically in connection with the market system and general purpose money, to which men have had differential access. Heen takes up the argument I presented in Chapter Three that: "Historically the male was the prototype of the independent person" (73).[1] Though men and women both may use money to gain independence, so central is independence to the meaning of manhood that money represents male independence, is a condition for it and a means of achieving it. Consequently, a man may use money in personal gift relations because money stands for his independence, "one of the most precious assets of the male person." In a gift relation then, to a certain degree,

...money from the man is standing for him as a person in the relation. It looks as if money can be transformed from something used

81

in the market to a gift which then actually 'becomes' the man himself. In some aspects of a social relation, a man and his money are in-
terchangeable...Such connections are not possible to draw in the
case of women. Women are not defined as the same type of independent persons in the first place, and secondly, money can seldom
represent the woman as a person in a personal relation (pp. 82-83).

It is, of course, possible for women to use money as a gift, but the meaning
of such practices is not symmetrical for women and men. Money does not
represent a concept of female personhood; it cannot affirm a woman's femininity as it can affirm masculinity in men. It remains important that a
woman be personally present in the gift relation (p. 83).

Heen is primarily interested in the ongoing, everyday transfers or
transactions of two types of values between the "spheres" of gift and market: internal values such as love and friendship, and external values such as
"economic values and success with regard to money and career" (p. 74).
The key distinction and the reason for there being "transaction barriers"
between the two is that "internal values acquire their worth mainly from
being outside the market sphere, and not being for sale" (p. 76). Nevertheless, transformations of these values from one sphere to the other occur all
the time between people and also within the individual according to intricate, gendered rules. She goes on to analyse how these cultural rules are
changing as women attain more "external" values and the degree of economic dependence on men declines.

From a similar perspective, I am interested in how community currencies also provide a set of circumstances in which rules governing transformation of values may change to allow for expanded notions of masculinity
and femininity. Next, I will identify some of the common understandings
within community currencies that help ensure that people follow through
on their obligations in gender appropriate ways. I am not referring to formal rules and expectations, which are made known through the newsletter, the membership agreement and personal contact with key people in
the group, but to informal expectations, which are made known, partly,
through stories passed from member to member. Scandalous stories focus
on extremes of behaviour to define and reinforce the general principles of

what is acceptable behaviour. Such stories are probably based on incidents involving actual members, but are embellished as they circulate. I heard two types of stories that enforce a gift attitude in LETS by informing members that certain forms of acquisitiveness are frowned upon. These stories have different messages for and about men and women.

The first type of cautionary story is about men who attempt to profit from LETS. In one LETS group, I heard versions of the same story from three different members about a skilled tradesman who charged his regular rate in federal dollars and an *additional* percentage of "green" to LETS members. In another LETS group a similar story was related by two members about a man who purchased an item from a woman for its regular retail price at 100% greendollars. The man re-sold the item at twice the regular price in greendollars. That he was able to do so indicates that the "market" value of LETS credits is about fifty percent of the federal dollar, even though members agree upon signing up that they will value greendollars as dollars. The man violated the group's agreement to uphold the value of the internal currency on par with the dollar, and he capitalized on the original seller's willingness to do so. A third example is a story a woman told me about exorbitant charging by a man for computer services to another woman. The woman paid $800 greendollars for a basic service that my informant believed she could have done on her own with minimal instructions.

The message of all of these stories is to beware of overcharging by men and to not trade with those men whose main motive seems to be the highest price possible. If you are a man, the message is to not treat the network merely as an opportunity for profit. The stories were repeated by men and women, and directed at everyone in the group, but they carry a secondary message about men. They suggest that men will attempt to exploit the advantages of membership in a gift community for individual pecuniary gain. Keep in mind that other kinds of gain in LETS are appropriate. Positive stories abound of all manner of accounted and un-(officially)-accounted gifts received through membership, such as a bicycle lent for a summer from one LETS member to another who was a newcomer to the city. Such personal gains are appropriate for boasting, but self-garnered pecuniary gains are not.

The second type of story is specifically directed at women. Based on my interviews, this type of story is rare compared to the stories of men, but it may have wider circulation. The following story was re-told by a woman member who heard it from someone else, and so on. The teller, Erin, I introduced earlier in the chapter. She passed on the story after describing the awkwardness of LETS trading with her friends. She first set it up by suggesting that it is one example of a general type of story she has heard:

> Erin: *And I've actually heard stories of other people saying that—there's one story about someone being offered cookies, and saying, 'Oh, thank you,' and eating some cookies that were being offered and then afterwards being told, 'Well they're fifty cents green each.'*

The first offence in this story was that the cookie provider did not inform the recipient that she intended to receive credit for the cookies. Had she done so, the cookies may have been refused in a way that gift cookies would have been difficult to refuse. The second and more serious offense, given the context in which Erin tells the story, was that selling the cookies redefined the relationship from one of friendship, in which the cookies were an intimate "currency of friendship," to one of balanced exchange appropriate to a conventional monetary transaction.

On first hearing, the story of the woman who charged for cookies seems to parallel the stories of men who over-charge. Both are taking LETS as a money system and attempting to attain the maximum price for their product. The difference is that in these stories acquisitiveness is expected in men. LETS asks men to moderate behaviour which is taken as commonplace for men outside of LETS. The message is that in LETS different norms for men prevail than in their conventional dealings. The stories also suggest that the switch from the dominant pattern is quite possible for men. Indeed, a number of men made it a point to say they are not motivated by money-making. Often men referred to the rural experience of barter, borrowing and mutual aid as an available cultural model of masculine gifting.

The story of the cookie sales-woman, on the other hand, is more scandalous because it tells of a woman who not only defied the norms of LETS, but also of her gender. The stories of men encourage change, but the story of the woman warns women *not* to change from their accustomed role as givers. It discourages women from using LETS to replace services they would normally provide in the name of friendship. Some women, in their trading experiences, have received similar discouragements from monetizing gift labour. For example, Cheryl, a former LETS member who now uses HOURS, had ongoing difficulty receiving credit for work she otherwise might have done as a neighbourly gesture.

> Cheryl: *I had trouble with providing services that were kind of informal, but where the person said, "Oh, thank you." And even though they contacted me because of LETS, they didn't acknowledge. Like, I was offering advice on things. They'd call up and take 45 minutes to an hour-and-a-half of my time and not credit it. Cause it's just advice.*
>
> MB: Your recourse is, when you get your statement, to call them up and say, "Hey, remember...?"
>
> Cheryl: *You see, I felt bad because the person I gave advice to is somebody I knew, and if they hadn't called me up through LETS, I would have given it for nothing. So I felt weird about it.*

"Just advice" in a market context can be known as "consultation," and can be highly paid. Yet Cheryl does not see herself as an expert, and the value of her time and knowledge is not culturally recognized. Cheryl's "bad" and "weird" feelings stem from her sense that because she was contacted through LETS in response to an advertised offer, she ought to have received acknowledgement for her service. However, she and the other member knew that in another context she would have given the advice for "for nothing." She was unable to redefine the exchange as one for which she could receive greendollars as a formal "acknowledgement," in addition to the "thank you."

These stories of asking for greendollars for cookies and advice suggest that, for women, receiving LETS credits may be especially disruptive of prior or assumed gift relations. This will be my argument in the remainder of the chapter: men more easily define their actions as gifts; women's gifts tend to be taken for granted. I will next illustrate these themes of definitional work through stories of four LETS members who desire to become "big" givers in the LETS community. As in the previous chapter, I present these stories as comparisons between matched pairs. First, I will describe Ron's purchase of cleaning services from Lesley, and Geraldine's purchase of craft work from Phil to compare a man and a woman negotiating LETS exchanges with members of the other sex. The second set of stories, of Caitlin and Kevin, reveals gendered issues of price-setting. The four stories suggest that men experience relative ease, first, in making gifts, second, in defining themselves as dominant in the gift relation, and third, in avoiding guilty feelings when negotiating and setting limits on their giving.

The Gender of the Gift in LETS
Ron: "A personal advantage thing"

Ron is an avid barterer who attributes his competence at making deals to growing up poor in the Maritimes, and to the influence of his mother, who could "squeeze a penny until it bleeds." He is in his late 40s, married without children. His overall livelihood strategy is intricate. He patches a dollar income from several sources, mainly, his home-based photography business and a disability allowance. In addition to his dollar income, he participates in LETS, he sets up complex three-way barter arrangements outside of LETS, and he routinely does "freebies." He keeps accounts in three currencies: cash, "trade" (such as used cameras and equipment), and LETS credits. To give an example of one three-way barter, Ron does bookkeeping for a massage therapist in exchange for her services, but he does not use these services himself:

> Ron: *As a matter of fact, [my dark room supplier] is starting to use her* (laugh). *He's got a very bad back so he's actually using her services, and I'm largely paying him in her services because he's using her services more than I am.*

For him, LETS is "a personal advantage thing." He likens his LETS account to a money account: "It's a Visa card. It's a bank account." Contrarily, he says: "Money is barter. I'm trading a promise to pay. If you read your dollar bill it's a promise to pay signed by the federal government...When I do a LETS transaction, I'm trading my labour or goods for a promise to pay from a third party. There is no difference." In other words, although Ron thinks of LETS as money, he rejects sharp distinctions between monetary and non-monetary means of livelihood, and he sees continuity between alternative forms of payment. As circumstances with his clients and associates change, he determines whether he will conduct business in cash, LETS credits, barter or gift exchange. He is highly aware of the extent of his reliance on non-monetary strategies, and spoke with pride of his ability to mobilize others' labour, coordinate complex exchanges and to make them work to his advantage.

When asked to describe a satisfying LETS exchange, he told of hiring Lesley to scrub a grease-splattered wall and floor in his kitchen. He described this exchange in the language of the gift. In a remarkable discursive feat, he conveyed the sense that the gift exchange was balanced; in addition to being highly pleased with the work she had done for him, he was also entitled to gratitude for what he had given her through their arrangement.

Lesley carried out no ordinary cleaning job. Ron described it as "killer work" and "heavy sweat type labour," comparable to scraping paint off a wall. She "took care of" the floor and wall over the course of six four-hour days. She and Ron did not openly negotiate how much her services were worth in greendollars. According to Ron, she did not quote him a price for the job or state her hourly rate or give him any message about what she expected for the work. As the job progressed, he "transferred an amount" into her LETS account. More specifically, in increments of GR$100, he gave her a total of $400 greendollars at his discretion. He only once referred to these amounts as payment, when he commented on his capacity for generosity: "I may have paid her more than I normally would have for that kind of a job because I had greendollars to burn at the time." He based the rate on what he thought commercial house cleaning services would charge, even though he also agreed with Lesley's reported pronouncement: "She says, 'You couldn't get Molly Maid to come in and do this.'" But he was assured that the amount was fair because "she's never complained about it."

Ron's relationship to Lesley helps clarify how he achieved a sense of balanced reciprocity in this exchange. She is a fellow Maritimer whom Ron has known as an acquaintance for several years. He thinks of her as a friend, and she is also a friend of friends. She works in the entertainment industry; Ron gloated: "I had a famous [professional] scrubbing my floors (laugh)." For the past two years he has worked as her bookkeeper. She pays him in dollars. He knows how much she earns, and he claims to have persuaded her to raise her professional rates. He also uses her specialized office equipment from time to time in a LETS greendollar exchange. Occasionally she invites him to dinner.

Ron explained why a "famous" professional woman whom he knows personally and professionally would choose to do heavy cleaning for him through LETS. As his story goes, he had mentioned to her in another context that he was looking for a cleaner in LETS. She was not listed as a cleaner, but offered to do the job. He described her offer almost as though it was her request that he was obliging:

> Ron: *She said, "Oh, at the moment I have some frustration I need to work off, and I have a large negative balance. How about I do it?" I said, "Sure." So in she came and did it.*

Later in the interview, Ron again emphasized Lesley's "need" to scrub, and his provision of a challenging project:

> Ron: *In her particular case, she just wanted to get some frustration out, so a good scrub would work and her house was immaculate. So she just needed another one to work on.*
> MB: So that's what was motivating her?
> Ron: *That's what was motivating her. It was an opportunity to both pay down her debt to the system and burn out some frustration.*

So, from Ron's perspective, he helped his friend with her emotional problem by offering her the "opportunity" to work for him. "It was exactly what she wanted at the time," he insisted again. In this way he deflected that component of her service which was a gift, particularly her availability, her symbolic levelling (or reversal) of their class difference and her acceptance of his discretionary remuneration. He spoke of their exchange as a fortuitous coincidence of wants, and a transfer of gifts. To balance his own account of himself as generous with his wish to be known as able to strike a good deal, at the end of his story he added: "And, *and*, I learned some really good cleaning techniques from her too, which I didn't previously know."

Geraldine: "Helping each other out"

Whereas Ron presents himself as magnanimous in his deal-making, Geraldine seeks to be generous through her acts of helping. She is a part-time home care worker in her 50s, unmarried with no children. She devotes much of her energy to social justice work. The opportunity to help other people, whether through offering her services or affirming others in their work, attracts her to LETS. For example, one of her most satisfying exchanges was giving Spanish lessons in her home to a doctor who works with a Spanish-speaking immigrant community. "It was very nice be-cause...it's like being with friends and helping each other out." When Geraldine makes purchases, she also enjoys the sense that even as a buyer she can "still help someone else in their work, in the things that they do and enjoy."

Geraldine told one story of an exchange with a man in which she did not have the satisfaction of feeling as though she helped the other person. She knows Phil through their joint volunteer work in community organizations. Geraldine had seen Phil do a simple craft for a group of children. The craft has negligible material costs, and so she offered to buy some pieces through LETS. But when Phil delivered the new work, she realized he had done far more intricate work than what she had expected. She was dismayed at her sense of having paid him too little in greendollars:

> Geraldine: *You could see the love that went into it and the amount of work. And I ended up giving him a [green] dollar per [piece] and now I feel like an idiot...But he accepted that, you know? But I feel very guilty about that one (laugh) because I think they were worth a lot more.*
>
> MB: How did you arrive at that price?
>
> Geraldine: *Okay, this particular individual never said this much or that much, you know. Just what would you like to give (laugh). And I guess at that time I found myself, you know, not having much money around and, you know, in a difficult period. And I wanted to give about ten [green] dol-lars and I did that but the [original craft that he had done] seemed a lot simpler. But when I saw these [pieces] after we contracted and he was re-ally deserving a lot more than that. He put more into them. I was going by (pause) contracting for simple [pieces], versus all the work that he did in*

painting every single one of them. So then I felt really bad about it, you know, guilty because I felt he deserved a lot more. So, I'm still guilty.

Twice I asked Geraldine to confirm that Phil had agreed to her price before he made the craft. She replied by elaborating on how she had arrived at her original price, and how Phil had given her something beyond her expectations. By asking to buy his craft, she had intended to give it recognition, and thereby "help" Phil in the manner she sees herself helping other craftspeople in LETS. But Phil had outdone her gift. His larger gift obligated Geraldine to reciprocate with further trading.

Geraldine: *I tried to make it up one time. We traded again. It was for ideas for games and activities. He's got lots of them. He gave me one or two ideas. But he asked for ten dollars and I thought, "Oh that's not too bad." So, I figured it was making up a little bit for that.*

For Geraldine, this one exchange was not enough to restore the balance in their relationship, and so she plans to make a demonstration of Phil's craft work at a LETS trading meeting: "See the beautiful, wonderful [pieces] he has done," she plans to tell people. "Oh, they are just gorgeous."

Unlike Ron, who was able to continue to transfer greendollars into Lesley's account until he felt he had somewhat exceeded the value of her work, Geraldine did not consider it within her power to balance the exchange with Phil. By accepting the gift and the guilt it produced in her, she allowed Phil to be the "big man" in the exchange. In both these stories, as is typical of gift exchange, the "seller" did not set the "price"—rather, a gift was offered (extraordinary gift acts of cleaning and craft work, in fact), and it was left to the recipient to respond with a counter gift that at least equalled or exceeded it. Neither Lesley nor Phil contested the greendollar amount they were given because a larger contest was underway in both transactions. In these cases the man prevailed: Ron in defining his counter gifts as balancing, Phil in seeing that Geraldine's sense of personal indebtedness extended over time.

Caitlin: Not wanting to ask too much

Caitlin is in her mid-twenties, single, and a recent university graduate in the social sciences. She now works for a small catering company. From the outset she entered LETS with a view to giving. In the first year she paid her membership fee as a donation, not expecting that she would use LETS, but wanting to support the organization. Gradually she began to find ways to participate. Pricing her labour, however, is her major difficulty in LETS. As she put it, "I'm not good at pricing things. I much prefer to let other people do that."

Caitlin offers baking, cooking and children's entertaining through LETS. She bakes often, and gives away about three quarters of her baked goods to friends. Her reasons for giving her baking away: "Because they're my friends. Because they appreciate it." When it comes to LETS exchange, however, she has no simple way of determining a price for her baking, and this is a source of considerable tension. Much depends on her relationship with the LETS member to whom she is selling. She usually allows the buyer to define the terms of the relationship and take the lead in negotiating the price:

> Caitlin: *If it's somebody that I just know through LETS, they might feel more comfortable saying, "No, I won't pay that much," or they might feel less comfortable and feel obligated to give me the price I ask for. It can go either way. You can feel the obligation to pay somebody what they ask for or you feel you know them well enough to say, "I'm not going to give you that [price]."*

As for Caitlin herself, "If I know somebody, I'm much more likely to say, 'Well, just buy the ingredients and I'll make it, but you don't have to pay for it.'"

She tells of a story of cooking for a fund-raising event for a volunteer organization that was a member of LETS. She had expected to be paid for her labour, but in the end was offered greendollars only to cover the ingredients. "It wasn't a big deal," she remarked. She felt she should have made her expectations known beforehand, but, she repeated: "It wasn't a big enough deal to say, 'Make a change.'" Had there been any negotiations at all about what she would receive for the cooking? I asked.

> Caitlin: *I probably could have. But I never would.*
>
> MB: Why not?
>
> Caitlin: *I just don't. Ever (laugh). It is really, really hard when it happens. I hate it. I hate negotiating a price with somebody. I don't know*

why. I guess with other people I don't want to do that because I don't know how much that really cost in terms of the tools and hours and what-not. And in terms of negotiating when somebody's buying from me, I don't want to feel like I'm asking too much. It's bad, I know.

MB: Why do you think it's bad?

Caitlin: *I don't want to worry too much about undercutting somebody else when I'm buying something from them, and I don't like to think that I'm charging too much for something. So it's sort of like, it puts them in a better position than me.*

Caitlin is ambivalent about putting others in a better position than herself. She does not like receiving too little reward for her work. She talked of instances where she would prefer to receive more for her baking and also for her children's entertaining. However, she also wants to appear to be generous and to be known for her generosity. One time she entered a negotiation to perform at a child's birthday party. She offered a price, which her co-transactor asked her to lower. She immediately consented, but then felt guilty about her original price: "It was like, 'Oh my goodness, how does she feel about me asking for that much money?'" Her preferred solution is to set prices with the help of friends:

Caitlin: *It's always like this big fight, where somebody is always saying, usually the person who makes it, "No, I can't charge that much!" And everybody else is saying, "You're not selling that unless you sell it for at least this much." And they're like, "Oh no, I'll sell it for this much less." So it's always like that.*

Other women LETS members told of similar price-setting strategies. For example, Julia has sold casual labour as a kitchen helper.

Julia: *It's an unusual thing for me to be selling anything so I had to adjust myself to being the seller, asking myself whether people really want what I have, whether it's a good value, whether my price is fair, I'm giving people good value. My tendency is to undervalue my time or my services, so my price was fairly low and it was only as high as it was because other people said, "Look, you gotta charge more than that."*

And Marion, likewise, does not like to price or sell her homemade preserves:

Marion: *It is so hard because I don't want [people] to feel that "She is trying to take advantage of my smiling at her." I want people to be happy to see me, not think, "Oh, she wants me to buy something I don't need."*

The performance of asking others to set the price allows the women to preserve their self-definition as givers and care-takers of others' feelings and interests in the exchange while also allowing them to seek fairness.

Kevin: Supporting the community

Kevin is in his early 30s, single and self-employed as a computer consultant, currently in a lucrative contract. He joined LETS because of his interest in social justice and economic alternatives. He continues to search for a greater degree of engagement in gift communities through his volunteer work for social justice groups, his housing cooperative and his involvement in LETS. He idealizes informal gift arrangements:

Kevin: *What I see as even better than a LETS system is something where—which already almost happens in the building I'm living in right now, in the co-op—is that people who I'm closest friends with, we just do stuff and we don't worry about it. There's no formal system of exchanging. "I have this many credits, you have that many. I have to pay you for services." We just do stuff. I know when I owe somebody, it's just like, "Okay, come on over for dinner." It's not even an "owe" thing, it's more if I see somebody that needs something, I'll offer to do it. There's no trading or any kind of negotiation or anything.*

Kevin's capacity for giving is most evident in the story of his purchase of graphic design through LETS. He maintains a web site for a natural food store and posts weekly specials in exchange for fresh produce. The arrangement had been ongoing for more than two years. It was complicated when the web site needed a graphic overhaul. Kevin found a professional graphic artist through LETS. He did not comparison shop, but hired the artist because she is a LETS member and fellow activist. He had not met her, but her name was familiar from newsletters, and he knew that she volunteers for social justice organizations Kevin also supports. Originally Kevin and the artist estimated that her work would be worth $200 to $250 greendollars. But the project took longer than she estimated, and she was doing good work, so Kevin asked her to do more, until finally she had done $500 worth of work, based on her professional hourly rate. Kevin thought it was fair to pay her this amount. When I asked about the process of working with her on the web site, his payment and her charges were not what he recalled first. Instead it was the satisfaction of seeing connections being made as a result of the work:

> Kevin: *This was part of a specialty site for [the food store]. So she was actually keen to do that because her mother is a gourmet cook, so she sort of got a chance to talk to her mother about some of the [unusual foods], so that was neat for her.*

Kevin did not recover the $500 from his client, the food store owner. He admitted with nonchalance: "So I guess, looking at it from a hard-nosed business point of view, I'm out 500 bucks." But, he rejects the hard-nosed point of view. The owner is pleased with the graphic art and the web site is attracting attention. Kevin regards the web site as a show piece: a gift work in itself. He hired and fairly paid a LETS member who, herself, does volunteer work for important causes. Within months he had raised his balance back to zero by doing computer services and casual work at $10 an hour for other LETS members. He admitted that at times he questioned whether he should raise his rates, but not as a matter of self-worth or the value of his time and skill (he can earn $100/hour for his paid consulting). Rather, he is willing to work at a nominal rate only for those members in LETS who are also giving to the community.

> Kevin: *I don't know if I should raise my rates though. Basically it was, I don't know, [there are] some people that maybe I wouldn't do the work for, that kind of work, just cause I don't feel like I'm doing it for the right reasons. Cause if it's just this guy selling his house to make some money for himself, I don't know if I would do that. Whereas [names of LETS members], I worked in their kitchen. Like I knew them, I knew they traded food, I knew that they do other stuff, and it's good for the community, so I feel, I just feel good about doing it.*

Kevin's pattern of gift labour is clearly intended to support a community that is involved in social causes and is connected through a web of gift relationships.

Comparing Caitlin's pricing conflicts with Kevin's nonchalance over his deliberate gift labour raises further questions about the "undervaluation" of women's work examined in Chapter Three. Here is an example of a man and a woman who consistently offer low rates and attempt to "put [others] in a better position than [themselves]." Should their low prices be taken as an indication that they undervalue their work?

Women LETS members refer to their own "undervaluation" of their work as an explanation for why they set low prices. Recall Julia's claim: "My tendency is to undervalue my time or my services, so my price was fairly low." Yet when men set low rates, "undervaluation" does not seem to be a fitting explanation. For example, when I questioned Geraldine why she felt bad for having given Phil the price he had asked, she momentarily considered whether Phil "underrated" himself or his work. She concluded that this explanation did not apply in his case.

MB: He had agreed to that though?

Geraldine: *He did, yeah, but then (sigh), knowing Phil, I mean, you have to know him. And then realize that he's not going to ask any more. Some people maybe have that. You have to be careful because they always underrate themselves in their work. So that's part of it. People maybe don't value their work as much. Well, not that he does, but I think he's a different individual, like in terms of relationships and his work. It's not that he undervalues his work, not Phil.*

Similarly, another woman LETS member, June, who received computer training from a man, reflected on whether his low price could indicate that he undervalued his work. Like Geraldine, she concluded that this could not be the case and the explanation must lie with the man's personality.

June: *We hadn't actually discussed his fee until the end of the session. And I was really surprised that he was charging that little.*

MB: Why do you think he was charging so little?

June: *I'm not sure? I mean this is a man that does a lot of volunteer work, so that could have something to do. I mean, I don't think he was being*

95

*self-critical or undervaluing his own abilities. But I just think, yeah, I
think it was probably his personality.*
MB: That it was something he wanted to give?
June: *Yeah, money doesn't have a lot of value to him. He wasn't in it for
money.*

Both transactions can be understood in terms of gift theory as gifts to the
group; in both cases, not only did the men's generosity gain them recognition and gratitude, it also propelled the women into fuller participation in
LETS (although Geraldine's participation was particularly guilt-driven).

The finding that men's low rates are taken as a gift and women's as a
sign of their "undervaluation" of self sheds light on the four cases in this
chapter: that in spite of the associations of the gift with the "feminine,"
men who enter community currency groups as a gift economy seem to have
greater ease in giving than do women. The gender of the gift, its subtle
double meanings for men and women, helps solve the riddle.

First, men's gifts outweigh women's because men are not expected to
make them; the Big Man is all the bigger for his exceptionality. We have
seen that, in LETS, cautionary stories are circulated and formal rules put
in place in efforts to check men's assumed proclivity to capitalize on the
group. So just by entering community currency groups with a desire to engage in the gift community, men are thought to be making a gift. Especially
when they are seen as foregoing money earnings by doing so, they are rewarded for putting aside the pursuit of "hegemonic masculinity." As I explained in Chapter Three in the case of Gil, oppositional masculinities are
available within the movement. My point here is that when a man is perceived to have willingly stemmed his presumed "masculine" attributes of
individualism, acquisitiveness, competitiveness and aggression, this is
taken as an achievement, as when Kevin casually rejects the "hard-nosed
business point of view." And so, in a group which valorizes giving to the
group, men's gift labour is more readily acknowledged and highly appreciated because it is thought to entail the renunciation of certain "masculine"
attributes that are not favoured in the gift circle but would be rewarded in
other contexts.

Women's gifts, on the other hand, are assumed and naturalized, and women are held to a higher standard of giving. When men demonstrate their generosity through low prices, they are thought to be making an esteemed *choice* in the group, whereas women are thought to have a tendency already to "undervalue" themselves. Low prices in themselves are not enough to make one a Big Woman. Women also overlay the exchange with additional gift work, such as showing concern for their co-transactor's interests and feelings. Such personal giving is compulsory for achieving a particular feminine status that is normalized in a group that valorizes the gift as "female." The compulsory aspect of women's giving may be what prevents women from claiming all their due "acknowledgement" in the form of greendollars. In my interviews there was evidence of men being more self-possessed in their giving, and women more self-effacing. Men seemed more able to proclaim their gifts, assert their generosity, feel entitled to recognition and gratitude. They were able to take satisfaction in the feeling that they had given of themselves, whereas some of the women felt either that they had not given enough or that they had "undervalued" themselves by not receiving enough.

The higher standard of giving is further compounded when women have less ability to give because of lower earnings or more demands on their time. To the extent that men have more material assets, they also have more opportunities to use community currencies as a vehicle for their giving. Even if material circumstances were equal, the accounting function of LETS is more likely to be considered antithetical to women's gifts than to men's. Prohibitions on using the community currency network for personal pecuniary interests are gendered. For men there are prohibitions on transferring the gifts of the group into the market as capital, while for women there are also prohibitions on transferring the unaccounted "currencies of friendship"—cookie-making and such favours—into community currencies. Those women such as Rhoda, Geraldine and Caitlin, who are most committed to defining their work as a gift, feel the most tension about accounting and pricing it. This problem of pricing relates most strongly to "women's work" that is conventionally done for "free." Lewis Hyde argues that even if gender discrimination were factored out, some types of work, "social work and soul work" specifically, would receive low wages because the gift element in the work cannot be fully commodified: "Any portion of gift labour in a job will tend to pull it out of the market and make it a less lucrative—and a 'female'—profession" (p. 107). This is true so long as the dualism between gift and market is upheld. The dualism is perpetuated by the expectation that women must refrain from monetizing their work in order to express its gift aspects, such as their care for the relationship. In a market culture, the values of the gift are preserved by differentiating them from money values and assigning their preservation to women. In this context, a statement that women "undervalue" their work may be, in part, the negative expression of their valuing of the gift relationship, and their insistence on money's role in demarcating separate gift and market spheres.

Most women in LETS resolve the pricing dilemma by drawing careful lines around their participation, so that "acknowledgement" through accounting does not threaten the gift element of their relationships or raise, for them, a crisis of gender. Community currency, as a special form of gift-money, therefore, does not eliminate the gender division of commerce, but softens the boundaries. As Jacquie put it, "Some things you do in the name of friendship and some things you do to value your services."

In the next chapter I will explore the "undervaluation" problem from the opposite side of the gift/money dichotomy by examining how women and men use community currency to "value [their] services."

Notes

1. Interestingly, Heen argues that although women appear to be more dependent on specific men, to be more identified through caretaking relations, and to be less integrated into the public sphere, their "independence" is of a different type than men's: women are more independent of the market. "Since women's identities are less tied up in how they manage their relation to the market and other arenas in the public sphere, women have a type of independence most men lack" (p. 73). She further shows how the gendered concept of "independence" obscures the ways in which men's social position is secured through women's "dependency" (p. 94).

Chapter Five

"What my Freedom is all About"
Women, Men and Money

THE PREVIOUS CHAPTER PRESENTED STORIES of women and men who understand LETS primarily as a gift network, with the "greendollar" credits serving only as means to formalize and enhance the circulation of gifts. Also introduced were those women who feel the accounting function in LETS conflicts too strongly with the spirit of gift relationships for them to participate comfortably. The gendered division of commerce between market and gift, I argued, accounts for why the monetary aspects of community currency trouble those who take on gift-work as a vital "feminine" imperative in a market culture. Although many men idealize community currency activity as a "feminine" gift economy, it is sometimes more difficult for women than men to receive greendollars while simultaneously defining their labour as a gift. The gift economy, therefore, provides the first part of an explanation for women's apparent "undervaluation" of their labour.

This chapter approaches the "undervaluation" question again, this time by looking at women's and men's relationships to money. It focuses on those women and men who understand community currency primarily as money in its function as a means of payment. As in Chapter Four, I will again draw most examples from the LETS interviews, because the finer price negotiations and higher frequency of personal and casual services being traded brought issues of undervaluation more strongly to the fore. I found that in all cases the men were relatively at ease with receiving payment for their work and negotiating prices to their advantage. The women presented in the main part of this chapter entered LETS with a desire to be paid for work they would have otherwise volunteered or performed in their

own household without pay. Revealing and acting on their desire for payment required considerable courage, as I will show, because it redefined relationships with their co-transactors and challenged some aspects of their
sense of self. These women reported feeling strong tensions and sometimes
a sense of empowerment when they used LETS to monetize domestic or
volunteer labour.

In previous chapters, I have been drawing parallels between the community currency movement and the much earlier Owenite case of utopian
socialist experimentation with money. Again, there is an important strand
of thought in Owenism that is helpful to understanding the present movement. Owen and his followers believed that achieving a classless society
would require breaking down the boundary between the market economy
and the family (Folbre 1993). In his views on the family, Owen clashed
sharply with his contemporary, Thomas Robert Malthus, and their prede-
cessor, Adam Smith. Malthus and Smith saw in the family a refuge from
the relentless competition of the market, a protected zone of benevolence
set apart from the prevailing situation of self-interested, individual striving. Owen shared this sense of the family as benevolent, but considered the
narrow interests of private families as the motive force for competition and
class divisiveness. This difference of views on the family was a manifestation of a more fundamental disagreement concerning the inevitability and
desirability of class stratification.

Owen's model of the cooperative society was the family writ large. His
feminist critics protested his lack of perception of the way paternal authority in the family makes it inegalitarian and a poor metaphor for cooperative society (Folbre 1993). While rejecting his paternalism, feminist
adherents of Owenism applauded his advocacy of birth control, the abolition of marriage, and the building of cooperative nurseries, kitchens and
washing facilities. Owen's schemes aimed to eliminate the gender division
of labour that relegated women to domestic tedium in secluded households. More radically, Owen recognized that the institutional and ideological separation of family and market has the effect of deepening gender and
class inequality. The labour note scheme was one of his pragmatic attempts
to alter these arrangements.

WHAT MY FREEDOM IS ALL ABOUT

Attempts to create communities across the boundaries of domestic and market relations with contemporary community currencies can have the contrary effect of unsettling class and gender hierarchies. Because most LETS and HOURS activity is located at this boundary, the tensions people experience as they use community currencies can provide insight into the relationship of the class structure to the structure of family and gender relations. Following Joan Acker (1988), I will argue that different types of money relations, particularly the wage relation, and personal relations of entitlement based on the gift, which organize the distribution of the wage, are among the key structures that maintain a separation of family and market. The separation is never uniform or complete, but I will show how decisions about which types of services should be purchased, self-provided within the household or received through gift networks can be, simultaneously, practices that uphold class and gender divisions.

In this chapter, a focus on women's tensions with pricing their work and asking for payment in contrast to men is my entry point to these larger questions of how money relations interact with relations of class and gender. I present findings from interviews in three parts. The first set of four stories demonstrates the prevalence of the "undervaluation" issue for women and its relative non-importance to men. The general pattern is consistent with other studies of gender and money, as I will show. I briefly consider how women's "undervaluation" has been analysed through the perspective of sex role/socialization theory.

The second set of stories further reveals how deeply gendered are issues with money. Not only do the emotional issues with money differ for women and men in my study; in most cases the tensions crystallize in opposite-sex exchange relationships. This second set of stories, however, highlights women members' awareness of their patterns with money, the consequences of these patterns for their lives and relationships and their intent to use the community currency to improve difficult relationships, including their relationship with self. The women see their attempts to demand and accept their rightful earnings as an aspect of personal growth. I touch on psychoanalytic theory to help understand the role money can have in the individuation process for women. Community currencies may provide opportunities for personal growth because they provide a new field in which to carry out struggles for fairness, recognition, reward and independence. As one woman declared about the changes she had made: "This is what my freedom is all about!"

These stories of change highlight the complexity of the underlying issues, and the inadequacy of single factor explanations for "undervaluation." They raise the question of what it is about community currencies that prompts and supports women to make shifts in the direction of reconciling their relationship to money. As in Chapter Four, where I discussed Bourdieu's question of what means have to be implemented to create the economic and social conditions for generosity, as in gift economies, here I put the parallel question of what institutional change would produce the economic and social conditions for more women to realize, psychologically and materially, their entitlements to, acknowledgment of, and fair reward for their work.

The two stories of the third set of cases suggest that the question of structure be addressed through attention to the location of LETS at the intersection of the public and the domestic. These last stories are of members who are willing to do domestic work for greendollars in the LETS network but unwilling to do the same work for wages. LETS, therefore, provides a site for observing how the distinction between paid and unpaid work mediates the relationship of gender to class inequality, and offers clues for theorizing how women's location in a gender/class system complicates their responses to money payment. One of these members complained of the feelings of inferiority produced by paid domestic work compared with the same work in LETS: "I don't like how powerful money can sometimes be." Significantly for my analysis of how structural arrangements produce "undervaluation," this statement was made by a man in a non-conventional, "role-reversed" marriage.

Gender and Money (I): Issues of Self and Relationship

Money themes in my interviews followed clear gendered patterns. In general they seemed to bear out popular stereotypes and findings of academic literature, revealing women to be less comfortable than men with the issues involved in setting prices and negotiating payment, whereas men, according to the literature, are relatively at ease with charging money, but have more difficulty with issues of relationship and intimacy. Members themselves made these observations when I asked about gender differences in trading. When asked whether women or men benefit most from LETS, Sandra explained that women do better because:

> Sandra: *Women are more social.*
>
> MB: So that makes them better traders?
>
> Sandra: *It makes them more into phoning people. It makes them more oriented to the whole concept. I shouldn't say women are more social. They are in a sense. It's not that it's bad...It's a really big generalization and it's not fair. But in the sense that they might be more networked or something. But they may be also more likely to undersell themselves. To take less money.*

The following stories of three women and two men illustrate the tendencies Sandra observed but hesitated to generalize because they so closely fit the stereotype.

Women's "Undervaluation" and Uneasiness with Money
Elaine

Elaine has received house cleaning services from more than one LETS member, and paid approximately GR$10/hour, which was the rate a few women were advertising for cleaning in the LETS directory. Elaine admitted she would have been willing to pay twice as much for cleaning. I asked her why the house cleaners were not then charging $20 an hour? She replied that one woman who had worked for her changed only GR$9/hour and refused to accept the GR$10/hour she offered. Elaine then gave a two-part explanation:

> Elaine: *If you were to go with federal money and look for somebody to clean, if you are paying $10 an hour, you're paying a good wage. And it sucks to say, but the reality is, if you are working as a domestic, a nanny or doing any kind of home care service, if you are getting $10 an hour, that's classed as a very good salary.*
>
> MB: So people are comparing their work in LETS with the federal economy and setting their prices according to that.

Elaine: *Yes. Because I know I do. But I think a lot of women who do use the system really undervalue what they have or what they can offer.*

The first part of the explanation was my focus in Chapter Three where I discussed obstacles to revaluation of women's work. Elaine suggests that gender inequality in the money economy is reflected in LETS as women set their prices according to women's low dollar wages for the same work.

The second part of the explanation is that women in LETS compare their prices to each other. Elaine, for example, expects that other women set their prices according to federal market equivalents because she herself does. That women set their prices in comparison to each other and to dollar prices does not imply that LETS is like a competitive, price-setting market. Interviews with women who clean house and LETS members who want to hire cleaners, as well as "Wanted" ads in LETS directories, confirm that demand for house cleaning in LETS is very high. As Elaine's story suggests, if women are competing with one another, they seem to be doing so in the manner of a gift tournament—an anti-market, actually—by tacitly refusing to exceed one another in earnings. Not to undercharge for domestic services would be to break with the way "a lot of women...use the system." It also would be to break with the expectation that a lot of women "really undervalue" their services.

Tamara

Tamara is a piano and voice teacher, in her late twenties, who has recently begun to do enough teaching to support herself without taking other part time jobs, although as she said, "It's tight. It's tight." She accepts HOURS for part of her fee, and occasionally barters her music lessons. We discussed the equitability of her most recent barter transactions. In one instance she agreed to accept home-baked goods from a woman student in exchange for a regular voice class. Soon she felt the student was giving her more than was fair. But even when Tamara told her she could bring less, the woman continued to bring baking.

In another ongoing barter arrangement, the opposite problem was occurring. This was an exchange of piano instruction for a small appliance and a piece of craft work. Tamara felt she had not received fair value, but she hesitated to ask for an additional thirty dollars in cash, the amount that would make the barter equitable.

> Tamara: *I have to think about, like, if I want to be like so—* (pause), *"Can you give me that thirty dollars cash?" Like I'm not sure how I feel about that, and I'm not good with asking for money, which is bad because I have to charge people. So I do feel a little bit uncomfortable. But I think that's just me. But the people haven't—like I'm sure they would give it to me, like no problem. It's not them, it's me.*

Tamara assumes that her discomfort with charging for her services is her personal problem. Being "not good with asking for money" is an area of deficiency particular to her, not a problem stemming from her relationship with her co-transactors and their treatment of her or a gendered social relation. She felt that asking for money would make of her something so wrong or bad she was unwilling to name it ("like, if I want to be like so—"). But, this created a dilemma because she also felt it was "bad" to be reluctant to ask for money, considering that the money was needed to make the arrangement fair to her and to keep her in business.

Emily

Emily is a stained-glass artist who accepts 25% of the ticket in HOURS. She talked to me about her difficulty pricing her work.

> MB: How did you learn to price your work?
>
> Emily: *Oh my goodness. It's completely difficult...It's really difficult to price your work. And, yeah, a lot of times, you know, almost always I've underquoted myself and I always feel bad. But I stick to my price. I never say more, I never say more. I always try to stick to it because you have to. But I've eaten a lot of hours that way because I didn't say enough money for a piece.*

Emily's desire to make money with her art and her frustration at repeatedly setting her prices too low affects her ability to identify positively with other women who seem to her to receive even lower prices for their work.

> Emily: *There's some people...who you know are making a dollar an hour by the amount of work they do.*

MB: Who's making a dollar an hour?

Emily: *Like there's one woman, she sells [hand sewn garments] for, like, $12 [an item]. Well, the material alone must cost half that. And it must take her a couple hours to make it...and then there's all her time at the market trying to sell the pieces. It's just like, "Oh," you know. I mean, you have to (pause) have some self-respect! But I'm past the self-respect, like, I need to make money doing this. I want to make money doing this! Not just a little bit here and a little there...But it's definitely hard, you know, to price things. It is really difficult to price things.*

Emily believes that women who charge too little lack self-respect. But she could not account for her own tendency "almost always" to "underquote" herself and "feel bad" towards herself.

These examples are illustrative of women community currency members' conflicts about money. Tensions arose even among women who readily acknowledged that they want and need money. The women often identified the issue as "undervaluation," which they saw as a problem of the self and a tendency characteristic of women. They rarely attributed "undervaluation" to the fairness of their exchange partners or the structures in which they made their pricing decisions. They tended towards being self-blaming, critical of other women and generally perplexed about why they felt so torn in their pricing decisions.

Men's Facility with Money

Among the men I interviewed there was a more visible spectrum of attitudes towards community currency as money. At one end are those men (and some women) who are drawn to community currencies for the possibility of practising the ideals of the gift in everyday material life. Such men, whom I described in the previous chapter, reject masculinist ideologies of individualism and competitive success, and are critical of the way these are achieved through conventional money dealings. As I will explain further in the next chapter, this group of men (as well as many women) sees in community currencies the potential to enrich, materially and spiritually, the local economy and their own lives by drawing together a large, diverse group with interpersonal ties based in ethics of community self-help and mutual aid. As for the actual greendollar or HOUR in circulation, for such members its moneyness consists only in its role in facilitating exchange, and its value, in the way it catalyses relationships.

In contrast, there are those men (and some women) who have joined community currencies for more pragmatic reasons: they see LETS or HOURS mainly as a means to increase their personal economy. Such members consider their LETS credits and debits, or the paper HOURS in their wallet, much as they would conventional money.

In spite of these more pronounced degree differences in idealism among men, the level of ease with monetary practices of pricing, charging and negotiating was remarkably consistent, and noticeably discrepant from many of the women. Although some men set low prices, and practised generosity in other ways as well, none described pricing decisions as difficult, nor did any second-guess their own rates. Like the women, all the men clearly desired to establish personal connections through community currency exchanges. For some, this desire had been worked out as a political philosophy of the gift community and was being acted upon in creative and sustained ways, while for others it remained a simple longing that found expression here and there. Whenever men described tension with money, it arose in relation to the way conventional money practices seemed to conflict with this desire for community or relationship. I will here tell of two men who took the most pragmatic approach to their participation in LETS, yet also sought closer connections, especially with women.

Keith: Leaving price unspoken

Keith, who I have already introduced in Chapter Three, is single and in his early 30s. When I first met him at a LETS trade fair, he was looking for someone to provide him with cooked meals through LETS. Later, in our interview, I asked if he had been successful at finding food. He had found one woman selling prepared food at a table, but he thought her price was too high. Then he met a second woman who also offered cooking:

> Keith: *Yeah, I talked to one other person...and I found out at the trade fair she does some cooking too. So we're going to do an exchange for something, (pause) well, something we both like, like to do.*

MB: What's that?

Keith: *I don't know. We're trying to negotiate what. Like she has certain things that she likes to cook and I have certain things I like to eat. So we'll try and find matches.*

At first, Keith described his encounter with the woman as though it was a classic barter situation: two people meet with a willingness to exchange; they talk until they find out what each has that the other wants. But here the "match" that Keith had in mind was a "negotiation" between what she likes to cook and what he likes to eat. He did not talk about what he would offer in exchange for her cooking, just indicated his readiness to receive it. As Keith presented the story, it would appear that the two were negotiating a gift exchange, lightly veiled in the discourse of barter. He was inquiring into whether his desire to be fed according to his likes matched her desire to feed him.

I then prompted him to redefine the prospective exchange as one that involved payment for services. He offered vague agreement, but did not take up the idea. I followed with a question about price.

MB: So that's the kind of thing—you're going to talk to her about the kind of food that you want to buy from her?
Keith: *Yeah.*
MB: And presumably you'll talk about the price too?
Keith: *Yeah, she didn't mention the price when we talked so I guess it's negotiable.*

Keith had left it up to the woman to "mention the price." When she left the issue unspoken, he did not ask. Price is not unimportant to Keith, as indicated by his complaint to me about another woman's over-pricing of food. In this case, however, he took the woman's omission of price to mean that "it's negotiable." At an earlier point in the interview he had made it clear that he found such negotiations unproblematic.

Most important, by telling me "she didn't mention the price," Keith resisted my challenge to the way he first framed the exchange as barter-cum-gift. He wanted me to know that she colluded in his construction of the exchange as gift-like. She did not say what she required as payment for her labour, and so he felt justified in his conclusion that price is of secondary importance to her wish to "exchange" her cooking for his eating.

Tom: "Kind of a social thing"

Tom is in his early fifties, divorced with no children. He describes his hobbies as fishing, hunting and outdoor activities. He is an electrician and has been employed through a trade union for most of his thirty year career. Two years ago he began working as an independent contractor with the aim of doing more business closer to home. Shortly after going independent he joined LETS for the local marketing opportunities it offers. He offers LETS members fifty percent of his price in greendollars. He estimates that LETS has given him approximately a quarter of his business so far, including referrals to non-LETS members who pay entirely in federal dollars.

In the interview Tom dwelt on his work history, earnings and the benefits and drawbacks of LETS participation for his business. He emphasized the monetary aspects of LETS involvement, considering whether various kinds of activities "pay off" or are "worth my time" compared with non-LETS opportunities. For example, it costs him significantly less to advertise his services in the LETS directory compared with the local newspaper. He can set up a table at a LETS community market for a fraction of the fee he would pay at a conventional home show. Because of the contact between LETS members, he also has better chances for referrals stemming from work within the LETS community.

In all interviews I asked members to compare work paid in community currency with similar work they had done for free and with work they had done for federal dollars. In Tom's case, his LETS offerings are an extension of his regular, primary paid profession, unlike many LETS services that are otherwise unpaid activities or activities taken up as a source of secondary income. Tom, therefore, hesitated to divulge stories of doing work for free or reducing his rate. Was he to "give somebody a break," he stressed, he would consider the business sense in doing so: "[The customer] can make it up by other means. Sometimes it's good advertising too." He described the detailed assessment he would make when considering a special arrangement with a customer who has difficulty making payment, such as whether the customer can refer other customers, provide repeat business or offer a specific service in return. Other considerations would include: how labour intensive the job is, how busy he is, the material costs of the job, how far he has to travel to the site, and the time the job takes. In emphasizing these calculations, Tom made it clear that he is not insensitive to the needs of others, but business imperatives do not allow him to make a gift of his labour.

Tom engages in barter, but cautiously, and again, with prior agreement on the way the other person will re-pay him. When giving examples of bartering his labour, his stories emphasized the specific arrangements he worked out in advance. He told a story to underscore the risk of barter relationships:

> Tom: *I saw a [barter] system...blow up in somebody's face a number years ago. It was a group of tradesmen, about six or seven of them. They were all young and they were building houses around the same time...There was a bricklayer, a carpenter, an electrician, a plumber, a heating guy. They all decided that they would exchange labour. It worked well except for the electrician. He didn't fulfill his commitments and [unfortunately for] the housing project, it ended up in a big fight. The carpenter ended up trashing someone's house...But it almost worked.* (laugh) *That was a good example of how not to run a barter network.*

This is a cautionary tale about informal systems of obligation. For Tom, the LETS system avoids the potential complications of barter: "This system is better because you're not obliged to any one person. You bank your money."

Even though LETS satisfies Tom's wish to avoid personal obligations, it presents him with another problem: he cannot easily spend his greendollar earnings. Because his LETS income is earned as part of his regular line of work, it is taxable in federal dollars. The importance of this income to his business contributes to the difficulty he has in spending: "I think of it as cash. I can't spend it frivolously." He has accumulated $1600 greendollars with the hope that he will be able to hire male casual labour in LETS at 50% greendollars to assist with some building work. So far he had not found anyone appropriate to the work. He recently tried to hire a man with a truck to help with some hauling, but was unsuccessful in this too. I will return to Tom's spending problem in the next chapter, consider what he means by spending "frivolously" and why this is a problem relating to his gender. For now, I want to clarify why Tom remains in LETS, in spite of not easily being able to spend his earnings. I asked if he would consider donating his LETS credits, considering the LETS proportion of his price as a pure discount that he would not recover except through additional contracts in slow periods and customer referrals. Donated credits are tax deductible under the rules of charitable giving. He said the work would not be worth his time unless he could benefit from the LETS income.

What does Tom get from LETS, if not others' services? In spite of his emphasis on business motives, one key difference between LETS and regular paid work is his relationship with customers. He mentioned these relationships first as one additional factor he takes into account when deciding to do a LETS job.

> Tom: *It all depends on how they treat you too. If you go in and they offer you a coffee or something like that. Because sometimes you go into places, I've worked in a place for hours without being offered a glass of water.*
> MB: Generally in LETS how do people treat you?
> Tom: *Excellent. They are very nice people to work for.*

For the most part, members are people who need his services and cannot afford to pay entirely in cash. He describes them as people "trying to get by," "trying to make ends meet." They are people with whom he identifies: "The majority of us," he said, "really need it." Tom cannot give his work away, but LETS provides a way to respond to others' needs with a minimum of risk. LETS also provides him with feminine and familial contact.

> Tom: *I've enjoyed meeting a lot of the people. They're the kind of people who you do a job for them and then you sit down. Like, I did one job for a woman and at the end of the day sat down and had a beer with the family and had lunch (laugh). It was great (laugh, pause). So, it's kind of a social thing too.*

At the end of the interview Tom again spoke warmly about how his LETS customers treat him. "They're the kind of people who you do a job for them and then you sit down with and talk to. Lots of times I've done a job for somebody and then sat down with the family for a couple of hours at a time." He again laughed, and then added heartily: "I'm supposed to be working!" Family involvement, in part, offset the problem of not being able to spend LETS credits on male labour.

Tom and Keith focused their interviews on the material opportunities they hoped LETS would provide, yet for both, LETS was also providing a way to seek intimacy, particularly as this could be experienced through food or sharing meals (DeVault 1991). Although LETS involvement did raise money-related issues—for example, Tom's concerns not to be cheated or obligated—the men did not experience difficulty with charging or negotiating as did the women. Their competence with these monetary aspects of LETS, however, overshadowed other areas of tension. Keith's search for cheap food seemed to obfuscate a deeper desire for relationship in which someone would care for his needs. Tom's feeling that he was "supposed to be working" and "banking his money" seemed to conflict with his enjoyment at being included in the family "for a couple of hours at a time."

Explanations of "Undervaluation" as Gender Difference

These broad patterns of gender difference in relation to money have been observed in other ethnographic studies, confirmed by survey research, and taken up in psychoanalytic literature. Much of this literature on money and gender[1] takes women as its focus, and attempts to explain observations that women have greater emotional conflict around money-making compared with men. It takes men's more positive orientation towards earning as normative and seldom problematizes men's patterns of interaction and emotional issues around money. In the following sections I present a sampling of studies that use ethnographic, quantitative, interview and clinical methods to observe gender differences similar to those I have described above. I have chosen these studies because they represent a range of analytical perspectives—role theory, socialization theory and psychoanalytical theory—that have been brought to the question of gender difference in relation to money. I will consider how well these explanatory frames contribute to my findings of gender patterns within the special case of community money.

112

Role theory, the idea that men and women think and behave more or less in conformity to socially-constructed sex roles, provides the first possible explanation of gendered money patterns. In a study closely relevant to community currency activity, insofar as it is "quasi-commercial exchange that grows directly from the home," Gretchen Herrmann observed gendered patterns in over 2,000 American garage sales (1995, p. 127). She found consistent, observable patterns in men and women's shopping, the gendering of objects for sale and the gendered division of labour of the sellers. For example, women selected items for sale as part of house cleaning and arranged them in neat displays; men posted signs, set up and dismantled tables. Her main finding was that "men are more concerned with money and their time, while women are more concerned with creating relationships through this informal trade (p. 128). Drawing on Deborah Tannen's research on men and women in conversation, she explained the pattern in terms of traditional sex roles. Tannen (1990) argued that men behave with a concern for status, hierarchy and power, attempting in interactions to maintain their independence and avoid failure. Women seek intimacy, consensus and community. These differences, according to Herrmann, stem from men and women's "socialization and disproportionate experience" as breadwinners and homemakers/care-givers (p. 143). In the garage sale study, men's behaviour directly reflected their bread winning role. Husbands either trivialized their wives' participation in sales because it embarrassed them in their role as primary breadwinner, or they became "super-involved," seeing sales as money-making enterprises. Women's garage sale activities, likewise, were an extension of their domestic roles. Women asked their husbands for help pricing objects, and, in general, were less interested in money-making than in the interpersonal aspects of the sale: emotional associations with objects and personal connections with shoppers.

Herrmann's study provides useful empirical backing to my observations, but a limited explanation. She argues that money is expressive of masculine goals of independence, power and success such that "male self-esteem is closely linked with the ability to make money" (Herrmann, p. 132). Sex role theory assumes that masculine and feminine behaviour are constructed in negative relation to one another. So, if money-making is a masculine preoccupation, it follows that the feminine response to money will be indifference or antipathy.

The problem of role theory is not its proposition that masculine and feminine constructs are binary, but that they are static and homogeneous. Role theory cannot account for variation or change. It assumes unitary individuals who passively assume sex roles that exist independently of them. Role theory would be confounded by the stories I present next of women who clearly do have positive pecuniary desires and a man who is in a domestic "role" and who dislikes the power of money.

According to Herrmann, individuals are socialized into male and female roles in childhood and adolescence. A quantitative survey of 605 students of a California university drew on socialization theory to explain gender differences in attitudes towards money. Analysis of this data on childhood and adolescent experiences revealed that:

> Money makes men feel loveable, happy, in control, and provides them with a feeling of self-worth. Men also envy those who earn a great deal of money. Women, on the other hand, are repelled by and consider immoral those who earn good incomes (Newcomb and Rabow 1999, pp. 865-866).

These results are based on factor analysis of 200 survey items that revealed two distinct constructs correlated with gender, suggesting an antithesis between men's (positive) and women's (negative) orientation to money. In addition to the results cited above, Newcomb and Rabow found that men regard people who earn a lot of money as responsible, rational and attractive, whereas women find rich people intimidating, and believe that they, themselves, would feel guilty about earning more money than their parents. The survey showed that although men and women do not differ in everyday money management skills, such as balancing chequebooks and paying bills on time, women feel more fearful and confused about financial matters than do men.

Newcomb and Rabow explain these gender differences in terms of separate socialization paths for sons and daughters. Their findings indicate that boys and girls differ in their early experiences with money, parental

114

teachings about money, and expectations of parents and self regarding future incomes and future financial independence. These experiences within the family lead men to have a positive evaluation of money for the self and a stronger desire for financial independence. They lead women to take a negative view of money, to have less desire for significant earnings and greater expectation of financial dependence.

Several items in the study reveal that boys more than girls were preparing for financial responsibility in their adolescent years. Boys were included in parents' discussions of finances, for example, a full year earlier than girls. This focus on the positive money lessons for boys seems to imply that girls were simply being left behind, neglecting to learn about money, or their parents failing to teach them. Newcomb and Rabow's position, however, is that boys and girls were receiving *distinct* trainings that put them on "separate money tracks" (p. 867). If girls were receiving an inferior version of the same money lessons their brothers got, we would predict them to have somewhat less confidence about money and, probably, weaker money management skills—to be lagging behind the boys on a generic "money track." But the finding was that gendered "money tracks" take girls and boys in divergent directions.

While Newcomb and Rabow provide evidence for sex role learning on money matters, their study assumes the passivity of girls and women in acquiring a predetermined set of gender-appropriate traits. Also, because their sex role theory conceives of gender as somehow fixed and not a relation, complicated by relations of class, race, generation, and so on, it is silent on questions of power. It cannot explain, for example, why parents would appear to be disadvantaging their daughters by not preparing them for monetary independence as they do their sons. To understand the feminine "money track" we need, first, to consider the negative lessons girls learn about money in light of other lessons they learn concurrently. Literature on adolescent girls has established that the most important of these lessons is about care-giving (Baines, Evans et al. 1991, p. 18).

Marge Reitsma-Street's (1991) study of delinquency in adolescent girls provides more complex analysis, which goes well beyond normative socialization theory by emphasizing girls' resistance to these lessons in the face of powerful agencies of gender enforcement that extend beyond the family. Reitsma-Street studied pairs of sisters in which one had a conviction in youth court and extensive contact with services for delinquent youth, while the other had no history of delinquency. Through analysis of interview records she discovered overriding patterns of commonality between the delinquent and conforming sisters that centred on the girls' desire and capacity to care for others, the costs of caring and the ways girls are "policed" to care.

The first lesson girls (re)learn in adolescence is that it is females who care. In a period when fathers and other male kin typically withdraw further from their lives, girls find themselves receiving care almost exclusively from women and other girls. Lessons about money are conveyed in this context of learning from other women and girls how to foster caring relationships. Reitsma-Street describes how, in open interviews, girls repeatedly and spontaneously mention the care they receive from other women and girls:

> They had lunch, sang, lived, and shopped with females; *they learned about money and getting along with others* from females; and they looked for help from and, above all, spent time with and talked with females (p. 112, my emphasis).

Girls discuss the female care they receive in relation to their own ability and desire to provide care for others. In this process of learning about giving and receiving care, money lessons are integrated with lessons in helping and getting along with others.

Girls' lessons in care, furthermore, teach them to restrict self-care to matters of dress and demeanour, and to direct their caring attentions primarily towards a boyfriend. To establish and maintain a relationship with a boyfriend, and potential husband, is the ultimate test of the ability to care. Success at caring, however, comes at a cost, as girls set aside their own interests to focus on the interests and needs of others, again primarily boyfriends. The emphasis on looking and acting nice detracts from girls' attention to their own basic health needs and increases their risk of disease, pregnancy, abortion and rape. More seriously for the long term, the tradeoffs and disasters arising from care and restricted self-care mean that girls

begin to forgo opportunities for greater financial independence in an economy where women are already at risk of dependency and poverty.

Reitsma-Street emphasizes that girls do not bear these costs without
resistance. She details the powerful practices and agencies that police caring in girls, which range from the pervasive evaluation of a girl's reputa-
tion, to violence and the threat of violence by males, to legal and judicial
systems that enforce feminine respectability and monitor girls' caring behaviour. Hence, it is in light of the emphasis on caring for girls that we can
begin to make sense of the finding that girls and boys follow separate
money tracks. Girls are directed onto a track that would make them
care-givers, as boys move towards increasing their earnings potential.

Newcomb and Rabow's analysis would suggest that a "caring track"
for girls more than distracts; it leads them away from a positive interest in
money. The finding is perplexing because even if money-making is subordinated to the desire to care, the ability to make, spend or give money
could be understood to increase the capacity to care. Just because girls and
women may define themselves, and be socially defined, as care-givers, why
should they not also embrace substantial incomes to the same degree as
men? The sister study provides a partial answer. Reitsma-Street found that
girls emphasize the emotional aspects of care—care as love and affection,
over the practical aspects—care as help, or care as labour to provide comfort and meet daily needs. While money may contribute enormously to *caring for* another, it is no substitute for *caring about* another (Baines, Evans et
al. 1991, p. 15), which, for the girls in the sister study, is the more important dimension of care.

When abstracted out of context, this distinction between "caring for"
and "caring about" recalls the work of the best-known socialization theorist on the familial gender division of labour. In Talcott Parson's formula-
tion, the feminine "expressive" function of the care-giving wife acquires
meaning through opposition to the masculine "instrumental" function of
the wage-earning husband (Parsons and Bales 1960). This type of theorizing is problematic, because the constellation of binary opposites that defines gender in the sex role/socialization tradition is also used to account
for the observed differences between women and men. Sex role theory be-

gins and ends with accentuated masculine/feminine polarities mapped onto the male/female dichotomy. The sister study is an example of research that goes beyond this circularity by exposing how dichotomous gender is constituted in discourse and practice, institutionally reified, reproduced and reinforced, as well as contested, negotiated and changed. By neglecting to focus on agency and power in the process of gender learning, Newcomb and Rabow's work reproduces static, binary conceptions of gender.

The following stories further challenge the sex role/socialization perspective by showing women attempting to embrace the "money-making" aspects of community currencies, struggling against old patterns and addictions, and seeking to change their relationships and sense of self.

Gender and Money (II): Women Negotiating Change
Annette: "Giving myself credit"

Annette is married and in her mid-20s. Her husband is a non-custodial parent. She works part time, studies for her degree part time, volunteers extensively with community organizations and, as a hobby, makes jams and chutneys. She was recruited into LETS by a friend who recognized that Annette already barters and gives away much of her jam. "In some ways the main attraction [of LETS] was being able to get rid of some of the stuff I had, and to get something for it." LETS also provided her the opportunity to have her work recognized, recognition she was not receiving as a volunteer.

> Annette: I was working [as a volunteer] with a lot of organizations which left me feeling very dissatisfied...I wanted to do something that would be literally a give and take, okay? Instead of always just give. So I figured with LETS I have a give and take, and it worked out very well because it really has its checks and balances in place...Before that I never really acknowledged that I wanted to have something in return...[With LETS] I have something tangible. I have an account with a balance.

Her LETS balance contributed to her attempts to restore a sense of balance in other aspects of her life: "my volunteering, work, school, my partner...I was just learning how important it was to start balancing stuff, and started

118

realizing that I have a lot more potential than I'd ever given myself credit for."

In LETS Annette achieved a greater sense of balance through recognition, appreciation and direct returns on labour that would have otherwise been unpaid. The establishment of balance in her LETS exchange has mainly served to enhance her capacity for further giving. For example, one of the main ways she has used her LETS account has been to buy Christmas presents for her husband and his children. She explained:

> Annette: *All [my husband's and step children's] Christmas presents from me were bought on the system with [greendollars]...I mean, it was very satisfying because here I am, I'm essentially trading something that I would have done anyway and I have my Christmas presents in return. And that to me felt like a really great sense of balance because finally there was something going on in both directions.*

If receiving LETS credits enabled her to give more at Christmas, receiving appreciation for her jams and chutneys, similarly, inspired her to make more and give more away.

> Annette: *It's nice to put in a lot of work to do something, but it's nice for it to be appreciated and to have people say, "Hey," you know, "got any more of this?"* (laugh).
>
> MB: *Do* you get appreciation from people who buy your stuff?
>
> Annette: *Yes! That's the best part. I mean, my family has gotten so used to having it that it's no longer special. It's just there. And, you know, I'm at the point where I don't eat it. A lot of the stuff that I make I cannot eat because of my diabetes. So I mean, I make a lot of stuff for other people, but I don't really have much for me. So when other people tell me how much they enjoy it, that's like, you know. I've been known to give people stuff when they do that.*

So for Annette, learning to "give herself credit" for her abilities has been a process of accepting credit from others, which she immediately converts into gifts. A man friend in LETS, in particular, is "very knowing of this" readiness of hers to give. The more satisfaction he shows in buying her food, the more likely she is to say, "You want this?...I'll just throw it in."

COMMUNITY and MONEY

Sandra: "What am I getting back?"

Sandra is in her early 30s and single. On the day of the interview she had been hired by a local TV station, ending a period of unemployment. She joined LETS for economic reasons: "I have no money," she put it bluntly. She initially saw LETS as an opportunity to extend her "purchasing power" and "get stuff" that she would not normally get. She attributed her financial situation to her personal choices, which she now disparaged.

> Sandra: *I've always done things that I liked, what I wanted to do. I've never done what is smart. If I was smart I would have become an IT professional, you know? So I guess I've never had a whole lot of money.*

She recalled how her father's attitude towards money—"There's no free lunch"—contrasts with her own pattern of volunteer work and giving. Like Annette, she has volunteered extensively for community organizations, music festivals and local musicians, especially doing event organizing and skilled desk-top publishing work. But she has now reached the point of deploring her own tendency to give.

> Sandra: *I just won't work for free anymore. Just cause of my background, I do a lot of community events, a lot of volunteer stuff. And I just can't give it away anymore, I can't give my time. It's like, "What are you going to do for me? What am I getting back?" You know? Or else, forget it.*

In spite of her resolve, in actual relationships, it was difficult to communicate her wish to receive something in return. Only recently she had again entered a barter arrangement that favoured the other party:

> Sandra: *I said, "Oh, I'll just give it to you for [a lesser service in return]." I shouldn't have done that. It was stupid. Do you know what I mean?*

She spoke about her volunteer work as though she were addicted to giving: "My challenge is to stop giving things away for free." But stopping has been a difficult challenge. She asserted her intention and, in the same breath, mentioned the one exception.

> Sandra: *So I could go to any organization and say, "How about if I do this for you." Right? And I've stopped that. Like I do a newsletter for an organization. I do it for free. It's a hell of a lot of work. But I'm learning from it, so I'll do it. But now I won't. That's the only thing I'll do for free.*

Her struggle to stop giving provided another reason to join LETS, beyond her lack of money. "The only thing I'll do now is barter. Or start to charge a little money." And her reason for charging a little money had to do with her self worth as much as her financial need. For example, she proposed to a women's band that she create a newsletter for them, something she would have done for free in the past:

> Sandra: *I wrote this e-mail to their manager saying, "Look, I've got to charge you because I have to start thinking of myself as a professional (? inflection) and I won't charge you much, but if I charge you nothing, I'm an amateur, right? So I was almost apologizing, but I have to start thinking of myself as a professional, so that means money.*

LETS provided a possible alternative to working for free or charging federal dollars. When a man friend produced a film, Sandra became excited about organizing a publicity event for the film's launch. She told her friend she would do the organizing, but then realized she did not want to do it for free. LETS presented itself as a solution, even though her friend was not yet a member. "I thought about it and I thought, you know what? It's going to have to be on the LETS system or I won't do it." For her, a LETS arrangement would satisfy her need for payment and professionalism while she offered her talent to her friend. But even the prospective LETS exchange caused her to worry about their friendship.

> Sandra: *I would probably undercharge him, I'd probably charge him 10 dollars an hour. The reason is that I'd feel guilty. I mean my work is probably worth [more]. Organizing-wise, I have three or four years experience at various different fundraising [events] and festivals. And I have a good number of contacts and stuff. It's probably worth 12 or 15. But he's a friend of mine and I feel guilty because then he's gonna hafta work off a lot and I feel bad if he has to work off too much. Which is not my responsibility, I shouldn't worry about that, but I do. So I figured I'd charge him 10 bucks an hour. But I'd be worried about how much debt he's racking up. Because then if he doesn't have something that he can sell for 60 bucks an hour, then he's going to have to work off a lot. Again his problem, but I always think about that. I shouldn't. You know?*

Sandra clearly has a strong sense of the market value of her work, but she felt guilty that she had decided not to make her services a gift of friendship. Here she openly reasoned why she would undercharge as a deliberate choice. As soon as she considered charging the friend for her work through LETS, she began perceiving him as unwilling to take responsibility for returning his balance to zero. Rather than asking him how much he valued the service and how willing he would be to reciprocate, she was tempted to continue doing the work for free.

June: "What my freedom is about"

June is in her 40s, single, and works full time as a researcher in a law firm. She house-sits for additional income. Eventually she wants to go into business offering holistic health services. She joined LETS first to hire tutors to begin learning business-related skills and then to take advantage of some of the services to businesses offered on LETS. Improving her computer skills is her first priority. She bought a computer with the expectation that she would get help through LETS. However, as soon as she signed up, it occurred to her that she could barter with her roommate, Gary, for the help she needed: "He had the computer skills that I was looking for, and he wanted food." Their barter began when she brought the new computer home. "He was helping me set it up and so forth, and I was cooking dinner." This was a loose arrangement, but they did have an initial discussion of what his time was worth in meals.

At first she believed the exchange was equitable, but it soon became evident that she had drastically undervalued her services relative to his. She had not taken into account the time and effort required in shopping and planning for the meals, or the inconvenience of being required to serve the meals at a regular time. Over time, she became aware that feeding him was too great a burden.

June: *And then, it was, like, I owe him three weeks of meals or something. And then, "Oh, I've got to go home again tonight and cook dinner. I don't want to do this anymore (laugh). This is what my freedom is all about!"*

The inequality of the exchange was not what was bothering June the most; it was the disparity in the types of services that were being traded. Cooking and serving meals is a personal service that requires a regular commitment and special attention to personal needs and preferences. For June, it did not feel comparable to the technical computer service that she was receiving in exchange. Having to render personal services for technical services seemed to put her in the role of wife. This is what made her most uncomfortable. She explained:

> June: *After a while I felt that this is, like, I might as well be married and have three kids. It was like, I had to come home every night from work to make dinner for this man that came home and sat himself in front of the television after work and waited to be fed. No! He's getting spoiled and dependent and I don't want this to happen in this roommate situation. I mean that's all it has been.*

The direct barter was uncomfortable because the type of relationship it established felt too dependent. June was emphatic that she and Gary are in a "roommate situation" and "that's all it has been." At first she found it awkward to look to LETS for computer help when the skills might have been available within the household from Gary.

> June: *It's pretty silly actually because here I am going out to somebody's house or phoning someone else to come into my house to teach me what I need to know about the computer when basically it's right there in front of us both. I've tried to, in my mind, sort through how it can work out to be more beneficial to both of us.*

In the end, she was unable to renegotiate a more equitable exchange. LETS became her way to discontinue the disadvantageous barter agreement and redefine her roommate relationship. When LETS members came to give her training, Gary was often present and talked to them about computers. June felt extremely awkward for having made this change, but as she reported: "He understands that I'm doing it because I don't want to feed him every day."

The Psychology of Women's "Undervaluation"

These stories of Annette, Sandra and June place women's ambivalence towards money in the concrete situations in which they must negotiate power in relationships, especially relationships to men. The situational and relational view of the undervaluation problem shows that gender cannot be reduced to categorical analysis of sex roles, although gender categories are invoked as part of the practice of undervaluation, as when Sandra contrasts her father's maxim, "There's no free lunch," with her pattern of "giving things away for free." Most striking about these stories is the connections the women made between money, the qualities they want to see in their lives and relationships—freedom, independence, balance, respect, recognition, fairness—and personal growth. The women describe how acknowledging and acting on these desires has been part of an ongoing and difficult inner process that has included "giving myself credit" and knowing "what my freedom is all about."

The types of answers psychoanalytic theory provides to women's ambivalence toward money often have to do with gender differences in the individuation process. In her psychoanalytic practice, Sheila Klebanow has also observed a dynamic having to do with "not quite being comfortable about earning money when one is a woman" (1991, p. 58). The problem for women is in the inability to see oneself as one's own effective power source:

> Part of the male persona, the sense of autonomy stemming from the ability to earn a living involves the perception of oneself as a power source. Perhaps in this sense men may have less neurotic conflict than women about the equation: money = power...Despite impressive professional and vocational attainments...for many women the power to have money as a result of one's own labor rather than through a relationship with a man is a concept not fully integrated (pp. 57, 59).

Various traditions of psychoanalysis offer different stories for why the male and female individuation process differs (Davies 1990). Nancy Chodorow's (1978) theory of psycho-gender development can be read as the story of what happens when it is primarily women who mother. Chodorow argues that because the infant's primary relationship is with a woman, acquisition of gender identity is more difficult for boys, for whom mother is perceived as opposite, than girls, for whom mother is perceived as more continuous with the self. While girls remain connected and identified with mother longer, for boys the developmental task of differentiating and separating from mother must begin earlier and be accomplished with more acuity. Consequently, girls and boys emerge into adulthood with different relational capacities: girls for care-giving and nurturing, and boys for independence.

In arguing that the female individuation process is not inferior or incomplete compared to the male, Chodorow departs from what has been the dominant tradition of psychoanalytic thought. Carol Gilligan (1982) takes up this latter point and argues that the mainstream of psychoanalytic theory takes independence to be the most desired end of individuation and makes the male process normative. The qualities associated with care-giving are thereby devalued and taken to be indicative of women's inferior moral development.

> Women not only define themselves in a context of human relationship but also judge themselves in terms of their ability to care. Women's place in man's life cycle has been that of nurturer, caretaker, and helpmate, the weaver of these networks of relationships on which she in turn relies. But while women have taken care of men, men have, in their theories of psychological development, as in their economic arrangements, tended to assume or devalue that care. When the focus on individuation and individual achievement extends into adulthood and maturity is equated with personal autonomy, concern with relationships appears as a weakness of women rather than as a human strength (Gilligan 1982, p. 17).

Money is important to this question of how to define psychological maturity because facility with money is often an expression of independence and autonomy, as it was with the women I interviewed for this chapter. So tightly linked are ideas of money, independence and psychological development that women's and men's behaviour with money is thought to reflect how the individuation process is unfolding for them (Rabow and Charness 1991). Following Gilligan's critique of the equation of personal autonomy with maturity, the challenge is to account for observations that women tend to have more "neurotic conflict" about money (Klebanow 1991, p. 57) without normalizing or elevating male psychology. Following Chodorow and Gilligan, I will argue that of most relevance to the psychological question is the sociological fact that women bear the major social responsibility for caring.

In contrast to Klebanow's concept of perceiving "oneself as a power source," Lewis Hyde (1983) writes of how, in gift communities, the gift is the power source (the *hau*) of the group. If women are living partly in the framework of the gift, they as individuals may indeed have difficulty seeing themselves as their own power source in an individualistic sense while tending the power source of the collectivity—the extended family, kinship and friendship networks, the community. The gift labour of caring that consolidates relationship may not foster autonomy, but does give rise to the experience of heteronomy, of relational power, relational selfhood, and connectedness (Friedman 1995).

From the perspective of the gift, psychological complications are bound to arise for women when the gift community is reduced in scale to the marriage dyad or nuclear family. The *hau* of the gift, of which Hyde writes, the increase that comes from its circulation, becomes distorted whenever the gift does not move. In nuclear family situations where women remain primarily responsible for the vital work of nurturing relationships, not only may they be unable to perceive themselves as a power source in Klebanow's sense, considering how such caring work is privatised, socially isolated and ideologically split off from "production," women may also be unable to experience power in the fruits of their gift labour. The skills that support positive interdependence in the gift community may, in nuclear units, present problems of submersion in relationship. In the dyad, desires for connection may be most sharply in tension with desires for independence. When it falls mainly to women to maintain gift relations under such structural conditions, issues of autonomy may be most likely to manifest in money-related neuroses and addictions.[2]

Margaret Randall's (1996) interview study and personal reflections on women's relationship with money resonates with Hyde's themes in that she, like Hyde, writes, "as an artist still learning how to value my own work while inhabiting a world in which money remains a metaphor for worth and control" (p. 203). She argues that feminist theory, the women's movement and individual memory work are helping women gain more control of money as they come to understand gendered childhood experiences.

Women, more every day...are examining the implications of having or not having money, coming to understand some of the traumas its discriminatory handling produced in our own early lives, and learning to avoid repeating these patterns with those we love...Through a process of coming together, sharing our stories, identifying hidden social patterns rather than isolated individual problems, and revising therapeutic disciplines, we are moving, fast, to a different public as well as private space. We are also beginning to discard the false divisions between these two previously very separate arenas...Such movement, such women's work, profoundly affects how we relate to money (pp. 36-7).

Randall's study shows this work of changing one's relationship to money, important as it is to individual healing and growth, cannot be undertaken at the level of the individual outside of relationship. The point of Chodorow's work on the reproduction of mothering and my discussion of the gift is that individual work is limited, also, until collective arrangements are changed. This is why LETS members see their daily negotiations as vehicles for personal transformation as well as political-economic change. I will now turn to a third set of stories to illustrate how the class/gender location of women and men affects money patterns. These last two stories of this chapter also show how community currency situations give hidden aspects of social location more visibility.

Gender and Money (III): The Meanings of "Undervaluation" in Context

June: Housekeeper or volunteer?

June found she had to continue to struggle for her "freedom" in the way she participated in LETS. Recall how she chose to use LETS credits to pay for computer services and avoid a relationship with a man that too closely resembled the personal caring services of a wife. But she chose to earn those credits through house cleaning at the rate of $10 greendollars an hour. Her first few LETS jobs she found laborious and unsatisfying.

She was unsure about why she had chosen to offer house cleaning, considering that, "It's not that I *love* doing it (laugh)." Initially, she felt it was work that she could easily offer to earn greendollars. She was right; there were more requests for her services than she expected and more than she could fulfill. Knowing she could readily earn LETS credits through house cleaning caused her more dismay than reassurance.

June: *I did not realize that. I'm not sure I even want to know that* (laugh).
I don't want to spend the rest of my life house keeping (laugh).

The demand raised fear that she could become trapped in a long term house cleaning role. She described one job that was particularly difficult because the house was messy and the woman of the couple who hired her was unable to clean because of an illness. This could have become a regular LETS job for June, but she declined. The couple's need evoked negative feelings of being "in demand."

June had difficulty explaining why she chose to offer house cleaning through LETS when she would not choose to clean house for federal dollars as a part time job, even if she were to spend the money directly on computer lessons, as she did in LETS.

June: *I wouldn't go and clean house for four hours on Saturday morning to earn forty dollars to, I don't know, go to the movie and dinner or something Saturday night. Or have a computer lesson once or twice a month.*

Her explanation helps clarify the differences between paid domestic work, domestic work in LETS and unpaid domestic work. Paid house cleaning, especially if done on a casual basis, is associated with the most subordinate class statuses. June stated:

June: *I have trouble understanding it. I know that, you know, I don't see myself—I've never considered earning extra money house keeping.*

She explained that when she joined LETS she was thinking primarily of what she could get rather than what she could offer.

June: *But when it's a service I can offer in exchange for another service it seems reasonable. [LETS] had things that I wanted to take advantage of, and to gain those things [cleaning] is what I can offer in exchange.*

Federal dollars can be used to pay for almost anything, and so it requires deliberate effort to earmark cash earnings from one particular source that are to be used for one particular purpose (Zelizer 1994). If June were to do house cleaning for cash to pay for computer training, she would have to differentiate that money from her regular income. Otherwise, it would appear that her regular income is insufficient to cover her needs, and she is compelled to do extra work for wages. LETS earnings, in contrast, are already distinct from regular dollar earnings, partly because there are limitations on how they can be spent. June could use her LETS earnings from house cleaning as a way to pay for some basic needs, and to do so would appear to be a creative choice and a voluntary undertaking. Paid house cleaning for dollar wages would not as readily appear to be a voluntary undertaking. June followed up these remarks by commenting on how volunteer work is more positively tied to her self-image.

> June: *I think if I was particularly just wanting to offer my services, I would be happy doing [house cleaning] on a volunteer basis. That's part of who I am. I would volunteer that service.*

June thinks of LETS somewhat more as an exchange of volunteer labour than a market. She seeks to place her house cleaning work in this "third sector" outside of market and domestic relations. Domestic services seem to her less devalued when performed voluntarily than when paid or performed in the household. LETS improves on the typical "third sector" situation by also providing tangible acknowledgment and returns. However, when personal dependencies are involved, such as June's experience working for the couple who had need of regular, ongoing house cleaning, domestic work in LETS reverts to being problematic to her sense of freedom.

Jonathan: Not liking how powerful money can be

Jonathan is in his late 20s, married without children. He is in a "role-reversed" marriage in that his wife is older than he, has more education and is the primary wage earner. He followed her to one city, where she upgraded her professional qualifications, and they then moved to another city where she got a permanent job. Since then Jonathan has not been successful finding work that is related to his studies, "Something where you come home and your hands are clean at the end of the day." He admits that his job search is not urgent: "Really, life is very comfortable when I think about it because my wife has a good job and there isn't a lot of pressure for me to work a lot of the time." But he does work a lot of the time doing unpaid domestic work. This he relates directly to his support of his wife's career.

Jonathan: *I kind of maintain her lifestyle, like help her. You know, cleaning the house and having meals ready and helping her with her work, and then in a small way she'll help me with my work...But, you know, I'm here in a very small town where there's not a lot of work and, um, I'm doing a lot of the house-y stuff.*

It was unclear how much Jonathan helps his wife in her profession, but he indicated that their couple strategy may be to have a two-person career until he finds work. He meets considerable pressure from other men who do not understand this family arrangement.

Jonathan: *A lot of men don't understand these things, and I found moving [here] and meeting older men and explaining to them, you know, "Hey [we moved here] because my wife got a job." They would immediately say, "Well, what do you do?" Because of the ways of traditional work they're expecting that my wife would almost be following me, but it's not like that. You know (laugh), she's got more schooling than me. She's got a better chance at a higher income. So, I follow her. Honestly (laugh).*

Like many of the women I interviewed, Jonathan uses HOURS as a way to redress the undervaluation of unpaid, domestic work, and counteract the ego damage of carrying on a shadow career while being unemployed "for months and months and months."

He had been speaking about his employment search when I asked if he thinks of his work for HOURS as a side business. He replied by reminding me that his domestic work is his primary activity.

Jonathan: *...[my work in HOURS] fits to my lifestyle. When I'm not doing this I may not be doing business. I may be supporting my family doing unpaid work, right? Because that's how my day fills up (laugh). I don't necessarily plan my week or whatever, but I turn around and look back and think, well it's gone. Time just goes. I don't sit and watch Oprah all the time, you know (laugh). We're getting things done and it's unpaid work, and society has very interesting attitudes towards unpaid work.*

Also, more typical of the women, he has chosen work in HOURS that is service-oriented and an extension of domestic work. His choice of offering in the HOURS directory emerged from what he already has "at home."

Jonathan: *I finally became involved with HOURS and I go home and I go "What can I do for HOURS?" And I see I've got all my window-washing equipment. I've got it at home. All I have to do was to provide the service, to advertise it, to offer it to people.*

Jonathan has done window washing for wages as a student summer job, but he would not consider doing the work if it were not for the opportunity to take part in HOURS: "It's sort of a regression to go back from office work to doing the windows work and without HOURS I wouldn't be doing it." Sometimes his HOURS customers refer him to neighbours or family members who do not have HOURS and want to pay for his services with federal dollars. On these occasions he enjoys receiving "money I can take to the grocery store." But the experience is often negative because of class and gender issues. One group of customers in a high end residential neighbourhood invited him back next year, but he doesn't want to return.

Jonathan: *White carpet in all these homes. So I'd rather not. I'd rather be in an informal [exchange]. Like, I do good work. I do work that I'm proud of. But I don't want it to be like a class issue or something. I don't want to be put down because I'm cleaning their house. And I think I don't get that feeling at all with HOURS people. I feel like equal when I go and clean their house and they're valuing me as a person. But other people just kind of look at the service. I don't know. I'll probably go back because I need the money, but that was my lingering feeling later on. It was like, well they could pay anybody to come here. Or not so much that but, they, you know, they're really ignorant. (pause) They could just throw their money anywhere. I don't like how powerful money can be sometimes. People can just pay a large amount and get something done because they can afford it.*

The money payment expresses a class difference and affects how Jonathan acts when providing the service.

Jonathan: *I [become] more humble and start creeping around the house and not feeling good about myself. Like, sure, I'm making money and stuff, but (pause) feeling that they almost didn't want me there. They just want it done...I would rather work for people who really appreciate that they've got a human coming in, somebody who's going to do the work. It's not a robot coming in.*

131

In the following passage Jonathan refers to "people" he cleans windows for in HOURS, even though these "people" are mostly, if not all, women. This was a consistent pattern of speaking about women. At another point in the interview he mentioned a "pregnant person" on his street. By referring to women as genderless persons, he may be reducing the gender conflict he feels in being a man who does domestic work. He talked about his enjoyment of entering their homes, being entrusted to see messes. He wants to include himself among those who enjoy domestic life.

> Jonathan: *I work for a lot of families and people are home with the kids...They are almost apologetic that "Oh, my house is like this, or I've got kids here, is that okay, or I've got things near the windows that I didn't manage to move before you could come." And people are apologetic. You know, it's nice (laugh), you know, when people are feeling a little bit guilty that they haven't done things for me.*

As much as he may enjoy domestic work, Jonathan wants his work to be recognized and valued. He talked about doing favours for people on his street: an eighty-year-old neighbour, the pregnant neighbour, and so on. He prefers work for HOURS to these neighbourly acts because of the recognition he receives.

> Jonathan: *HOURS is sort of a formal way of doing favours sometimes. Because if you just go and do random acts of kindness or just go and clean something for somebody, you don't know if it's reciprocated appreciation, but with HOURS they're putting something out. They are saying, "I value this because I'm giving you HOURS," and [you know that] it was something they wanted. They came and asked for it to be done. They might have advertised and said, "I need somebody to come and do this work."*

So Jonathan's emphasis was not on the financial or material benefits of HOURS, but on the work experience, being paid and appreciated, and the social aspects of participating in HOURS.

"Undervaluation" and Social Relations of Distribution

These final stories of June and Jonathan's willingness to perform domestic work for community currencies but not for cash provide clues to the relational context that produces "undervaluation." Different forms of payment for the same work can indicate vastly different work relations. This idea is best illustrated by Marilyn Waring's "parable" of the man who marries his maid (Waring 1988; Brandt 1995). How money may be gotten, from whom, in what form and in what amount always matters because it is not the money itself, but the relationships through which money is socially produced which create the material and psychological conditions of our lives. The same work of window washing that, when done for HOURS, makes Jonathan revel in being a valued part of the domestic matrix of cleaning and child care, when done for federal dollars, makes him feel diminished and inferior. Different relationships are established through the two currencies.

Recall the attempts of Owen and the utopian socialists to remove the boundaries between the domestic and the market as a strategy for egalitarianism. Community currency activity is located right at these boundaries. June and Jonathan, for instance, situated their house cleaning and window washing for community currency in relation to a dichotomy between work that is marketed and work that is volunteered or performed domestically without pay. The diagram on page 134 depicts the institutional structure that makes that dichotomy so relevant. In the figure, "total economic activity" is organized according to the circumstances of money changing hands.[3] The formal economy is designated by money exchange, which measures and makes visible productive activity. The complementary economy is the non-measured economy in which productive and reproductive work is invisible to official economic indicators. Community currency activity relates to both sides of this structure. As a parallel money system its function is to measure work. Such work may be an extension of the domestic sector, as when members like Jonathan and June offer window washing and house cleaning services, or it may extend the petty competitive sector, as when self-employed members like Tom and Tamara charge a percentage of their price in federal dollars for work that is their regular source of income. The diagram illustrates how community currency activity blurs distinctions between market, voluntary and domestic sectors because it involves both private, market distribution, on the one hand, and personalized inter- and intra-household distribution on the other, work for income and work for self-consumption.

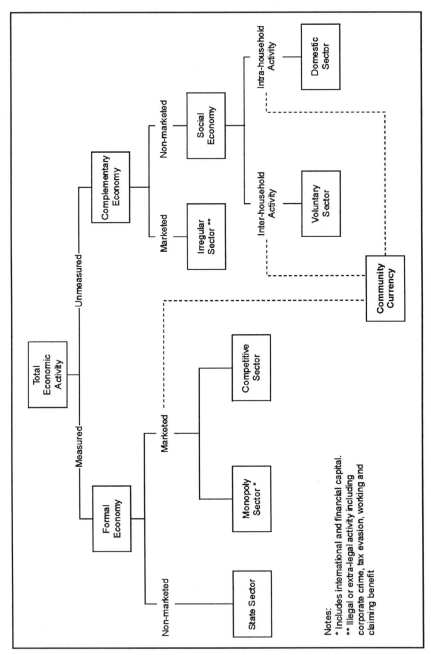

Community Currencies within a Model of Economic Institutions
(Adapted from Wheelock 1992, p. 18, and Pacione 1997, p. 1185)

WHAT MY FREEDOM IS ALL ABOUT

Joan Acker's essay, "Class, Gender and the Relations of Distribution" (1988) is helpful to understanding the implications of community currency's intermediacy to the domestic and formal economies. The essay belongs to a body of feminist work that attempts to reconcile "Marxist analyses of political-economic structure with feminist analyses of women's place" (p. 473). Acker departs from "dual systems" theory, the idea that capitalism and patriarchy are distinct, interacting systems of exploitation and oppression, because the "dual systems" perspective assumes a gender-neutral class structure. She, instead, theorizes the connections between class and gender through analysis of social relations of distribution of the means of survival, which in capitalist societies mainly consist in the wage and personal relations of distribution within and between households, supplemented by state transfers. Each of these ways of organizing money transfers, Acker argues, have the interacting effect of reproducing women's dependence. Even though new kinds of wage work are available for some women, "dependence is a core constituent of the reality of class in the lives of many women" (p. 477).

Gender is an organizing principle for the three main relations of distribution Acker identifies: the wage, personal gift relations and state transfers. Both men and women's wage is insufficient for the reproduction of working class labour, but women are the worse off: women's wage is less than men's, employment is less stable and more women are at the bottom of the wage scale. "Economic independence is impossible for most women under such conditions," Acker observes. "Many women experience the consequences of these structural conditions as personal failure" (p. 483).

The distribution of the wage to the unwaged takes place in the context of marriage and kinship relations, and entails performance of unpaid work that is entirely different from work in the marketplace in that "no connection exists between monetary rewards and amount of work, skill, experience, or effort" (p. 486). The expectation that gift relations are based in "love, duty and commitment" obscures that they are economic relations, and makes them difficult to negotiate. Personal relations of distribution are based on the entitlement of wives to husbands' support and husbands to wives' domestic services within the "spirit of sharing, commitment and sexual mutuality that many people expect to find in marriage" (p. 487). Women have little control over the conditions of their material existence or unpaid work when they are dependent on the personal distribution of the wage within the family. Moreover, conflict over money appears as interpersonal conflict, not related to the underlying structural conditions that produce these forms of dependence. For the same reasons, money conflict is also internalized.

> Dependence can be conceptualized as part of the processes or relations that constitute the society as a whole, rather than as an aspect of family structure. Dependence experienced as fear, powerlessness and loss of self is often the individual consequence of this system of distribution...The structural roots of women's ambivalence about their self-image are located in a societal arrangement that makes many women economically dependent on men (p. 489).

The independence and autonomy that money is thought to confer (Klebanow's equation money=power) is not available to most women through the wage. The dependent status even of middle class, working women within marriage is evidenced by statistics showing that following divorce economic welfare declines for most women, but for men tends to improve (Finnie 1993, p. 205).

These arguments about women's class experience help explain why payment in community currency and payment in cash carry different implications for the very same work, and also lend insight into women's "undervaluation." Paid domestic work, the lowest waged women's work, is personalized service that entails personal dependence on the employer for the wage. In LETS and HOURS, domestic work is not coerced through market dependence, which is why June likened it to volunteer work and, as Jonathan explained, the work relationship is usually between people of similar class status. Work for neighbours, friends and community members takes place through a set of relations distinct from wage relations and marriage/kin relations, and so does not reproduce the same kinds of dependence.

Community currency activity can be personally transformative when it allows for renegotiation of dependence in relationships. Price and "undervaluation" are key aspects of the definitions that must be negotiated. June placed a limit on her willingness to do house-cleaning when she perceived her customers were too dependent on her services. Jonathan withdrew when he felt he was not being personally appreciated by people with money who cared only about the work contract and not the person of the worker. If either had simply raised their price, they would have changed the understandings that locate them in a space between personal and market relations.

These observations suggest that undervaluation in community currencies is complex. If women charge too much they risk breaking with other women or disrupting relationships with men; but, most important, they also risk having their exchanges resemble devalued, feminized, low wage service work. The structural location of community currencies presents opportunities for negotiating price in ways that blur the gift/money, domestic/market dichotomies because exchanges may be constructed in more or less gift-like or exchange-like ways. This allows women to attempt to transform situations of invisible personal service and obligatory caring in the pattern of the gift into situations where the value of the work is formally accounted and negotiated, but important gift associations are retained all the while. It equally allows men to attempt to create a sense of giving within a structure of reciprocity, to enter community and enjoy a personal quality in their work relationships without becoming "feminized" by dependency or generosity.

Margaret Randall writes of this innovative potential of community currencies at the conclusion of her book on women's relationship to money:

> In essence, these [local currency] economies have allowed people some respite from the feelings of greed, competition, scarcity, powerlessness, and inequity engendered by our conventional money system...Women, and others who have been exploited and manipulated by economies of greed...make excellent authors of change. And each community programme gives new range to their creativity and to the ethics of caring that for so long have been used against them (Randall 1996, p. 167).

COMMUNITY and MONEY

By taking gender struggles over issues of power and intimacy, entitlement and obligation outside of nuclear family relationships, community currencies expand the space for artful interpersonal negotiation. The spaces of experimentation they create are small, and pertain to the smallest aspects of gendered relationships. Nevertheless, they can be sufficient space for members to begin to assert, among other things, what their freedom is all about.

Notes

1. A somewhat larger body of sociological literature on money and marriage examines allocation of money within the household, the role of money in the balance of marital power, and monetary outcomes of divorce (Cassierer and McGuire 1993; Singh 1994; Vogler and Pahl 1994). These works are less relevant to my questions of gender relations at the community level, except for one key insight. The notion that money is inherently corrosive of human relationships has its strongest experiential basis in domestic conflict over money, not marketplace transactions (Rabow and Charness 1991). LETS and HOURS advocates promote the potential of "convivial currencies" to transform *impersonal* market relations. The prevalence of domestic money conflict, however, suggests the need to transform *intimate* money relations. As I will argue, community currencies potentially could address both problems of impersonality and intimate conflict by moderating tensions between the wage relation and gift relations of distribution.

2. Margaret Randall comments insightfully on money-related addictions: "Money is something like food, in that we need it to survive, and so total abstinence is also not the answer. People with eating disorders are constantly running into the dilemma: we cannot give up eating as others might give up drinking or smoking or using drugs. I'm not suggesting a pecking-order of difficulty here. I'm just saying that when the dis-ease thrives around something with which we must come in contact many times a day, healing may require a different process" (p. 199).

3. My adaptation of Wheelock's diagram emphasizes how monetization symbolically bifurcates the economy and how community currencies bridge divisions between measured and unmeasured, marketed and non-marketed activity. Other ways to conceptualize the economy as a whole, such Hazel Henderson's layer cake analogy and Hillka Pietilla's concentric circle diagram, emphasize the interdependence and interpenetration of economic "spheres" and the relationship of human institutions to nature (Henderson 1991; Waring 1988).

Chapter Six

"A Very Social Thing"
Consumer Politics and Community

COMMUNITY CURRENCIES ARE MORE OFTEN promoted as sources of alternative employment than as opportunities for ethical spending, yet for
some members, this is their main attraction. Political scholar Eric
Helleiner, analyses community currencies as a green consumer movement,
comparable to the fair trade, consumer boycott and voluntary simplicity
movements: an instance of "a political movement that seeks to challenge
the priorities of global neoliberalism in the contemporary age by altering
the consumption patterns of individuals" (2000, p. 49). He describes how
community currencies respond to the neoliberal creed of globalism,
de-politicization of money, and radical individualism specifically by fostering: "a more localised sense of economic space, the capacity of local communities to manage money actively to serve political goals, and a more
communitarian sense of identity" (p. 37). As the political/managerial elite
presses for global economic integration, Helleiner explains, local currencies advance "small is beautiful" localism and decentralism. These goals
originate in green political thought, which is deeply concerned with questions of the scale of social organization. As Helleiner points out, however,
localism and decentralism can sometimes "dovetail" with the neoliberal
programme of reducing the role of the state, leading to such possibilities
that, for example, local currency earnings could substitute for government
benefits and services that had previously been basic entitlements. The consumption-based political strategy, Helleiner argues, is the factor that introduces the awkward alignment of greens and neoliberals on local self-
reliance.

Local currencies seek to promote change through a mechanism that
neoliberals themselves endorse: the voluntaristic behaviour of indi-

139

viduals acting as consumers in the economy. In this way, the local currency movement highlights a limitation of the use of consumption as political tool: it seeks to promote social change by playing within the set of rules and terms that neoliberals have sought to establish as the new terrain of politics (p. 51).

Even though local currencies potentially "pose a very radical challenge" to "the global neoliberal agenda and its associated values of individualism, mass consumerism, globalization and laissez-faire economics" (p. 50), Helleiner concludes that the consumer movement approach to these issues is politically limiting.

This chapter takes up Helleiner's themes and examines the potentials and limits of community currencies as a consumer movement. One challenge to evaluating the movement's political strategy is that, although community currencies may be considered a countermovement to market dominance, traditional oppositional movement models of social change do not apply. As Lyndon Felps, bioregionalist and co-founder of Dillo HOURS in Austin put it, the political strategy of HOURS is to create positive alternatives to the current economic order and, thereby, "underthrow the system" (1997). The quiet, casual and creative tactics involved in this "underthrowing" conceal just how radical a challenge community currencies may pose.

The movement's potentials could be assessed in a couple of ways. One way would look at the *limitations of* community currencies as an oppositional movement. The other would look at the *limitations on* community currencies as a constructive project. The first approach would ask how far-reaching and positive would be their impact if community currencies were to fulfill their goals in terms of membership, acceptance and circulation. This is Helleiner's question as he evaluates the movement's political strategy. The second approach would consider what limits the movement in practice, not only from meeting its current potentials, but also from continuing to formulate more radical agendas. This has been my main undertaking in the book: to identify the practical, gendered constraints as people try to make change in their own lives and communities. In this chapter, I continue in the same manner by discussing Helleiner's arguments about the *limitations of* consumer politics, while also emphasizing how gendered patterns of consumption place *limitations on* how well community currencies carry out these politics and move beyond them. I start with a brief history of gender and consumption to set the context for understanding how community currencies relate to consumer politics today. I then go on to discuss how the gendered separation of production and consumption hampers LETS and HOURS from realizing larger potentials, not only in the field of consumer politics, but in their endeavour to create distinct subcultural communities.

The Gendering of Consumption in Historical Perspective

Louise Tilly and Joan Scott's (1978) history of women's work in England and France relates changes in the mode of production to changes in family arrangements, particularly women's place in family livelihood strategies. Tilly and Scott tell a story of how the transition from an economy of household production to the "family wage economy" and, later, the "family consumer economy" entailed the spacial and temporal separation of production and consumption. In the family economy of the early modern period, households were relatively self-sufficient units of production and consumption. Much of the household's need for food, clothing, shelter and tools were provided directly through the labour of its members, who also earned money for materials through small-scale cottage industry and, for those without access to land or a trade, wage work. Household composition constantly shifted to ensure that the availability of labour balanced the number of mouths to feed. With urbanization and the spread of the factory system, wage work increasingly replaced forms of livelihood based in agriculture, craft and guild. The wage economy located production in capitalist enterprises, while the household became the site of consumption of the means of life purchased by the wage. Women became responsible for the daily and intergenerational work of reproducing labour, that is, restoring workers' capacity to perform the next day's factory work and raising the next generation of workers.

In the twentieth century, through processes of structural change that were by no means even or regular, the wage economy intensified. Fordist mass production and mass consumption furthered the decline of women's production for direct consumption. The "demise of domesticity" (Kessler-Harris and Sacks 1987) is one phrase used to describe changes in women's reproductive roles, as households became increasingly dependent on services provided through market exchange (de Grazia 1996). Consumer durables entered every home, and so did a whole range of specialized products for use with washers, refrigerators, furniture, toilets, and so on. "Ready-made" consumable commodities substituted for "home-made" cooking, baking, sewing, knitting, gardening and preserving (Firat 1994). Tilly and Scott argue that the transition from the "family wage economy" to the "family consumer economy" increased the demarcation of separate spheres of production and consumption, and positioned women even more distinctly as consumers. For all levels of the working class, they write:

> ...as the family economy became a family consumer economy, the woman's position as financial manager of the household expanded. The primary source of her status in the family (and in the community) came from the wife's ability to provide for the needs of the household by carefully managing the money contributed by others...A woman's major domestic responsibility continued to be the management of household finances, a consequence of her role as chief consumer for the family (Tilly and Scott 1978, pp. 204-5).

Feminist historians have since contributed complexity to the story Tilly and Scott tell, showing that the division of production and consumption did not take place as a linear or uniform process; women everywhere experienced it differently according to their position in the matrix of family, class and race relations (de Grazia and Furlough 1996). Nevertheless, the gendered separation of spheres of production and consumption is also a discursive reality in western modernity such that even the majority of women and men whose lives do not fit the pattern still live in relation to these basic ordering constructs (Parr 1990). To call the separation a "discursive reality" is to say that the story and the social relations and institutions it pertains to are mutually constitutive.

Even though Tilly and Scott's history is specific to place and has been complicated by more recent social histories, the narrative line of the story of the separation of production and consumption is familiar to modern western social history. It fits within a meta-narrative that holds that modern social order originated through the differentiation of previously merged unities (Jenks 1998). The modern discipline of economics, for example, arose through the new perception that the social and the economic constitute a duality (Polanyi 1957). In modern economic thought, where this differentiating pattern prevails, bipolar categories appear to describe the domains of social life, and also to correspond with the gender dichotomy (Nelson 1996).

Karl Marx developed his analysis of the separation of production and consumption as a critique of this differentiating pattern in classical political economy. Marx showed how the emergence of production and consumption as separate domains coincided with the severing of exchange value from use value. The identification of two forms of value resulted from organizing commodity production for the extraction of capitalist profits, which had the effect of obscuring the underlying unity of economic processes. Marx began the *Grundrisse* by pointing out that in situations of production for direct use or for simple exchange, the processes of production and consumption are merged—"consumptive production," he called it. Capitalist manufacture consumes materials and worker's labour power in the parallel process of "productive consumption" (1973, pp. 90-1). From these observations, he proceeded to analyse production and consumption (and distribution and exchange) as moments in a single process hat are rendered distinct and opposed as a result of specific relations between classes of people, principally owners and workers.

In cultures where processes of production and consumption are more obviously integrated, so are concepts of work and leisure. The more such concepts become polarized, the more they tend to be associated with the male-female dichotomy, while the categories of sex and gender collapse into an identity of female-feminine and male-masculine. Gender divisions of labour are premised on these associations. Productive work is "male," and has value and importance. Shopping and other "female" consumptive activity is defined as non-productive, non-work and leisure. So, as Fuat Firat explains, the feminization of consumption is a historical process that links changes in economic organization, economic discourse and gender representations:

The female—specifically, in visual culture, the female body—became the representation of the feminine, which was the *ideal* consumer in western culture. She "went shopping" while he worked. She spent his money or earnings. Her frivolity in buying and consuming became a major topic of jokes in the culture. She was such a consumer that he had always to restrain her appetite for consumables (Firat 1994, p. 210).

In spite of this devaluing of consumption in association with the feminine, there is a debate about whether women's position as consumers has been, in some ways, empowering. The "empowerment" argument refers to recent political developments through which demands for consumer entitlement have emerged as a form of citizenship claim (de Grazia 1996). Consequently, traditional politics of collective action rooted in solidarities of class and other collective identities are being displaced by more individualistic and politically centrist "lifestyle" movements. The "empowerment" position points out that consumer roles have brought women into the public spaces of the urban downtown. Consumer interests have placed women at the forefront of certain political and environmental movements on actions ranging from consumer boycott campaigns in the West, to food riots in "developing" countries undergoing financial austerity programmes. In commercial cultures where the consumer sphere now challenges the political sphere as an arena of public protest, consumer movements offer women all the more opportunity to exercise the power of consumer "choice." So while, on the one hand, women's shopping is a devalued, trivialized aspect of domestic labour, on the other hand, consumer roles have opened up to women a larger range of identities, "lifestyle choices" and avenues of political participation.

The contrary view, that consumer politics are not emancipatory, argues that, in the end, they hold no promise of liberation from the dominance of the market system itself. This position is rooted in concern that consumer movements contribute to the subordination of politics to the market. In other words, the fear is that politics, as state/civil society relations, are losing ground to politics as consumer preference. Consumer politics cannot address those issues of health, welfare and ecological protections, justice and equality that require market regulation. Moreover, the challenge of restricting corporate dominance requires concerted action, given the resources and skill of marketers in appropriating the underlying impulses of even the most critical social movements and selling the ideas in re-packaged forms. As Firat argues:

> The modern market system...is able to marketize the expressions of feminist, postmodernist, and other countercultural movements. The market system has, indeed, proven to be very resilient in its ability to co-opt many a countercultural movement's expressions by emptying them of their original meanings and translating them into images/products that are marketable (Firat 1994, p. 218).

Consider the "back to the land" movement: attempts to withdraw from consumer culture by re-establishing family producer households. Because of the individualism of the movement (Jacob 1997), even such anti-consumerist acts lend themselves to being constructed as an "alternative lifestyle" choice. Marketers seize on the desire to reject consumer culture and fashion the latest consumer products, from trucks to bread machines, as emblems of simplicity, self-sufficiency and the homestead.

It is from the perspective of this debate about whether progressive politics are those that seek to wield power through the market or to regulate it that Eric Helleiner evaluates community currencies. As I mentioned at the start of the chapter, Helleiner identifies community currencies as a consumer movement, and considers this orientation as limiting their political potential in the long run. My study supports his characterization of community currencies as largely consumption-focused, but also provides evidence that, at their most effective, LETS and HOURS are more of a cultural than a consumer movement, which would place them a step outside the frame of the debate. Movement leaders also would describe community money as a tool to promote local self-reliance, the goal being to avoid excessive dependence on either the market system or the state. Community currencies create the kind of local ties that further the potential for community-based livelihoods—a process Paul Glover describes as "making community while making a living." Unlike the back to the land movement, this re-localization of livelihoods with community currencies is a collective process. The cooperative aspects and the goal of creating community, in potential at least, take LETS and HOURS beyond being a movement of individuals acting in/against the market through consumer protest.

As I have been arguing throughout the book, however, community currencies have always been hampered by features of the gendered economy. This is true of their effectiveness as a consumption-based movement, and also of their ability to reconnect consumption and production in more cooperative and self-reliant communities rather than in individual "homestead" lifestyles. As in previous chapters, I will illustrate the tensions at play by drawing on the much earlier Owenite experiment, where it would appear that gendered consumption was also a limiting factor. The Owenite example takes us back to the setting of Tilly and Scott's history: early nineteenth century London, when the large scale transformations in the gendering of production and consumption that I have just described were well underway.

Historian J. F. C. Harrison recounts explanations for the failure of the Equitable Labour Exchange that had been published in the 1830s. Among the reasons was a single issue regarding women's participation. Harrison gives it relatively little weight, merely noting: "It was also claimed that the members' wives objected to shopping at only one store" (1969, p. 207). Although Harrison provides only this keyhole glimpse into the possible shape of gender relations at the labour hour bazaars, this single statement on the gendering of consumption relates to the issues at hand. I am not about to argue that women in LETS and HOURS object to restricting their shopping, although possibly some women and men do not join community currencies for this reason. The reference to women and shopping introduces a more complex argument for how the gendering of consumption limits community currencies as a consumer movement, and as a farther-reaching movement for alternative livelihoods. This small clue to the failure of the Labour Exchange does not directly parallel the contemporary experience, but it does suggest the importance of understanding LETS and HOURS through the history of "women's shopping."

Of first note is that Harrison's statement places Owenite women in the roles of wives and consumers. It identifies "the members" as men, and erases women's status as producers for the bazaars, even though feminist historians affirm that *thousands* of women workers sold goods, such as clothes, buttons, shoes, lace and gloves, through the Labour Exchange (Taylor 1983, p. 88). Harrison's small detail also identifies women as complainers, and implies that their quibbles about shopping, in part, foiled a remarkable endeavour. Harrison does not identify the reasons for women's objections, such as concerns about quality and selection. The remark is similar in sentiment to other men's commentaries on the collapse of Owenite communities in the U.S. that took women's "complaints" as contributing to the downfall of the experiments and as blameworthy rather than as constructive and insightful (Harsin 1984). Reports of the day suggested that women were at fault "for ruining good Owenite experiments simply because they could not understand what utopian living was all about" (Kolmerten 1990, p. 171).

The comment about women as shoppers in the bazaars is interesting, not just because it blames women for the failure of the labour note scheme, but because it exposes a larger cause of failure in practical Owenism: the failure to observe gender imbalance and inequity in its everyday manifestations, such as in patterns of reproductive labour in which women are shoppers. This is important because among the parallels I have been drawing between Owenism and the community currency movement is that both profess gender egalitarianism. The mantle of egalitarianism can hide gender oppression, as when Owenite men took the issues raised by real-life women as private peeves, and not as valuable critiques of unequal arrangements (Kolmerten 1990, p. 101).

Most commentary on the Owenite experiments, including Harrison's, discusses their failure not in reference to particular categories of people involved, such as "member's wives," but in terms of the gap between ideology and what was practically realizable at the time (Polanyi 1957; Heilbroner 1967, p. 105; Harrison 1969, p. 207; Taylor 1983). Writing of the labour exchanges, Owen himself commented on the necessity of adapting their design to existing realities: "The National Equitable Labour Exchange does not come up to the expectations formed by its well-wishers; and yet it is the nearest approximation we can make to the Rational System, being at the same time obliged to admit a part of the irrational, or old system" (cited in Royle 1998, p. 54). The statement about shopping complaints by "member's wives" is interesting, therefore, in how it illustrates a crucial aspect on which Owen's vision had to be compromised. As I have noted in Chapter Five, Owen's writings advocated the abolition of marriage and of sexual divisions of labour within single family households. His utopian communities would have had women and men fulfilling a variety of work roles within arrangements that would have negated distinctions between producers and consumers, and corresponding gender divisions. The comment about women's shopping, therefore, attests to the scope and direction of historical processes at the time, against which utopian socialist countermovements could not hold sway.

Finally, Harrison's remark about the Owenite women's objections to shopping at only one store can be read as the comment of a western male historian writing in the late 1960s. The lesson Harrison seems to be drawing from his 1830s sources is about the failure of labour hours to change consumption patterns. Because he gives no reason for women's objections, one implication of the remark is that labour hours had failed, particularly, to limit women's consumerism. These were hardly Owen's central concerns,[1] but reflect concerns about "consumer culture" that arose in the 1950s and continue to motivate today's anti-consumptionist movements. Whereas Owen, the former factory owner, primarily aimed to dignify men, women and children as producers, today's community currencies are promoted as opportunities for meaningful work *and* more ethical alternatives in people's roles as consumers.

Seen as a consumer movement, community currencies advance a double agenda. First, they promote local shopping, and ethical or "green" consumer choices, including reduced consumption, repair and re-circulation of used goods, and do-it-yourself skills. Second, they promote monetary reform by providing choice in currency. At the present level of LETS and HOURS organization, they hardly pose a threat to the federal dollar; but, at least in theory, the two types of currency, local and federal, can be thought to compete. In some Third World contexts such as Thailand, authorities have banned local currencies, perceiving that they could undermine the national currency system. In the following three sections I will discuss how community currencies can be a vehicle for consumer politics, first, in the specific ways they are used to express certain political values and, second, just in that they are chosen as an alternative to the national currency. In the third part I argue that LETS and HOURS have political potential beyond the arena of consumption.

Consumer Politics of Directed Spending

Some models of local money other than LETS and HOURS are more decidedly organized as a consumer movement. I will describe two before turning to a discussion of consumer practices with HOURS. First, in the Berkshire region of Massachusetts, the town of Great Barrington has seen several special purpose notes organized through SHARE (Self-Help Association for a Regional Economy) in association with the E. F. Schumacher Society. The first were Deli Dollars, which helped finance the re-location of a popular Main Street restaurant. The deli owner, Frank, sold vouchers for a ten dollar lunch at the new location. His customers paid eight dollars for the notes and, within thirty days, raised $5,000 for Frank's move. Building on this experience, SHARE organized several issues of store notes, including Berk-Shares, which had the participation of seventy stores and the local Chamber of Commerce. Susan Witt and Robert Swann (1995) explain the political significance of store scrip such as Deli Dollars in a small town whose economic base is threatened by malls and large chains.

> Deli Dollars started a consumer movement in the Berkshires. The Berkshire Farm Preserve Notes, Monterey General Store Notes, and Kintaro Notes that followed gave Berkshire residents a way to vote for the kind of small independent businesses that help to make a local economy more self-reliant (pp. 13-14).

The Toronto Dollar is a second local currency model with a consumer-focused design. Like the Berk-Shares, Toronto Dollars are issued when consumers purchase them with federal dollars, but unlike the Massachusetts scrip, they are backed by a reserve fund in federal dollars. Also unlike the Berk-Shares, they circulate in an urban commercial centre where they are accepted not only by small independently-owned businesses but also by mall merchants and franchises of large corporate chains. Their primary purpose is to unite customers and businesses in support of local charitable causes by creating a special convertible token. It works as follows: consumers receive Toronto Dollars in exchange for Canadian currency and spend them at par, as they would cash, at participating restaurants, farmer's market vendors, grocery stores and retail businesses, as well as for professional services. Businesses either re-spend them with other businesses at full value, or redeem them at 90 cents on the dollar. The 10% of Canadian dollars that will never be drawn on for redemption provide the backing for issuing an additional 10% of Toronto Dollars to those purchased by the consumer. That is, for every ten Toronto Dollars purchased by a Toronto Dollar shopper, one additional Toronto Dollar is issued as new currency, and designated for community services. The additional Toronto Dollars are set aside in a Community Fund which, on regular, highly celebrated occasions, is granted to community agencies. The recipient organizations may spend the Toronto Dollars for programme needs, use them to create paid positions, or distribute them directly to beneficiaries (in the form of bursaries for low income college students, for example), who would spend them at participating businesses, as would shoppers who had purchased the dollars. The Toronto Dollar is promoted as an opportunity for consumers to contribute to local charitable causes just by shopping with a special community money and spending no more than they would Canadian dollars. The benefits of participation to merchants include positive publicity and the loyalty of the Toronto Dollar shopper.

Berkshares and Toronto Dollars enter circulation when consumers exchange federal dollars for them. Similarly, with HOURS (but not LETS), it is possible for some people to participate solely in the role of consumer by purchasing HOURS with federal dollars from designated businesses that accumulate a large supply. I will use Lenore's case to explain how this form of involvement works. Although Lenore advertises that she is available to teach a second language, she has not been receiving requests for this service. Also, her two part-time jobs and care of four children allow her little time to offer lessons should she receive requests. And so she participates in the HOURS economy only by shopping with them at the farmer's market and other businesses in town that accept them. In this way she hopes to stimulate trading by re-circulating HOURS that were lying unspent. Lenore's decision to support HOURS by shopping with them is a political form of consumer action: every act of support for HOURS represents a withdrawal of support from the conventional economy:

> Lenore: *I'm kind of at the edge of the [HOURS] system. Just trying to support it rather than actually using it.*
>
> MB: What is it about the system that you want to support?
>
> Lenore: *Well it's kind of the diametric opposite of the multinational, oppressive, corporation-type economy.*
>
> MB: Which you don't want to support?
>
> Lenore: *Right. And I do my very best not to.*

If HOURS were only a movement in support of local shopping, they would not serve as well Lenore's objective of opposing "the multinational, oppressive, corporation-type economy." She could more easily use federal dollars to shop at the farmer's market and support local small businesses, self-employed individuals and those looking for supplemental income. By choosing HOURS, Lenore is supporting a system of currency that symbolically reinforces the interdependence of consumers and producers in the region where she lives to a degree that dollars do not.

To clarify the role of HOURS in the relationship we need to see it also from the perspective of producers. Ellen and Dan are vegetable farmers who accept Lenore's HOURS at the local farmer's market. They see little direct benefit from HOURS, but are, nevertheless, enthusiastic about what HOURS symbolize: a consumer ethic of "buy local," on which they depend as farmers. Dan explains:

> Dan: *It's not really an easy thing to use, but it is a constant reminder of where our income is coming from and how we can keep it local.*

Ellen agrees that they gain little from their involvement in HOURS, but they have larger reasons for participating. She and Dan speak of the importance of tangibly marking their relationship to consumers.

> Ellen: *I like the idea of it [HOURS]. And I really want to support the idea...Since we're constantly trying to encourage people to buy local products, not only [our produce], then it just makes sense that we belong to it.*

Dan: *Yeah. Right. We're tied because the only place we sell [our produce] is in [town]...So as part of the community we have to take HOURS and encourage other people to use them.*

MB: So, even if the material benefits to you are not all that great, it's promoting a community ethos that is about shopping locally and... [Dan: *Right*] [Ellen: *Yeah, yeah*]...keeping money in [this region].

Dan: *Think locally, act locally. That kind of thing.*

Ellen: *That's the main reason that we're [involved], you know. And with being farmers it's so much more obvious because for the farmers to not be supported locally is just terrible... There would be competition from California, the competition from large agri-business and all. The local farmers can't make it if there's not some awareness and there is, luckily, a lot in [this community], of "Buy Local." You know, if you have two choices at [the grocery store] of California celery and local celery, people are going to, hopefully, there's a lot of people who are going to buy the local just because it's local. That's really important for farming.*

MB: How much do you think HOURS contributes to that awareness?

Ellen: *I think it contributes. Like I said, I think it's a reminder. It's not so much a matter that in actual, practical terms that it contributes, it's more a reminder.*

Dan: *Yeah, they're a hassle.* (All laugh).

In spite of their enthusiasm, farmers such as Ellen and Dan and small merchants may have weak incentives for participation, considering the "hassle" of returning the HOURS into circulation. When Dan receives an HOUR he thinks more about its circulation than what it can buy: "It's more how I'm going to return it into the community."

Lenore and others acting in the role of consumer are often aware of the transaction cost they pass on to producers:

MB: What's your experience been like shopping with HOURS?

Lenore: *Well, I mostly do it here at the Farmer's Market. And I always have a little bit of a niggling feeling that, "Oh, these small little vendors are getting too many HOURS and they actually need the money"* (laugh). *So I feel a little bit* (soft voice), *"Is it okay?". And they always say, "Yes."*

But, (soft laugh) *because these are small, local crafts people and vegeta-ble people and I want to support them. But, I do, I want to support the sys-tem as well.*

Emily has similar feelings when she purchases plants and vegetables at the Farmer's Market.

MB: How is it when you approach [the vendors] with HOURS?
Emily: *Oh, it's fine. It's definitely fine. But you definitely have that feel-ing like, "Oh, sorry." And I don't know why, but you feel that way.*

The consumer politics of HOURS succeed because the relationship of local consumers and producers is so important to both parties that the addi-tional work involved in marking it is undertaken in good spirit. When there is such an identifiable division between those who produce and those who consume, however, imbalances arise within the HOURS network. Producers of food and high demand services accumulate too many HOURS and are unable to find sufficient outlets for, as Dan put it, "[re-turning them] into the community." If producers are unable to re-spend HOURS, the currency system will stagnate. Gendered patterns contribute to this problem. The two preceding examples of Lenore, and Ellen and Dan illustrate the typical case in which the chief consumer is a woman. In spite of the fact that Dan is more vocal about the difficulties of re-spending HOURS, Ellen and their children are the ones who spend most of them at the farmer's market and food co-op.

The gender division of labour whereby women mostly shop is only one source of gender imbalance in the production/consumption relation. The structure of employment in the wider economy also constrains women's participation as producers on the community level. Alice Kessler-Harris and Karen Brodkin Sacks (1987) describe the context in which women, like Lenore, are less able than in the past to act as producers in a parallel economy such as HOURS creates:

The suburbanization of their communities together with the growth of a service sector that provides women with both jobs and con-sumer services reduces the strength of informal kin and neighbor-hood support networks. Unlike earlier income-generating activities and jobs, new jobs for women conflict in time and space with family and community life. As wage-earning women pass into these jobs, community-based, informal economic activities can be expected to break down (p. 78).

Lenore exemplifies the situation of women whose political commitments would lead to fuller participation if the demands of paid work combined with family responsibilities permitted, and if their positioning in service sector roles did not limit the productive offerings they could make in the local economy. I will return to these issues of the gendered economy in the last part of the chapter.

Consumer Politics through Choice of Currency

Only a few people in HOURS can participate just as consumers by exchanging dollars for HOURS; most people must earn before spending. In LETS, for all members, earning and spending must be balanced over time. When functioning well as a currency system, LETS and HOURS are poised to do more than promote local shopping. In providing an alternative to the federal dollar, they give members such as Lenore a way to express their critique of the conventional money system and "vote" for a different model. Central to this critique is how LETS and HOURS challenge the basis for the issuance of national currency. In the conventional economy, almost the entire money stock (97 to 98 per cent) comes into circulation through banks in the creation of commercial, consumer and public debt. As Michael Rowbotham (1998) argues, the basis of the money supply in debt, particularly mortgages (accounting for 70 per cent of the money stock in the U.S.), results in fundamental insecurity and competitiveness because it creates a double calling on money: for circulation and for debt repayment with interest. The situation of chronic money scarcity incites aggressive economic behaviour because the economy must grow to keep pace with the growth rate of debt. In the United States, private and public debt has expanded by 1,000 percent in the past 33 years, according to Margrit Kennedy (1995, p. 31). Rowbotham (1998) and Kennedy (1995) argue that the system of credit-money redistributes income from the poor to the rich, not only because the poor carry more debt, but also because in-

terest on debt is passed on in prices of commercial goods and public services. Taking these hidden interest charges into account, Kennedy
presents figures from Germany showing how the low- to lower-middle income households pay more interest than they receive, while households of
the tenth income decile receive about double the interest they pay, and the
wealthiest one percent collect from fifteen to two thousand times more
than they pay. She argues that if money were understood as a public service, the redistributive effects of compound interest would be recognized
more readily as a form of exploitation:

> This is a different and far more subtle and effective form of exploita-
> tion than the one Marx tried to overcome. There is no question that
> he was right in pointing to the source of the "added value" in the
> *production sphere*. The *distribution* of the "added value," however,
> happens to a large extent in the *circulation sphere*. This can be seen
> more clearly today than in his time. Ever larger amounts of money
> are concentrated in the hands of ever fewer individuals and corpo-
> rations. For instance, the cash flow surplus, which refers to money
> floating around the world to wherever gains may be expected from
> changes in national currency or stock exchange rates, has more
> than doubled since 1980. The daily exchange of currencies in New
> York alone grew from $18 billion to $50 billion between 1980 and
> 1986. The World Bank has estimated that money transactions on a
> world scale are from 15 to 20 times greater than necessary for financ-
> ing world trade. (p. 27).

Local economies compete for scarce investment dollars and public services
even as financial and currency markets expand because indebtedness and
the chance to make money from money compel governments, consumers,
corporations and financial dealers to put their money where it can get the
highest rate of return. David Korten (1997) recounts a conversation with
the Malaysian government minister in charge of forestry: "In explaining
Malaysia's forestry policy he observed the country would be better off once
its forests were cleared away and the money from the sale was stashed in
banks earning interest. The financial returns would be greater" (pp. 14-15).

For ordinary consumers, spending on the cheapest imported products is a comparable form of short term financial thinking induced by pressures to stretch the dollar. As Rowbotham explains, prices do not carry information about the longer term economic costs of spending on imported goods. As liquidity drains from the local economy, reduced purchasing power creates more dependence on cheap imports at the cost of local enterprise.

Community currency is designed to stay local and circulate, and so it avoids the compulsive drive for the cheapest prices and highest rate of return that conventional credit-money generates (Milani 2000, p. 167). Geographical limitations on spending and earning benefit local producers in the first instance; and as Thomas Greco (1994) puts it: "[Local currency's] narrow range of circulation makes it more likely that the spender will be able to earn it back. Local currencies, thus, stimulate local production and employment" (p. 47). HOURS member Gil compares the effects of HOURS and dollars on spending decisions in this way:

> Gil: *I see [HOURS] as a potential for people who are trying to live an alternative lifestyle, trying to put their money into better things and building a community. It can foster that. And I think [with HOURS] you can direct where your money is going that way. Whereas if you have dollars, it might not work that way. You work hard for dollars, you're going to want to put that money into the cheapest cost you can.*

Community currency cannot be used for dollar loan repayments or cheap imported goods, it must be re-spent locally, and (for LETS) its supply is not scarce, but sufficient to the exchange requirements of users. As a result, it is less restrictive of the inclusion of ethical criteria in spending choices. Often people remark that with LETS or HOURS they buy products they could not have afforded according to their dollar budget calculus, or they find themselves willing to pay more than the conventional market price. Local money can *only* buy local art and handcrafted goods, locally grown food, holistic health services, lessons, repair work, used goods and all other manner of personal assistance, from accounting to yard work. The sufficiency of supply of community currencies invites a re-thinking of the notion of "choice." The dollar's scarcity directs consumer "choice" towards cheap prices. Restricting money to the local community currencies open up a new range of "choices" and spending criteria. Gil explains:

Gil: *There's a machine shop that's taking HOURS now. And to me that could be very valuable. I had an old table saw from 1929 that I picked up at a garage sale. It needs to have the bearings re-done. It would cost $125 to get it done, and you could get an okay table saw for $250. So, is it worth it? With HOURS it could be worth it and have this old... You know, it can't cut a lot of wood, but it could do the simple stuff that I need for cheap. For $125. So it makes that exchange happen.*

"[Making] that exchange happen" is important to Gil for reasons beyond the usefulness and money value of the saw, although these are also key. The exchange keeps an old tool in use and resists the ecologically destructive throw-away culture. By extending the life of the saw, Gil also reminds himself of how his work extends a way of life in his community.

Beyond Consumption: Building Community by "Supporting the System"

Returning now to Helleiner's question of whether choice of currency is an effective response to the challenges of marketization, I will consider once again the apparent affinity of greens and neoliberals on matters of localism and decentralism. As Helleiner reminds us, neoliberal theorist Fredrick Hayek was also an advocate of consumer choice in currency through the denationalization of money (Hayek 1990 [1976]). Hayek's proposals for multiple privately issued monies were aimed to subvert the state's ability to regulate the money supply in the interest of national projects. Community currencies advance a quite different agenda with a localism that is not anti-national. They have always been conceived as complementary to the national currency, competing as currency of choice only in local commerce. And so, although they do circumvent more conventional parliamentary approaches to monetary reform, they should not be thought merely to reinforce the market system as the mechanism for social change. Their politics extend beyond the market arena, first, in the way they educate and politicize members about money, second, in their promotion of alternative taxation and financing of local services, and third, in the way they make the notion of community an organizing principle.

Community currencies contribute indirectly to monetary reform, first, through popular education about money. LETS and HOURS give members a new understanding of how money works. Earlier I mentioned Judith, a LETS member who felt she had not learned much about money through her formal education even though she had once enrolled in economics in university. "Until I was on the LETS I didn't really understand money," she said. This is a common experience. A survey of the largest LETS in Australia, Blue Mountain LETS, confirms that experience with LETS helps demystify money in general. Of the 73 percent of members who said LETS had changed their life, meeting new people was the most common life change. "Change in attitude to money" was the second most common transformative experience (Chadwick 1995). Furthermore, Judith's changed understanding of money had politicized her. She spoke of wanting to "get up on the soap box and get everyone's attention" to try to communicate the critique of federal money she is continuing to work out.

> Judith: *I guess mutual funds is my next big target because this concept of everybody investing is ludicrous because if everybody invests, everybody can't also collect (laugh)...And 18 percent returns on mutual funds, who is paying that price! You know. And I want to diagram that. I really want to see and find out where that's coming from and going. Were you ever taught about money in school? how the economy really works? And forget economics with supply and demand curves and all that kind of that stuff. I took economics at [university] and I just quit.*

The second way community currencies could potentially go beyond consumer politics is through the various proposals leaders have made for contributing to public financing on the local level. Some argue that for it to serve as an agent of localism, it should be integrated into municipal governmental finance. Local money could improve the capacity of local government to provide services if it were accepted as an optional means of paying municipal taxes, fines and fees. Local currency is already considered taxable income but not an acceptable means of payment of taxes. The "backing" of local government acceptance would greatly expand and strengthen the local currency and make it easier for main street businesses to accept it, as they would be guaranteed a way to spend it. In turn, accepting revenues in local currency could boost government revenues by reducing the number of people who default or evade taxation. In the long run, a vigorous local currency system could raise personal incomes, create a stronger tax base and serve as a resource for local governments to fulfil their public services commitments.

There is yet a third way in which the politics of community currencies go beyond the actions of individuals vis-a-vis the marketplace. Helleiner's discussion of LETS as a consumer movement assumes an opposition between only two arenas of politics, state and market; but HOURS and LETS take up a third type of focus on community-building. He is correct to suggest that the consumer-focus of LETS is non-consumerist: "Consumption behaviour is used not to reinforce a sense of possessive individualism, but rather a sense of communitarian values that often rejects materialism as a value" (p. 47). Valuing community has a feeling aspect that the money symbolizes. Helen Luke's (1995) essay on money and the feminine draws these connections between money and community from the perspective of a Jungian psychologist. She speaks of "earning and paying" rather than "getting and spending" to reinforce that our material existence (getting and spending) depends on the quality of our social relationships (earning and paying). Attention to how we act with money can bring consciousness to the human qualities of our exchange relationships, an awareness we can also recognize in others.

> We can usually tell by the atmosphere of a store whether the owner cares for the values of exchange in his money dealing or whether he cares only for money itself. Of course, no matter what the general state of affairs is, one may come across individuals anywhere in whom this beauty shines. I suppose every woman among us can remember instances on her shopping trips when she has been served by a saleswoman who is truly concerned, not just to sell her any old thing, but to find the coat or the dress that is exactly right, and this is accomplished for obviously personal as well as business reasons. We come away not only delighted with our acquisition but with a feeling of real exchange between people, and the money which passes is for the moment truly connected to that for which it stands. (Luke 1995, p. 52)

This attitude of caring for the values of exchange, which is sometimes present in regular commerce, pervades community currencies. LETS and HOURS members speak of how they want more than advantageous trading; they also want to connect meaningfully with other people. LETS member Louise states:

> Louise: *For me, I value [material] things, like I don't want to get just two dollars for something. I would really like to get more than that, but not a monetary thing...I like to go to somebody's house and see where they live, for one thing, and see who they are and talk to them. And knowing that they're in LETS, I'll probably be seeing them again...And people in LETS seem to be open to meeting you. I like to get...a piece of a person's life, and I would give the same too. And I feel on a certain level in LETS that people have that sort of interest in each other.*

As I have already discussed elsewhere in the book, in many cases the desire for interpersonal connections is what motivates involvement. Vince, who I will talk more about in the conclusion, became involved in HOURS because "it really made me feel like part of the community." He expressed excitement similar to Louise about the way people in HOURS take an interest in one another.

> Vince: *Every time you use HOURS, even the other people who use HOURS are, you know, you hand over some HOURS to buy something and, "Oh, what do you do for HOURS?" and you start talking to them and, you know, and strike up a deal. You don't get that spending [federal] currency, you don't get (higher pitched voice): "Oh, what did you do for that?" (laugh) You know, it's a really—, everyone I've dealt with in HOURS, they really are like that.*

Jonathan revealed a similar interest in knowing his neighbours in more than one facet of their lives. He reflected on how doing favours is an opportunity to foster good feelings, and to develop closer relationships.

> Jonathan: *That's something I value, is community. And neighbourhood favours come from that because not only are you doing the work, but you're in touch with the person, you know how they are that day, you know about their ailments, you know about their needs.*

Jonathan then explained how HOURS trading develops through such interaction. In my interviews I was curious about how people seek out opportunities to spend HOURS, and so I asked Jonathan to describe his experience at HOURS bazaars with this question in mind. Our conversation quickly turned back to the theme of community.

MB: You say that people at the bazaars asked, "What do you do?" [Is that] because they want to know how they might be able to spend their HOURS?

Jonathan: *Well, no. They're curious. If you are involved in HOURS, how are you involved in HOURS? It's a piece of the puzzle. It's a very social thing, I think, that they are viewing it that way.*

MB: Oh, you think it's a social thing. It's not like they are going around figuring out...

Jonathan: *Not how to spend HOURS money, but "Who are you and why are you here? What's your angle? Why are you involved? What do you have to offer?" Things like that. I think it's more personal. And then I think business develops out of that.*

For Jonathan and members like him, spending is not the focus; relationships are. Political organizing around the feeling-values of community does not in itself take LETS and HOURS beyond a consumption-based movement. The desire for community is highly susceptible to being marketized, particularly as money frees individuals to live in "communities of choice." Market researchers identify "communities of consumption" (de Grazia 1996, p. 280) and sell people on living in "lifestyle communities." There is one sense, however, in which the pursuit of community in LETS and HOURS goes beyond consumption. I have been describing how community currencies reconnect processes of production and consumption, first, in that the local money marks and fosters these local connections, and second, in that every member must balance both activities. Production and consumption come together in LETS and HOURS also simply in that members "produce" their own currency. For this reason, when LETS and HOURS members, as a community, "consume" the local currency by choosing it over the federal currency, they differ from people who would "consume" currency under Hayek's proposal for a "free" banking system.

Members distinguish these "moments" of production and consumption of currency when they differentiate between the "community" and the "system."[2] Their desire for community is closely related to their interest in "supporting the system," but these are not identical. The "community" consumes the system's product and pays its costs. In LETS, these costs are usually administered in the form of a small transaction fee. When Jacquie barters directly she continues to register the exchange through LETS because she wants to "support the system" with the service fee.

> Jacquie: *I really believe that we should be going through the LETSystem because they're the ones who have kind of brought us together more or less, and that percentage fee is much needed (laugh), you know?*

In HOURS, one way to "support the system" is to provide solid backing for the currency in goods and services. For example, Michael does this by offering canoeing lessons:

> Michael: *I am one of the few people who will accept HOURS, 100%. Which is to say, I really want to support the system. It's not just like a cute little adjunct.*

Sometimes members feel tensions between "supporting the system" and just being in community. Judith, for example, questions whether the community should pay for the system and its product.

> Judith: *I would rather do direct [barter]...If you really believe in the LETS concept and you want to promote your LETS to the community, you know, justify its existence, you'll put those trades through. And you're paying that [transaction fee] to put them through. But then the LETS itself can say, "Well we traded this many dollars this year, and there's been this many sales and purchases," and stuff like that...Once people have made the contact, they're going to by-pass the LETS, they're gonna trade directly... So pretty soon there will be no need for that LETS to be there. This whole network of people know each other now and all do the direct trading and don't put it through the LETS. So the LETS in a sense is accomplishing a lot in networking these people, but there's now no method of tracking it.*

Kevin was attracted to LETS because it expanded his "small circle of friends" with whom he enjoys barter relationships. Now that he has become close to some LETS members, he has questions similar to Judith's:

Kevin: *I'm just [wondering], like, when we do direct exchanges—I did one the other day with somebody—I was wondering whether I should charge [greendollars]. I charged her something and she charged me something, and it was like, "Okay, should we bother?" because it was just about even. We are going to enter it into the system. The problem is that the system needs the input to keep going. And we wouldn't have LETS without the system anyway. So, it's kind of weird. Like when you get a lot closer to somebody and do a lot more trading, it just seems like an unnecessary drain. It's like, what do you need this for?...I guess the issue is more, you can't be good friends with everybody and do that for free for everybody. At least not in today's world (laugh). So in terms of expanding the system or getting stuff more specialized, or stuff that isn't between a small circle of friends, I guess it makes sense to still be part of that system and to contribute the overhead into the system to pay for it.*

Kevin and Judith began by questioning the sustainability of "the system" without the willingness of "the community" to pay for it. They then recognized the impossibility of "the community" in the absence of "the system." Kevin concluded his reflection saying: "Now that I look at it (laugh) the local currency thing is pretty crucial to the sustainability of the whole thing." "The community" and "the system" are interdependent. This is the strongest way in which community currencies reconnect production and consumption. While it would appear that members are choosing a particular community or choosing a particular currency in a consumer fashion, actually they are producing themselves as a community as they consume their own product. As Gil put it: "In some ways I look on it as our money. And...we can create this system the way we want it."

The Problem of Gendered Consumption

In spite of Gil's optimism, there are obstacles to fulfilling the largest potentials of the system. Here I will return again to the gender divisions in production and consumption, earning and paying, in the wider economy and focus on how these manifest as gender imbalances in LETS and HOURS. Gendered consumption is reflected, first, in role divisions between couples, second, in the difficulties of individuals to achieve balanced accounts, and third, in the imbalance of "male" and "female" offerings.

Take first the example Sam and Alice. Sam's hobby is bee-keeping. Alice packages the honey and comb, as well as her own cinnamon and chocolate honey spreads. They both sell the honey together at LETS trading fairs. Alice thinks of their LETS account like a joint bank account, "only better," because they have a high positive balance. I asked her how she and Sam use the LETS credits they jointly earn. She began to detail how they spend as a couple. Most of their spending is done at the trade fairs, she explained. They both arrive early and, just as the trading is beginning, she checks every table for items she wants. "Generally I make most of the decisions for the purchasing unless Sam sees something he wants," she concluded. The same pattern holds for trading through the directory.

Alice: *When the [newsletter] comes in some time between the day it comes in and about 3 to 4 days afterwards I usually go over it with a highlighter, highlight everything that interests me, mark down notes. I've now, since I receive it on e-mail, I just print it up so I get a hard copy, put it in a duo-tang, highlight the things that I want, and because it's printed off e-mail there's enough space to write comments beside it. So for all those that I call and I want information I always indicate: "Called. Date. Left message. Spoke to them. Made arrangements. Blah, blah, blah," and you know, do it that way.*

There have been a lot of products on the system that have interested me and, you know, you call and you leave a message and you never hear back from them. Sometimes it takes 3 or 4 calls, but you just do what you can. So, (sigh) generally that's how it's done.

If I think there is something that would be of interest to Sam I usually mention it to him. But he, you know, some point after I look at it, kind of looks at it, sees whether or not I've highlighted any Christmas gifts for myself, or things that we should consider for his mother, or whoever. And then essentially looks at the stuff, whether or not there's anything specific that he needs and then [I] go about it.

In this narrative, Alice reveals the extent of her responsibility for decision-making about the joint account, and the labour-intensiveness of spending and procurement in LETS. She also indicates how she involves Sam in the process by giving him opportunities to oversee her decisions and ensure that she has included "gifts" for herself among her purchases.

A similar pattern held for another LETS couple whom I interviewed together. Janet and Patrick also hold a joint LETS account. Patrick earns most of their greendollars through his locksmithing business. He marvels at Janet's ability to spend them. Rather than recognize what she does as work, he justifies their division of labour by attributing it to Janet's particular talent for shopping on the LETS.

> Patrick: *Janet's better at spending the money than I am* (laugh). *She can find things without any problem.*

In response, Janet also downplays the work and describes how spending greendollars differs from federal dollars for reasons I have already laid out: they buy different items: spending is not constrained by budget pressures.

> Janet: *I spend them more readily than I would cash. But I get good value for what I spend, and I buy a lot of things I wouldn't normally buy. I try different things. But if I had to fork over cash, I'd do a little less than I do…It's just that there's so much that is available for greendollars that isn't available for cash, and it's stuff that I wouldn't normally try. And I've made a lot of friends, and done a lot of things I wouldn't normally do.*

Janet's ability to spend is linked to her willingness to make friends and do what she would not normally do. As I have been arguing, new patterns of spending involving closer relationships are fundamental to how community currencies work. The examples I have presented so far suggest the skills needed to make them work are "feminine."

In fact, my interviews with couples show that the division of labour whereby the man mostly earns and the woman mostly pays is so ingrained that, even in Jonathan's household, which was largely "role-reversed" (the wife was the sole breadwinner and Jonathan "supported her lifestyle" by doing domestic work), the traditional pattern applied to Jonathan's HOURS earnings and, according to him, their regular income as well. His wife was the financial manager and chief shopper.

Jonathan: *What happens is I earn the HOURS and my wife spends them. It's the same with most of our money. Right?* (laugh) *Except she basically earns most of the money and we jointly sort of share the money. But the discretionary money I think, she goes, "Okay, that's a good project. Let's endorse that." She's got the final kick on the discretionary money. But she loves to spend the HOURS money. That's hilarious.*

Gender divisions are most obvious among heterosexual couples, but even looking at individuals, gendered patterns still show up as unbalanced accounts. Women more than men tend to experience difficulty earning. For some women, not knowing how they might earn through community currencies—being unable to identify skills they can offer—is a barrier to joining. Other women find the skills they do offer are less valued than services typically provided by men. Difficulties in paying are also gendered. Women more than men tend to feel reluctant to let their accounts go below zero.[3] Consider Donna, a tea room and gift shop owner in her 50s.

MB: You get your account statement every month from LETS. Are you in the positive?

Donna: *Oh, yeah. I don't believe in going in the red. I don't know why because it doesn't bother me to owe MasterCard or Visa, but it just, I don't know, it just bothers me, I couldn't do it.*

MB: What's the difference between being in the red in LETS compared to using your credit card?

Donna: *I don't know. I guess it's almost like, I feel it's like I owe money to a friend or a relative, or something.*

By refusing to "go into the red," Donna shows her regard for LETS members as similar to friends and relatives. It may be the closeness of such relationships, or their permanency, that makes her reluctant to complicate them by the feeling that she "owes money." Her hesitance to feel monetarily indebted to friends limits her to always having to stay in the black and to earn before spending, a pattern that could not hold for many LETS members.

Men are more likely to have difficulty spending for other reasons. Recall Tom's frustration at not finding satisfactory ways to spend his balance of close to $1600 greendollars because he feels he "can't spend it frivolously." Part of the problem for Tom is that "frivolous" spending is feminizing. Another problem is that the range of services offered through LETS is unbalanced. He described a failed attempt to spend some of his greendollars for a job he needed in relation to his work as an electrician.

Tom: *A week ago I tried to hire a truck to move a stove. There were three listed for greendollars. I couldn't get anybody. I could get one, but I had to wait until they were finished work in the evening and I had to do it during the day on a specific day. One person advertised and didn't call me back. And the other person, I think he just wasn't there. The directory changes.*

Women and men both experience the sheer work involved in arranging exchanges on LETS. Married couples tend to designate this work as women's. The problem is compounded for single men, such as Tom, because of the predominance of personal services that women tend to offer. To give another example, Mark, a deli owner, has accumulated hundreds of dollars worth of HOURS. He is waiting for an opportunity to spend them on labour for a special event at the deli. Until this is organized, he is uninterested in spending HOURS on items other members have advertised in the directory. He mentioned, in particular, the preponderance of "women's" services:

Mark: *I just knew that there would only be so many times that I would use them to get ear candling or something* (laugh). *No offence to ear candlers* (laugh), *but...*

Even if such services were attractive to men like Mark and Tom, it would require of them concerted effort to spend their small hoards of HOURS and greendollars on these lower priced items. Hiring labour would seem a good way to re-circulate their currency, if only they had the organizing skills to bring about the right occasion or the connections to recruit willing workers. The longer they wait, leaving HOURS and greendollars unspent, the more trading stagnates in the entire network, and the fewer opportunities they will have to spend in the longer term.

These three types of imbalance—the inability of some individuals to balance their accounts and avoid over-accumulation, imbalances in the division of labour between couples, and imbalances in the types of services available across the network—reflect gender divisions in the wider economy. One source of the problem, as I have explained, is the predominance of women in the service sector and their distance from other valued producer roles. This situation, going further back, is linked to the large scale historical processes whereby consumption work was feminized. As in Owen's day, people often fail to recognize and address such gendered patterns as systemic issues. Instead, problems are seen as reflective of the personal failures of individuals or the failure of LETS or HOURS as models for change. Nevertheless, community currencies are positioned to create new awareness and systemic change because a re-balancing of consumption and production is a condition for their success. Not everyone can participate as a couple with complementary skills, and so this re-balancing would necessarily entail that members achieve a more balanced alignment of the gendered aspects of work, shopping and exchange. Community currencies, therefore, support change along these multiple dimensions, as the stories of the final chapter will now show.

Notes

1. Owen always advanced a broad programme for the uplifting of the working classes. He is credited with founding the consumer cooperative movement in Britain (his lasting legacy, according to Polanyi). Even so, he considered the Equitable Labour Exchange a single facet of his trade union organizing, whose larger objectives included improved wages, education and housing.

2. "System" is part of the LETS acronym, and so members frequently refer to the items available "on the (trading) system." They also refer to the accounting and administrative functions as "the system." Even though HOURS transactions are not centrally recorded, there is still administrative work involved in printing the money, regulating its supply, monitoring its circulation, publishing the list of backers, informing and expanding the number of users. Consequently, HOURS users also refer to these functions as "the system" in the same way as LETS members. In my interviews, six out of eleven HOURS users made twenty-four references to HOURS as "the system." Thirteen out of sixteen LETS members made ninety-three references to LETS as "the system."

3. As explained earlier, in LETS it is necessary that some accounts show a negative balance and others are positive so that the system of accounts as a whole balances. The system is functioning well when individual balances regularly fluctuate above and below the zero point.

Chapter Seven

"There's a Flow to it"
Gender Balance and Balanced Accounts

THROUGHOUT THE BOOK I HAVE BEEN making reference to Owen's labour-money experiments as a parallel to present day community currencies. There is one aspect in which the comparison becomes problematic, and that is in how short-lived the Owenite communities and the Equitable Labour Exchange really were. In spite of their failure to take hold over the long term, historians continue to find the Owenite projects interesting, not just for what they tried to do, but also for the reasons they failed. Owen historian J. F. C. Harrison among others, emphasizes the difficulty of introducing such extensive changes as the Owenites attempted under the circumstances that prevailed at the time. For the Labour Exchange, just as for the utopian communities, he argued, it was "impossible for the system to become insulated from the pressures of the commercial world outside" (Harrison 1969, p. 206).

For feminist historian, Barbara Taylor (1983), the utopian socialist analysis of gender oppression, and the overall direction of Owen's prescriptions for a "new moral world" of class and gender equality, have provided an enduring socialist feminist vision. Like Harrison, she describes how the Owenite schemes were unrealizable because of practical circumstances of the day, including the inadequacy of pre-Marxian social analysis. Nevertheless, she argues, the cause of women's emancipation suffered a set-back when "scientific socialism" pursued a narrower programme of proletarian revolution and suppressed the feminist agendas that had been active within Owenism. For Taylor, the significance of Owenism, and the aspect that must be revived and carried forward, is the utopian style of the movement which encompasses multiple agendas for social change:

In the end the case for our cause—for feminist socialism—must become the case for Utopianism itself, for a style of socialist endeavour which aims to transform the whole order of social life and in so doing transforms relations between the sexes. This was the Owenites' endeavour in which, hampered by their own difficulties and those of their times, they failed. We must not. (p. xviii).

In this book I have been considering community currencies similarly: as utopian social experiments. They have already exceeded the Owenite precursors on many criteria of "success," including numbers of participants, longevity and replication of the models. By most assessments, however, community currencies have fallen short of their proponents' two highest aims: shoring up the local economy and reducing poverty and unemployment. Some anticipated, following Jane Jacobs' (1984) work on the economies of cities, that local currencies could help compensate for the failure of national currencies to provide "feedback control" for cities and regions (Dobson 1993; Swann and Witt 1995; Solomon 1996). To function this way, as a "skin" buffering regions from macro-economic fluctuations (Linton and Greco 1987), local currencies would have to account for a greater level of economic activity than they currently do. Even though a few individuals rely extensively on their local currency earnings, the number of members and the overall level of participation in most schemes remains lower than their founders had hoped. New Zealand likely has the highest rates of participation in LETS, with 0.1% of the population involved in 1991 (Boyle 1999, p. xx). The participation rate in the UK is approximately 0.03%, or one out of every 2,980 (Williams, Aldridge et al. 1999). The level of community currency involvement in Canada and the U.S. is substantially lower.

The second broad aim of the movement, which has not yet been fulfilled as hoped, has been to reduce unemployment by connecting local needs with under-used capacities and resources. As I have explained, advocates look to non-scarce accounting currencies like LETS and community-managed currencies like HOURS to provide a stimulant to employment and a new source of purchasing power, especially for people with low and fixed incomes. Here again, the record so far has been modest. A survey of

Stroud LETS in England, for example, showed that LETS income amounted to only 1.8 percent of total household income on average, and 4.6 to 7.2 percent for the low-income members (Williams, Aldridge et al. 1999).[1] These supplementary incomes undoubtedly are important to their earners in the low-income category, 70% of whom say that LETS has improved their material standard of living. Given the relatively low numbers of participants, and the fact that the poor and unemployed are only slightly over-represented, such findings do not as yet confirm LETS as a single-intervention solution to poverty, for those hoping it could so prove to be.

Evaluation research that focuses only on how close community currencies come to reaching these large goals misses their significance as utopian experiments. The purpose of such experiments is to organize around a set of shared values and, by doing so, to identify the limiting conditions that exist at present and the conditions that would make it possible for the group's ideals to become more widely manifested. The symbolic significance of such experimentation is not lost on the mainstream media, which has given extensive coverage to local currencies. The Ithaca HOURS web archive, for example, lists more than five hundred references to feature stories and reports in print and electronic media about Ithaca HOURS.[2]

Like the historians of Owenism, I have turned my focus from evaluating community currencies' official goals to examining how the wider context of the gendered economy has constrained how far individuals can carry through new forms of interpersonal and community exchange relationships. Observing the gendered aspect of economic relations has helped explain the limitations the movement faces as a serious economic innovation. My analysis has highlighted the clash between community currencies and specific gendered patterns in the conventional money economy, patterns of valuing human activity, of gift labour, of monetary negotiation, and of the splitting of production and consumption into separate, specialized activities.

The finding that gender relations are a sticking point for the movement presents one major implication: conventional gender arrangements will need sustained attention if LETS and HOURS are to advance on a transformative path. Convivial economic relations within healthy communities depend on gender equity and balance. The question becomes, what would gender balance look like within LETS and HOURS, and what kinds of strategies would best foster it?

The complexity of gender relations in community currencies that I have documented calls for a diversity of strategies. The authors of *A Male/Female Continuum* (Pierce, Wagner et al. 1998), to which I referred in Chapter Two, would support this conclusion. They advise and work with large organizations that have come to recognize the need for a "power equity" approach to issues of gender, race, class and sexuality. Their key insight is that "paths to colleagueship" are necessarily different for men and women, and for those starting at different points along a spectrum of gender relationships.

Bronwyn Davies (1990) makes a similar argument for the need to support the coexistence of different "feminisms" whose philosophies and approaches may seem contradictory. Davies is influenced by Julia Kristeva's (1986) essay, "Women's Time," in which Kristeva identifies three "generations" or "tiers" of feminism that are now interwoven in the same time period: liberal feminism, radical feminism and a third strategy that seeks to challenge gender projects themselves. All three feminisms are already evident in the community currency movement. Liberal feminism—seeking "access to the male symbolic order" (Davies 1990, p. 502)—captures the aim of revaluation of "women's" work, which I described in Chapter Three, and also the efforts by women to negotiate fair prices for their labour, which I analysed in Chapter Five. Many women and men, however, are dissatisfied by limiting feminist goals to equality and fairness on "masculine" terms. Davies' understanding of radical feminism—the "celebration of femaleness and of difference, separation from the male symbolic order" (p. 502)—describes the agenda of shaping LETS and HOURS as "feminine" gift economies. As I argued in Chapter Four, the celebration of the "feminine" in this way has contradictory outcomes for women. Although it appears to elevate "women's" work, it does so by reversing the hierarchy, while leaving the dualistic structures, categories and evaluative dimensions of gender unquestioned. In Chapter Four I showed that men who were able to achieve the valorized "feminine" attitudes of gifting received greater recognition and reward than did women, who were expected to "undervalue" their own contributions.

Davies' third feminist approach is less easy to conceptualize because it involves reconstructions of gender that would make available less dualistic ways of being and relating. For Davies, shifts at the third tier would entail:

> ...a move towards an imagined possibility of "woman as whole," not constituted in terms of the male/female dualism. Such a move involves confronting one's own personal identity with its organization of desire around "masculinity" or "femininity." The desired end point of such a confrontation is to de-massify maleness and femaleness—to reveal their multiple and fragmented nature and remove from the meaning of maleness and femaleness any sense of opposition, hierarchy, or necessary difference. This is not a move towards sameness but towards multiple ways of being. (p. 502)

In LETS and HOURS some members' gender practices reflect an ability to live their politics at this third tier. Such members' stories can illustrate the kind of "imagined possibility" of wholeness Davies describes. I will conclude the book by presenting stories of three LETS and HOURS members, all woodworkers, who have used community currencies to support changes in their livelihoods. Compared with others, these members seem to have achieved remarkable degrees of balance in their earning and paying in LETS and HOURS. Concerns about getting and spending local money are secondary to their relationship to their work and the pleasure they take in exchange relationships. As one of the men said of his account, he has discovered that "there's a flow to it." These members tend to take a spiritual outlook towards work, time and money, and communicate an understanding that their balanced accounts are collective, not just individual, achievements. Importantly for my arguments in the book, their ability to get their needs met while doing work they love seems to go along with their capacity to integrate the "masculine" and "feminine" of the community currency experience. The political significance of such achievements by relatively few lies in the stories they make available and how these stories, to use James Hillman's phrase, continue to "possibilize the imagination" for themselves and others.

I will compare two men, Michael and Vince, from two different HOURS communities, with a woman, Beverly, who is a LETS member. There are significant differences in socio-economic, family and personal attributes between the men and Beverly. The men are both in their mid- to late-twenties, university graduates, unmarried and childless. Beverly is in her mid-fifties, college-educated, divorced, a mother of four and receiving social assistance. These three make an interesting comparison because, in spite of clear differences in social location, there are interesting similarities in their livelihood strategies beyond the basic similarity that all three happen to be self-employed woodworkers: Michael builds canoes, Vince is a carpenter, Beverly is a woodcarver.

Michael, Vince and Beverly all described feeling that their work for LETS or HOURS is meaningful and fundamentally expresses who they are. They all have been enjoying increased local currency trading and federal dollar earnings, as well as receiving other forms of recognition. They took these successes, in Beverly's words, as "affirmation that that was where I should be." They had all taken risks and foregone various other sources of security in order to pursue their craft. Michael made a dramatic choice to turn away from the material security of a well-paid job. Vince had made a conscious commitment to protect the most creative elements of his woodworking from commercialization. Beverly spoke to me of a more gradual personal transformation through which she had begun to experience a sense of abundance and a loosening of the ways her material poverty had been restrictive in the past. All three described coming to embrace an understanding of security that allows for a psychic and creative life undominated by the need to make money. As Vince explained:

Vince: *When you are a craftsperson...it's probably your craftsmanship that drives you, not making money. Because making money, it's very hard to make people things and you can't think about the wage you are making, ah, because it's depressing. You just have to say, "I will make this and see how much I can get out of it," and go from there. So money, getting money out of it isn't the motivation in the first place. It's trying to make a living by doing what we love to do. But we are doing what we love to do. So getting every last penny we can isn't terribly—it's important but it's not the focus.*

The sense of security for these three members derived from a faith in the "flow" of money and time, the sufficiency of the means of life, and the abundance of gifts. In their orientation towards money they seemed to live out Helen Luke's teaching that "real freedom from anxiety" requires facing fears of the loss of security and "giving a fundamental consent to insecurity" (1995, p. 54). Their trust seemed to be born out in the balanced flow of paying and earning they all achieved in HOURS or LETS, and in the way their ability to benefit from community currency exceeded the majority of users. Most interesting, their achievement of balanced accounts was linked to indications of the balanced ways these members integrated the gendered aspects of their inner lives and their relationships.

Michael: Being true to himself

Michael accepts HOURS for canoeing lessons and guided trips. He spends them enthusiastically at restaurants, the farmer's market and for business-related services and supplies, including local, ecologically harvested wood. His main dollar income is from a new small business building canoes, which, at the time of the interview, he had been running for just over a year. He is willing to accept partial payment for a canoe in HOURS. After graduating from university, he had been employed in a number of jobs in the social work and education fields, until he finally left a secure, well-paid "semi-administrative" position to start his company. I will let him tell the story, beginning with his description of his salaried job:

> Michael: *Had a free cell phone and all the perks...I'd been working there about a year and just thoroughly unhappy with it. It was enough money really. I had [a retirement savings plan] even, you know. Felt like I was Mr. Middle-class. But I wasn't really thrilled.*
>
> *I had built a couple of canoes and loved it. You know, I've always loved to build and to make stuff. As I look back I see that so much of my identity, you know, my personal feelings about who I am, is really tied into the making of things, you know, that that is just crucial for me.*
>
> *So I made up this great plan about a year ago and said "Okay, I'm going to wait a while, save up some money and pay off some debts and I'm*

going to be really logical and reasonable. Six months from now, I'll kind of
assess the situation. Then maybe I'll make some plans to leave.

The next morning I went in and quit. Had $200 in the bank. Owned a
power drill. It was like, "I'm starting a company building canoes!"

I didn't have a place to work. Had a lot of money due in bills monthly.
My personal fixed expenses were quite a bit higher than they are now. But
just really said, you know, "You can fish or cut bait. How much faith are
you going to have?" basically was the way I decided to do it.

I just had the feeling like if I don't do this, something is just going to eat
away at me. I'm just not going to be true to myself, really. So that no mat-
ter how much I may have to get creative financially or business-wise, or
whatever, that's all worth it because there is no way I can sell myself, sell
myself out, as I felt like I had been doing. Because I was very good at the
work that I did. Very good. I had all sorts of accolades and praise and
raises. And people thought I was super. But, like I said, something in my-
self knew that it wasn't a real expression of what I wanted.

Michael continued to tell a series of stories about synchronous events that
contributed to the start-up of his business. One of these stories was of how
he found his workshop and arranged to barter his labour for the rent. His
landlord owns apartments, and Michael does casual work, such as painting, which they agree to value at $15 an hour. He and the landlord keep
track with a running ledger of credits and debits, and no cash changes
hands between them. Michael's ability to tolerate a degree of insecurity,
which is to say, his larger sense of security, not only enabled his change of
career, it has also contributed to the workability of his barter arrangement
and other such small improvisations. I asked about his account with the
landlord, and he elaborated:

MB: Do you make sure it balances every month?
Michael: *Well, that would be nice, but no, I owe him a few hundred*
bucks right now and he knows that and I know that and it's fine. The
work will get done.
MB: Have you been in a positive credit situation with him in the
past?

Michael: *Oh, yeah, definitely. I have had times where I do a mess of work and I've paid two months ahead. It hasn't been that long. Not quite a year, but having seen it go up and down I've sort of realized that that's just how it is. There's a flow to it.*

Vince: You get more tomorrow

Like Michael, Vince is self-employed. He graduated with a bachelor of science degree and went to work as a builder and carpenter. He does craft work and renovations for HOURS, which he spends at restaurants and among other artists and craftspeople. Vince has a history of barter, which he thinks was partly influenced by his father, "a pretty serious do-it-yourself-er," and to his family's weekend projects, including building the family home, that required "a very cooperative attitude towards labour." Vince shares Michael's sense of security. In the following passage he speaks of the flow of favours and of time.

Vince: *I think I've always, I don't know, traded things with people. Favours, you know, "I'll do this for you; you do that for me." You know, you don't write it down, you just kind of keep track. "I'll help when you're doing—"... Just a community feeling, you know. That's what neighbours and friends do for one another, they help out. The thing about time is, you get more tomorrow. You know, you never run out of it* (laugh).

Vince's greatest pleasure in using HOURS is the satisfaction of using his talents to produce something of value to another person. In the following speech he begins by explaining why he and his business partner make things to sell for HOURS.

Vince: *We feel good taking HOURS and supporting the whole system. And we want people to have something to spend them on. And it's fun. It's fun making something. That's why I do it. They say, "Oh my goodness, this is beautiful." That's why I do it. I really get off on that, you know. I may have a big ego, but, I like making something beautiful and having someone else think it's beautiful too. That's exciting.*

Vince's enthusiasm for earning HOURS by making beautiful things equals his enthusiasm for spending them. Not only has he been able to "use HOURS on [regular purchases] so I can save my dollars for things that you need to buy with dollars," he has also taken pleasure in using HOURS to get "stuff I wouldn't normally get."

As I showed in Chapter Six, shopping with community currencies is typically "women's" work, and the ability to use them well, to pay freely not only for money-saving items but for whatever is on offer in the community that has worth, is thought to be a "feminine" capacity. Vince and Michael, therefore, stand out among the men. The emphasis of my analysis all along, however, has not been to identify male/female differences but to show how individuals relate to and negotiate gender divisions.

Listening closely to Michael and Vince's accounts of how they achieve a balance of earning and paying in HOURS, we can hear them call attention to the same gender patterns in evidence in others' experiences. In their cases, however, they demonstrate their ability to hold together attributes that are conventionally split. In the following passage, for example, Michael uses his tone of voice to dramatize his sense of the contrast between a "feminine" way of shopping with HOURS and a "masculine" way of reckoning with market money.

> Michael: *I know that when I use HOURS there is sort of like a whimsical feel to it, that's like,* (higher pitched voice, faster and louder than his normal speaking voice) *"Hey, it's HOURS."*
>
> (regular voice) *Like it doesn't feel like money in a way. Like I don't have that guarded feeling of like,* (lower pitched voice, slower than his normal speaking voice) *"Ooh, I'm down to my last, you know, couple of bucks."* (regular voice) *It's sort of like,* (higher pitched voice, louder, faster) *"HOURS, yeah, I'll get flowers at the Farmer's Market. It's only HOURS."* (regular voice) *Like, it doesn't somehow register that you're spending money. It's sort of like, oh, you just get it. There's neat stuff and you can get it and, okay, cool.*

By marking the contrasts in this way—describing himself as entering a "whimsical," "feminine" arena when he shops with HOURS, and departing from the "guarded," "masculine" feeling-terrain he usually associates with dollars—Michael acknowledges that his actions take place within a polarized gender order. He, simultaneously, reveals his desire to transgress and transcend it.

Vince conveys a similar message that the style of business dealing he eschews contrasts with the "sense of community and very intimate interaction with people I deal with" in HOURS, and that the contrast is gendered. He told me: "Most people I work for [in HOURS] end up being my friends." I asked him how these friendships come about and he explained:

> Vince: *If I make something for someone...I really try to get some understanding of what the person is looking for...If you asked me to build something for you, I'd really try to get an idea of what you're looking for, what your aesthetic might be. What would you find pleasing, what would you like? And it goes for a picture frame to a house.*
>
> *I work very hard at that. And I like that. I like really* (pause) *I treat it like an art. I'm making you something, you know? And so, I guess I get personally involved...Instead of just going* (exaggerated low tone of voice), *"Oh, you'd like a table? Okay, I'll make it this big, and put some legs on the bottom of it for you. There you go."* (regular voice) *You know?...I get to know the person, I think about them, and I brood on it a little bit, I do a sketch and I come up with something that I think will suit them, them personally.*

Using a deeper, more "manly" voice to mock a standardized, quick and impersonal way of relating to work and clients, Vince also mocks a type of masculinity that goes along with it. By contrast, he takes delight in the personal; he takes time to "brood" on his work. And so Michael and Vince indicate that certain aspects of successful participation in HOURS, namely shopping and befriending, are feminizing, but that they, themselves, have achieved a comfort with the "feminine," which they wanted to assert unmistakably in the interview with me through their words and intonation.

Beverly: A lovely way to beat the system

Most notable about Beverly is the extent of her use of LETS and the difference it seems to have made to her quality of life. I met her at a LETS trading fair. Her wood carvings were attractively displayed on a covered table, except for one that she wore on a ribbon around her neck. It was a small, round-bellied figure of a woman holding an orb above her head. "I call her 'Abundance,'" she said.

In our interview Beverly told me several stories before I asked about her trading: stories of her struggle with a bout of depression ten years ago following a divorce and a move to a new town with four children, aged 3, 7, 10 and 12; stories of how she came to take up woodcarving and discover that she has a talent for it; and stories of how she became involved in LETS and began to use it as an outlet for her carving. I knew from her table at the LETS fair that her work sold well. When I asked about her account, she indicated both how skillfully she uses it and how important it is to her in light of her dollar income.

MB: Are you able to spend your greendollars without much trouble? I know some people who are successful at earning have this problem of not being able to spend because the things they need are not available, or they don't have time, or for whatever reason. They end up building up a huge positive balance.

Beverly: *Mine is fairly balanced...I'm not even sure where I am and I'm not concerned about it because I know that it keeps balancing out one way and another. So I don't really keep track of it. When I get my slip with the [newsletter] each month it's a surprise to read the total at the bottom because I have not kept track of it. I don't concern myself with, "Am I in the red or in the black." I just keep on doing it because I know that I'm going to keep on selling stuff. And there's so many things that I can get in exchange.*

MB: How carefully do you keep track of your bank account?

Beverly: *The real money? (laugh) I'm real, real careful there. Yeah. Yeah. Yeah, because you can't go into the red there. In fact when I was in the bank the other day I was just checking when I got my bankbook back and it said "Balance $1.86." A dollar-eighty-six! And it's only the 17th of the month! How can this be? (laugh) So I had a little cushion account that I could take some from and put it into the "Pay Bills" account. But if I hadn't noticed it at that time I would have been in trouble.*

With the LETS money I don't have to keep that careful watch on it because, as I say, there are those people who always buy from me...so I don't have to be anxious that I'm not going to balance out somewhere along the line.

The list of things she has received through LETS includes food, clothing and shoes, pottery, jewellery, accounting, publicity, plumbing, carpentry, hauling appliances, physical therapies such as massage, and various kinds of household help. She has purchased services that she urgently needed but did not have money for, such as a brake job on her car, as well as items that were less urgent, such as a computer for her children and a night in a Bed and Breakfast with her cousin:

> Beverly: *My cousin had never been to a B. & B. before. Neither had I. We just treated ourselves and luxuriated in the wonderful [B. & B.]. And so we'll do that again in the summer when she comes.*

In the stories of each purchase Beverly conveyed a sense of gratitude. She also expressed some awe about the positive openings that were coming about as her carving gained attention and "a following." The story she most wanted to tell was of a Lifework seminar she had wanted to attend in British Colombia. The seminar leader had offered to waive the fee and pay for half of her accommodation if she could pay the other half and the cost of travel. She doubted it would be possible: "With my particular financial situation, [it was] farthest from anybody's mind that I could possibly handle something like that." The money had to come from completely different sources than her regular income, which was already stretched to cover basic expenses. She told stories of fundraising in her church, finding a new venue for her carving sales, making unexpected carving sales, and receiving an anonymous donation until, finally, she concluded: "It did all come in."

It is not difficult to see how the fluid balance of Beverly's LETS account is linked to her achievement of gender balance in her life generally. First, it is evident from her pattern of trading that Beverly has formed fruitful trading relationships with both women and men in LETS. Unlike many women, she has been particularly successful in acquiring men's services. Second, interestingly, when describing her family background, she associated her "way of managing with money" with her mother and connected her love of woodcarving—her vocation—with her father:

> Beverly: *Even my earliest shopping trips would be to [a thrift store]. I remember going with Mom and having a great time finding bargains there...*

181

I've always been drawn to wood. My dad is a carpenter and as kids we'd go out into the woods and gather interesting pieces of wood, and he would clean them up and make lamps or things to hang on the wall.

In telling these memories Beverly, like the men, called attention to gender divisions of production and consumption, and demonstrated how she integrates them.

The most telling indication of gender balance is the contrast between Beverly and Donna, the woman in the previous chapter who fears feeling indebted to the LETS community, and other women I have described in earlier chapters who have difficulty setting prices. Beverly is unusual in her high degree of comfort with asking and receiving, as the story of raising money for the Lifework seminar illustrates. Now that she has returned from the seminar, she is giving talks to her church and carving club about her experience. She reciprocates to the LETS community similarly by introducing more people to LETS. She described her pitch to me with much laughter and enthusiasm, adding: "Those of us who are in it and who do well with it can talk other people into it."

Michael, Vince and Beverly have managed to incorporate community currencies into their livelihood patterns in ways significant to their well-being and enlivening to the entire money network. In presenting their stories I have mainly focused on individual attributes, arguing that their success in balancing earning and paying has required that they overcome the limitations other members have experienced in relation to the constraints of gender identities. Achieving balance has required of the men that they come to terms with any fears of being feminized by shopping. It has required of Beverly that she confront doubts that she can "handle" what it takes to pursue her "lifework."

It would be important to understand how such members' social position contributes to their pursuit of balance, although small numbers do not allow for a conclusive analysis. Two characteristics all three have in common are suggestive, however. First, all are self-employed, skilled artisans who enjoy autonomy in their work. Second, they all live in non-nuclear family arrangements and outside of heterosexual marriage where they can be less implicated in intimate gender divisions of labour. Although not all single, self-employed people in my study participated at the level of these members, these factors may facilitate the ability to direct their livelihoods away from the "family consumer economy."

Michael, Vince and Beverly represent the boundary of what is currently possible within LETS and HOURS, and so it remains to reflect on the political meaning of what the community currency movement achieves through them. That these individuals' choices are political is clear. The men have made conscious decisions as much as possible to abandon middle-class family consumer roles and masculinities in favour of the satisfactions of creative work and personal exchange relationships. Beverly did not reject consumer culture in the same way as the men; it was no longer available to her following her divorce when she was raising her children on a low income. It was not for Beverly to renounce the system, but to overcome it. As she explained: "I love to try and beat the system, and LETS is a lovely way to do that."

These cases show that at their cutting edge, community currencies are not primarily about ethical action in the market, although they do advance ethical alternatives to corporate work and commerce. Neither are they primarily about pressuring the state for regulatory action, although their educational effects could build support for monetary reform and, if taken up, they could become a tool for municipal government to deliver services and revitalize the local economy. Community currencies, in their current manifestation, represent a third political strategy, a "lovely" means of acting in the arena of culture and community, where struggles for gender emancipation and economic well-being are worked out, however imperfectly, in exchange relationships between members. Such experiences can be invaluable for the persons involved, but their enduring contribution is in the way these stories can create new imagined possibilities the more widely they are told.

Notes

1. At the time of the survey Stroud LETS had a membership of 326, n = 94.

2. See http://www.lightlink.com/hours/ithacahours/

Bibliography

Acker, Joan (1988). "Class, gender, and the relations of distribution." *Signs: Journal of Women in Culture and Society* 13 (3): 473-497.

_____ (1990). "Hierarchies, jobs and bodies: A theory of gendered organizations." *Gender and Society* 4 (2): 139-58.

_____ (1992). "From sex roles to gendered institutions." *Contemporary Sociology* 21 (5): 565-569.

Agarwal, Bina (1992). Gender relations and food security: coping with seasonality, drought and famine in South Asia. *Unequal Burden: Economic Crises, Persistent Poverty and Women's Work.* Edited by Lourdes Beneria and Shelley Feldman. Boulder; San Francisco; Oxford, Westview Press: 181-218.

Armstrong, Pat (1996). The feminization of the labour force: harmonizing down in a global economy. *Rethinking Restructuring: Gender and Change in Canada.* Edited by Isabella Bakker. Toronto, University of Toronto Press.

Baines, Carol, Patricia Evans and Sheila Neysmith (1991). Caring: Its impact on the lives of women. *Women's Caring: Feminist Perspectives on Social Welfare.* Edited by Carol Baines, Patricia Evans and Sheila Neysmith. Toronto, McClelland & Stewart.

Beesten, Michelle (1997). "Ithaca HOURS: Where Household Need Meets Political Innovation." Department of Rural Sociology, Cornell University. Ithaca, New York. M.A. Thesis.

Benello, George C., Robert Swann and Shann Turnbull (1989). *Building Sustainable Communities: Tools and Concepts for Self-Reliant Economic Change.* New York, The Bootstrap Press.

Beneria, Lourdes and Shelley Feldman, Eds. (1992). *Unequal Burden: Economic Crises, Persistent Poverty and Women's Work.* Boulder; San Francisco; Oxford, Westview Press.

Bielby, William T. and James N. Baron (1986). "Men and women at work: sex segregation and statistical discrimination." *American Journal of Sociology* 91 (4): 759-99.

Block, Fred (1978). *The Origin of International Economic Disorder: A Study of United States International Monetary Policy from WWII to the Present.* Berkeley, University of California Press.

BIBLIOGRAPHY

Borsodi, Ralph (1989). *Inflation and the Coming Keynsian Catastrophe: The Story of the Exeter Experiments with Constants.* Great Barrington, MA, The E.F. Schumacher Society and the School of Living.

Bourdieu, Pierre (1997). Marginalia—Some additional notes on the gift. *The Logic of the Gift: Toward an Ethic of Generosity.* Edited by Alan D. Schrift. New York, Routledge.

Bowring, Finn (1998). "LETS: An Eco-Socialist Initiative?" *New Left Review* 232 (November/December): 91-111.

Boyle, David (1999). *Funny Money: In Search of Alternative Cash.* London, Harper Collins.

Bradley, Harriet (1999). *Gender and Power in the Workforce: Analysing the Impact of Economic Change.* New York, St. Martin's Press.

Brandt, Barbara (1995). *Whole Life Economics: Revaluing Daily Life.* Philadelphia and Gabriola Island, BC, New Society Publishers.

Brittan, Arthur (1989). *Masculinity and Power.* Oxford and New York, Basil Blackwell.

Buchan, James (1997). *Frozen Desire: An Inquiry into the Meaning of Money.* London, Picador.

Carruthers, Bruce G. and Sarah Babb (1996). "The color of money and the nature of value: greenbacks and gold in Postbellum America." *American Journal of Sociology* 101 (May): 1556-91.

Cassirer, Naomi and Gail McGuire (1993). *Cashing in on love: the struggle over money and power in marriage.* Association paper, American Sociological Association.

Chadwick, Martin (1995). Blue Mountain LETS, econ-lets archive, http://www.mailbase.ac.uk/list/econ-lets.

Cheal, David (1988). *The Gift Economy.* London, New York, Routledge.

Chodorow, Nancy (1978). *The Reproduction of Mothering: Psychoanalysis and the Sociology of Gender.* Berkeley, Los Angeles, London, University of California Press.

Claeys, Gregory (1987). *Machinery, Money and the Millenium: From Moral Economy to Socialism, 1815-60.* Cambridge, Polity Press.

Clark, Gordon L. (1999). The retreat of the state and the rise of pension fund capitalism. *Money and the Space Economy.* Edited by Ron Martin. Chichester, England; New York, John Wiley & Sons.

Cockburn, Cynthia (1983). *Brothers*, Pluto.

Cole, G.D.H. (1933). Note on a 'Free Money' experiment. *What Everybody Wants to Know about Money: A Planned Outline of Monetary Problems.* Edited London, Victor Gollancz.

Connell, R. W. (1987). *Gender and Power.* Stanford, Stanford University Press.
_____ (1995). *Masculinities.* Berkeley, University of California Press.

Crawford, Tad (1994). *The Secret Life of Money: How Money Can be Food for the Soul.* New York, Allworth Press.

Davies, Bronwyn (1990). "The problem of desire." *Social Problems* 37 (4): 501-516.

Davies, Glyn (1994). *A History of Money: From Ancient Times to the Present Day.* Cardiff, University of Wales Press.

de Grazia, Victoria (1996). Empowering women and citizen-consumers. *The Sex of Things: Gender and Consumption in Historical Perspective.* Edited by Victoria de Grazia and Ellen Furlough. Berkeley and Los Angeles, University of California Press.
_____ (1996). Establishing the modern consumer household. *The Sex of Things: Gender and Consumption in Historical Perspective.* Edited by Victoria de Grazia and Ellen Furlough. Berkeley and Los Angeles, University of California Press.

de Grazia, Victoria and Ellen Furlough, Eds. (1996). *The Sex of Things: Gender and Consumption in Historical Perspective.* Berkeley and Los Angeles, University of California Press.

DeVault, Marjorie L. (1991). *Feeding the Family: the Social Organization of Caring as Gendered Work.* Chicago and London, The University of Chicago Press.

Di Leonardo, Micaela (1987). "The female world of cards and holidays: women, families, and the work of kinship." *Signs: Journal of Women in Culture and Society* 12 (3): 440-453.

Dobson, Ross V.G. (1993). *Bringing the Economy Home from the Market.* Montreal, Black Rose Books.

Dodd, Nigel (1994). *The Sociology of Money: Economics, Reason and Contemporary Society.* Cambridge, Polity Press.

Douglas, Mary (1990). Forward. *The Gift: The Form and Reason for Exchange in Archaic Societies.* Marcel Mauss. London, Routledge.

BIBLIOGRAPHY

Douthwaite, Richard (1996). *Short Circuit: Strengthening Local Economies for Security in an Unstable World.* Dublin, Ireland, Lilliput Press.

Erickson, Bonnie H. (1998). Social Capital and its Profits, Local and Global. Paper presented at the Social Networks and Social Capital International Conference, Duke University.

Felps, Lyndon (1997). Dillo HOURS: A Local Currency in Process. Paper presented at the E. F. Schumacher Second Decentralist Conference, Williamstown, Massachusetts.

Ferber, Marianne A. and Julie A. Nelson, Eds. (1993). *Beyond Economic Man: Feminist Theory and Economics.* Chicago, University of Chicago Press.

Finnie, Ross (1993). "Women, men and the economic consequences of divorce: evidence from Canadian longitudinal data." *Canadian Review of Sociology and Anthropology* 30 (2): 205-241.

Firat, A. Fuat (1994). Gender and consumption: transcending the feminine? *Gender Issues and Consumer Behavior.* Edited by Janeen Arnold Costa. Thousand Oaks, Sage.

Fisher, Irving (1933). *Stamp Scrip.* New York, Adelphi Company.

Folbre, Nancy (1993). Socialism, feminist and scientific. *Beyond Economic Man: Feminist Theory and Economics.* Edited by Marianne A. Ferber and Julie A. Nelson. Chicago, University of Chicago Press.

Foucault, Michel (1984). *The History of Sexuality.* Harmondsworth, Penguin.

Friedman, Marilyn (1995). Feminism and modern friendship: dislodging the community. *Feminism and Community.* Edited by Penny Weiss and Marilyn Friedman. Philadelphia, Temple University Press.

Galbraith, John Kenneth (1975). *Money: Whence it Came, Where it Went.* Boston, Houghton Mifflin Company.

Gerson, Kathleen (1993). *No Man's Land: Men's Changing Commitments to Family and Work.* New York, Basic Books.

Gilbert, Emily and Eric Helleiner, Eds. (1999). *Nation-States and Money: The Past, Present and Future of National Currencies.* London and New York, Routledge.

Gilligan, Carol (1982). *In a Different Voice: Psychological Theory and Women's Development.* Cambridge and London, Harvard University Press.

Glover, Paul (1995). *Hometown Money: How to Enrich your Community with Local Currency.* Ithaca, Ithaca Money.

Greco, Thomas H., Jr. (1994). *New Money for Healthy Communities.* Tucson, Thomas H. Greco Jr. Pub.

Gregg, Richard (1963). *The Big Idol.* Ahmedabad, Navajivan Publishing House.

Guggenbuhl-Craig, Adolf (1982). Projections: Soul and Money. *Soul and Money.* Dallas, Spring Publications.

Harrison, J. F. C. (1969). *Robert Owen and the Owenites in Britain and America: The Quest for the New Moral World.* London, Routledge and Kegan Paul.

Harsin, Jill (1984). Housework and utopia: women and the Owenite socialist communities. *Women in Search of Utopia: Mavericks and Mythmakers.* Edited by Ruby Rohrlich and Elaine Hoffman Baruch. New York, Schocken.

Hayek, F. A. (1990 [1976]). *Denationalisation of Money—The Argument Refined: An Analysis of the Theory and Practice of Concurrent Currencies.* London, The Institute of Economic Affairs.

Heen, Hanne (1995). Money, gifts and gender. *Labour of Love: Beyond the Self-evidence of Everyday Life.* Edited by Tordis Borchgrevink and Oystein Gullvag Holter. Oslo, The Work Research Institute.

Heilbroner, Robert L. (1967). *The Worldly Philosophers: The Lives, Times, and Ideas of the Great Economic Thinkers.* New York, Simon and Schuster.

Helleiner, Eric (2000). "Think globally, transact locally: green political economy and the local currency movement." *Global Society* 14 (1): 35-51.

Henderson, Hazel (1991). *Paradigms in Progress: Life Beyond Economics.* Indianapolis, Knowledge Systems.

Herrmann, Gretchen M. (1995). "His and hers: gender and garage sales." *Journal of Popular Culture* 29 (Summer): 127-145.

Hewitson, Gillian J. (1999). *Feminist Economics: Interrogating the Masculinity of Rational Economic Man.* Cheltenham, UK; Northhampton, MA, Edward Elgar.

Hillman, James (1982). A contribution to soul and money. *Soul and Money.* Dallas, Texas, Spring Publications.

BIBLIOGRAPHY

Hochschild, Arlie and Anne Machung (1989). *The Second Shift*. New York, Avon Books.

Hudson, Alan C. (1999). Off-shores on-shore: new regulatory spaces and real historicla places in the landscape of global money. *Money and the Space Economy*. Edited by Ron Martin. Chichester, England; New York, John Wiley & Sons.

Hyde, Lewis (1983). *The Gift: Imagination and the Erotic Life of Property*. New York, Random House.

Ingham, Geoffrey (2000). 'Babylonian madness': on the historical and sociological origins of money. *What is Money?* Edited by John Smithin. London and New York, Routledge.

Ironmonger, Duncan (1996). "Counting outputs, capital inputs and caring labor: estimating gross household product." *Feminist Economics* 2 (3): 37-64.

Jackson, Mark (1995). Helping Ourselves: New Zealand's Green Dollar Exchanges. *ANZAC Fellowship Report*.

Jacob, Jeffrey (1997). *New Pioneers: The Back-to-the-Land Movement and the Search for a Sustainable Future*. University Park, Pennsylvania, Pennsylvania University Press.

Jacobs, Jane (1984). *Cities and the Wealth of Nations: Principles of Economic Life*. New York, Vintage Books.

Jenks, Chris, Ed. (1998). *Core Sociological Dichotomies*. London, Sage Publications.

Jennings, Ann L. (1994). "Toward a feminist expansion of macroeconomics: money matters." *Journal of Economic Issues* 28 (2): 555-565.

Kennedy, Margrit (1995). *Interest and Inflation Free Money: Creating an Exchange Medium that Works for Everybody and Protects the Earth*. Philadelphia, New Society Publishers.

Kessler-Harris, Alice and Karen Brodkin Sacks (1987). The demise of domesticity in America. *Women, Households and the Economy*. Edited by Lourdes Beneria and Catharine R. Stimpson. New Brunswick and London, Rutgers University Press.

Kimmel, Michael (1987). The contemporary 'crisis' of masculinity in historical perspective. *The Making of Masculinities: The New Men's Studies*. Edited by Harry Brod. Boston, Allen & Unwin.

_____ (1996). *Manhood in America*. New York, The Free Press.

Klebanow, Sheila (1991). Power, Gender and Money. *Money and Mind.* Edited by Sheila Klebanow and Eugene L. Lowenkopf. New York, Plenum Press.

Kolmerten, Carol A. (1990). *Women in Utopia: The Ideology of Gender in the American Ownite Communities.* Bloomington and Indianapolis, Indiana University Press.

Korten, David (1997). Money versus wealth. *Yes! A Journal of Positive Futures.* 2: 14-18.

Kristeva, Julia (1986). Women's Time. *The Kristeva Reader.* Edited by Toril Moi. New York, Columbia University Press.

Lambek, Michael (2001). "The value of coins in the Sakalava polity." *Comparative Studies in Society and History* 43 (4).

Lang, Peter (1994). *LETS Work: Rebuilding the Local Economy.* Bristol, Grover Books.

Lee, R. (1996). "Moral money? LETS and the social construction of local economic geographies in Southeast England." *Environment and Planning A* 28: 1377-1394.

Lietaer, Bernard (1997). Beyond greed and scarcity. *Yes! A Journal of Positive Futures.* 2: 34-39.

Linton, Michael (1999). The Community Economy, http://www.gmlets.u-net.com/explore/comecon.html.

Linton, Michael and Thomas Greco (1987). The Local Employment Trading System. *Whole Earth Review:* 104-109.

Lomnitz, Larissa and Ana Melnick (1994). Middle class, social networks, and the 'neo-liberal' model: the case of the Chilean school teachers 1973-1988. *Artful Practices: The Political Economy of Everyday Life.* Edited by Henri Lustinger- Thaler and Daniel Salee. Montreal, Black Rose Books.

Luke, Helen (1995). *The Way of Woman: Awakening the Perennial Feminine.* New York, Doubleday.

Lustinger-Thaler, Henri and Daniel Salee (1994). The quest for a politically effective language of everyday life. *Artful Practices: The Political Economy of Everyday Life.* Edited by Henri Lustinger-Thaler and Daniel Salee. Montreal, Black Rose Books.

Luxton, Meg (1980). *More than a Labour of Love.* Toronto, Women's Educational Press.

BIBLIOGRAPHY

Malinowski, Bronislaw (1935). *Coral Gardens and their Magic*. New york, American Book Company.

_____ (1961). *Argonauts of the Western Pacific: An Account of Native Enterprise and Adventure in the Archipelagoes of Melanesian New Guinea*. New York, E.P. Dutton & Co.

Mander, Jerry and Edward Goldsmith, Eds. (1996). *The Case Against the Global Economy and for a Turn to the Local*. San Fransisco, Sierra Club Books.

Marx, Karl (1973). *Grundrisse: Foundations of the Critique of Political Economy*. New York, Vintage Books.

Mauss, Marcel (1966). *The Gift: The Form and Reason for Exchange in Archaic Societies*. London, Cohen & West, Ltd.

McMichael, Philip (1996). *Development and Social Change: A Global Perspective*. Thousand Oaks, Pine Forge Press.

Meeker-Lowry, Susan (1996). Community money: The potential of local currency. *The Case Against the Global Economy and for a Turn to the Local*. Edited by Jerry Mander and Edward Goldsmith. San Fransisco, Sierra Club Books.

Milani, Brian (2000). *Designing the Green Economy: The Postindustrial Alternative to Corporate Globalization*. Lanham, MD, Rowman & Littlefield Publishers.

Milkman, Ruth (1987). *Gender at Work: The Dynamics of Job Segregation by Sex during World War II*. Urbana and Chicago, University of Illinois Press.

Mitchell, Ralph and Neil Shafer (1984). *Standard Catalogue of Depression Scrip of the United States: the 1930s*. Kraus Publications.

Moore, Henrietta (1994). " 'Divided we stand': sex, gender and sexual difference." *Feminist Review* 47 (Summer): 78-95.

Nelson, Julie A. (1996). *Feminism, Objectivity and Economics*. London and New York, Routledge.

Newcomb, Michael D. and Jerome Rabow (1999). "Gender, socialization and money." *Journal of Applied Social Psychology* 29 (4): 852-869.

Nozick, Marcia (1992). *No Place Like Home: Building Sustainable Communities*. Ottawa, Canadian Council on Social Development.

Offe, Claus and Rolf G. Heinze (1992). *Beyond Employment: Time, Work and the Informal Economy*. Cambridge, Polity Press.

191

Pacione, Michael (1997). "Local Exchange Trading Systems as a response to the globalisation of capitalism." *Urban Studies* 34 (8): 1179-1199.

Parr, Joy (1990). *The Gender of Breadwinners: Women, Men and Change in Two Industrial Towns, 1880-1950.* Toronto, University of Toronto Press.

Parsons, Talcott and Robert F. Bales (1960). *Family, Socialization and Interaction Process.* Glencoe, Ill., Free Press.

Pateman, Carole (1988). *The Sexual Contract.* Stanford, Stanford University Press.

Pierce, Carol, David Wagner and Bill Page (1998). *A Male/Female Continuum.* Laconia, NH, New Dynamics Publications.

Polanyi, Karl (1957). *The Great Transformation: The Political and Economic Origins of our Time.* Boston, Beacon Press.

_____ (1968). The economy as instituted process. *Primitive, Archaic, and Modern Economies: Essays of Karl Polanyi.* Edited by George Dalton. New York, Doubleday & Company: 139-174.

_____ (1968). The semantics of money-uses. *Primitive, Archaic, and Modern Economies: Essays of Karl Polanyi.* Edited by George Dalton. New York, Doubleday & Company: 175-203.

Rabow, Jerome and Michelle Charness (1991). "Women and money: identities in flux." *Humanity and Society* 15 (3): 254-275.

Randall, Margaret (1996). *The Price You Pay: The Hidden Cost of Women's Relationship to Money.* New York, London, Routledge.

Reitsma-Street, Marge (1991). Girls learn to care; girls policed to care. *Women's Caring: Feminist Perspectives on Social Welfare.* Edited by Carol Baines, Patricia Evans and Sheila Neysmith. Toronto, McClelland & Stewart.

Roberts, Susan (1994). Fictitious capital, fictitious spaces: the geography of offshore financial flows. *Money, Power and Space.* Edited by Stuart Corbridge, Ron Martin and Nigel Thrift. Oxford; Cambridge, Basil Blackwell.

Roberts, Wayne and Susan Brandum (1995). *Get a Life!* Toronto, Get a Life Publishing House.

Rotstein, Abraham and Colin Duncan (1991). For a second economy. *The New Era of Global Competition: State Policy and Market Power.* Edited by Daniel Drache and Meric S. Gertler. Montreal and Kingston, McGill-Queens University Press.

BIBLIOGRAPHY

Rowbotham, Michael (1998). *The Grip of Death: A Study of Modern Money, Debt Slavery and Destructive Economics*. Charlbury, Jon Carpenter.

Royle, Edward (1998). *Robert Owen and the Commencement of the Millennium: A Study of the Harmony Community*. Manchester and New York, Manchester University Press.

Sachs, Wolfgang (1995). One world. *The Development Dictionary*. Edited by Wolfgang Sachs. London, Zed: 102-115.

Savdie, Tony and Tim Cohen-Mitchell (1997). *Local Currencies in Community Development, or Too much Mngwotngwotiki is Bad for You*. Center for International Education.

Siltanen, Janet (1994). *Locating Gender: Occupational Segregation, Wages and Domestic Responsibilities*. London, University College London.

Simmel, Georg (1991). *The Philosophy of Money*. London, Routledge.

Singh, Supriya (1994). Women, marriage and banking. *Women, Money and Power*. Edited by Chris Black. Australian Women's Research Centre.

Solomon, Lewis (1996). *Rethinking our Centralized Money System: The Case for a System of Local Currencies*. Westport, Praeger.

Stack, Carol B. (1974). *All Our Kin: Strategies for Survival in a Black Community*. New York, Harper & Row.

Strange, Susan (1994). From Bretton Woods to the Casino Economy. *Money, Power and Space*. Edited by Stuart Corbridge, Ron Martin and Nigel Thrift. Oxford; Cambridge, Basil Blackwell.

Swann, Robert and Susan Witt (1995). Local Currencies: Catalysts for Sustainable Regional Economies. Great Barrington, MA, E.F. Schumacher Society.

Tannen, Deborah (1990). *You Just Don't Understand: Men and Women in Conversation*. New York, Ballantine.

Taylor, Barbara (1983). *Eve and the New Jerusalem: Socialism and Feminism in the Nineteenth Century*. London, Virago.

Thorne, L. (1996). "Local exchange trading systems in the United Kingdom: a case of re-embedding?" *Environment and Planning A* 28: 1361-1376.

Tilly, Louise A. and Joan Scott (1978). *Women, Work, and Family*. New York, Holt, Rinehart and Winston.

Vaughan, Genevieve (1997). *For-Giving: A Feminist Criticism of Exchange.* Austin, TX, Plain View Press.

Vogler, Carolyn and Jan Pahl (1994). "Money, power and inequality within marriage." *The Sociological Review* 42 (2): 263-288.

Waring, Marilyn (1988). *If Women Counted: A New Feminist Economics.* New York, San Francisco, Harper & Row.

_____ (1999). *Counting for Nothing: What Men Value and What Women are Worth.* Toronto, Buffalo, University of Toronto Press.

West, Candace and Don H. Zimmerman (1987). "Doing gender." *Gender and Society* 1: 125-51.

Wheelock, Jane (1990). *Husbands at Home: The Domestic Economy in a Post-Industrial Society.* London and New York, Routledge.

Williams, Colin, Theresa Aldridge, Roger Lee, Andrew Leyshon, Nigel Thrift and Jane Tooke (1999). "The potential of the social economy in tackling social exclusion: some lessons from Local Exchange and Trading Schemes (LETS)." *Journal of Community Currency Research.*
www.geog.le.ac.uk/ijccr/

Wilson, Valerie (1999). *The Secret Life of Money: Exposing the Private Parts of Personal Money.* St. Leonards, Australia, Allen & Unwin.

Zelizer, Viviana (1994). *The Social Meaning of Money.* New York, Basic Books.

Index

A

accounting currency 5

alternative lifestyle 145,156

artisans 20,62,64,182

B

"back to the land" movement 145

barter 1,6,10-16,18-19,21,35-36,44,
53,63-64,84,86,104-105,108,110,
118,120-123,162-163,176-177

Berk-Shares 149

bread winning 59,65,113

C

capitalist 64,135,141,143

caring xii,12,34,56-57,59,69-70,73,
81,116-117,125-127,137,160

Civil War 40

commercial barter networks 6

community currencies vii,ix,xi-xiii,
1-4,10-11,14-20,22-29,31,34-35,
37,44-45,47,52,73,75-77,82,97,101
-102,106-107,118,132,137-141,145-
146,148-149,156,158-161,163,165-
166,168-173,178, 182-183

community currency movement
14,20-21,25-26,28,30,58,68,75,
100,147,172,183

community development initiatives
4

community market 109

competition
17,21,41,68,72,100,137,152

consumer politics
141,144,149,153,158

consumption xii-xiii,15,133,139,
141-146,148-149,153,161-164,
168,171,182

conventional viii,xii,3,5,21,23,25,
27,34,43,45,47,51,53-54,59-60,
62,65-67,78,84,97,102,106-107,
109,137,151,154,156-157,171,
178

cult of familism 73

currency of friendship 79,84

D

debt 41-42,88,121,154

Deli Dollars 149

dependence 37,42,44,46,63-66,68,
81-82,98,102,113,115,117,124-
126,135-136,138,145,151,156

desire viii-xi,3,19,25,28,44-45,
47,49,54-56,61,64,67,69,78,
85,96,99-100,105,107-108,112,
114-117,124-126,145,160-162,
173,178

discrimination 33,57,97

distribution 36,71,101,133,135-
136,138,143,155

Dobson, Ross 17,23,43,77-78,170

domestic skills vii,16

domestic work viii,26,51,58,73,
102,128-130,132,136,165

dual career couples 34

E

E. F. Schumacher Society 149

earmarking 38,43

economic man 28,70

economic thought 36,143

egalitarian ideals 45,56

egalitarianism 45,51-52,54-55,
60-61,63,66-67,133,147

Equitable Labour Exchange
19,52,146-147,168-169

ethical 78,139,148,156,183

ethics 17,62,71-72,78,106,137

F

family 1,13,25,28,37,53,57,59,
65,73,100-101,111-112,115-
116,119,126,130-131,136,138,
141-142,145,153-154,174,177,
181-183

family economy 73,141-142

fathering 66

favours viii,1,13,17,74,79,97,132,
160,177

federal dollars 6,51,66,83,109-110,
121,128,131,133,149-151,165

Federal Reserve Act 40

feminine x,xii,21,26,32,57,69,73,80,
96-97,99,111,113-115,117,143-
144,159,165,172-173,178-179

feminism 26,172

feminist historians 147

feminist ideals 25-26,63

Fisher, Irving 14-15

food 6,9,24,48-49,51,80,93-94,107-
108,112,119,122,138,141,144,
153,156,181

friendship viii,79,82,84-85,97-98,
121-122,126,179

G

garage sales 113

gender ix-xiii,2-3,16-17,21-22,
24-34,37,42,44-49,52-53,56-59,
61-64,66-67,69,73-75,77,80-82,
84,86,96-102,104-105,111-117,
123-124,126-127,131-132,135,
137-138,140-143,146-147,153-
154,163-164,166-167,169,171-
173,175, 178-179,181-183

gender ascription 17

gender attributes xiii,30

gender balance 172,181-182

gender difference
29,46,52,61,112,114,124

gender division of commerce 98

gender equality xii,45,49,67,169

gender patterns xii,30,46,112,178

gendered institutions 28

generosity viii,13,71-73,77,87,92,
96-97,102,107,137

Gesell, Silvo 14

gift economy xii,17,26,68-70,73-75,
77-79,96,99,102,172

gift labour 73,85,95-96,98,126,171

gift relations 69,72-74,78,81,85,95,
98-99,126,135,138

Glover, Paul xiii,7,17,19,145

gold standard 40

gold value 40-41

greendollars 6,9,11,78-79,83,85,87,
89-91,94,97,99,102,109-110,119,
127,163,165-167,180

INDEX

H

hegemonic masculinity 33,66,80,96

HOURS vii,xi-xiii,2-4,7-13,15-16, 18-20,22-24,26-30,32,34,43-46, 50-56,59-63,65-67,74,77,85,101, 104-105,107,130-133,136,138, 140-141,145-146,148-154,156- 157,159-162,164-168,170-175, 177-179, 183

house cleaning 87,103-104,113,127-129,133

I

indebtedness 90,155

independence 63-66,81,98,102,113, 115,117,124-126,135-136

individuation 101,124-125

interest xi,3,5-6,9,15,25,28-29,40- 41,43,45,56-57,70-71,73,77,82, 93,97,100,113,116-117,130,144, 147,154-155,157,160,162,164, 167,169,174-175,181-182

Ithaca HOURS 7-9,19,50-51,60, 171,183

L

labour hours 18-19,22,47-48,52-53, 56,58-59,61-62,67-68,148

labour markets 27,59

LETS vii-viii,xi-xiii,2-7,9-12,14-17, 20,23-24,26-28,31,34,43,45-49, 51,59-60,74-75,77-81,83-104,107, 109-112,118-123,127-129,136, 138,141,145-146,148-150,154, 156-168, 170-175,179-183

LETSystems 75

Lévi-Strauss, Claude 74

Linton, Michael 4-5,7,19,23,43,75,170

local alternative 24

M

male/female xii,3,25,31,33-34, 173,178

Malinowski, Bronislaw 70,76

manhood 64-66,81

manual work 50,56,62

market money 38-39,75,178

market society 68-69,73

masculine x,xii,21,32,47,57,64-65, 67,73,75,84,96,113-114,117,143, 172-173,178

masculinity 32,65,82,179

material life 71,106

Mauss, Marcel 70-72,76

minimum wage 46,50,54-55

monetary scarcity 40,42,44

multi-currency societies 37

municipal government 15,158,183

N

national currency xii,1,5,38-40,52, 149,154-155,157

negotiation viii,xiii,1,24,27,35,91- 93,99,108,127,136,138,171

neighbours 2,13,74,77,131, 136,160,177

New Deal 15

New Harmony 18,52

New Lanark 18,68

non-market 37-38,71,138

non-modern 36,38

O

occupational restructuring 25

opposite-sex exchange 101

Owen, Robert 18-21,52,55,68,100, 133,146-148,168-171

Owenism 19-20,68,100,147, 169,171

P

parallel currency 25

paternalism 33,100

payment viii,x,xii,1,7,9,22,35-38,41- 42,46,48,53-54,56-57,61,69,76-77, 80,87,94,99-102,108-109,121,131- 132,136,154,156,158,175

pension funds 39

Polanyi, Karl 19-20,36-38,68,70-72, 143,147,168

political alternative 24,68

pricing viii,47,53,69,80,91,95,97-98, 101,105-108,113

pseudo-currencies 37

psychoanalytic theory 101,124-125

public service 155,159

R

reciprocity viii,xii,10,12-14,18,21,26, 71,77,80,87,137

re-circulation 43,148

Republicans 40

revaluation viii,45-47,49-54,57,59, 61,67,69,104,172

S

Schumacher, E.F. 2,44,149

self-employment viii,19

Self-Made Man 64,66

sex roles 113-114,124

sex segregation 57-58

shopping xiii,59,113,122,144,146- 148,150-152,154,159,165,168, 178-179,181-182

social experiments 170

socialization theory 101,112, 114-115

stamp scrip 14-15,22

suburbanization 153

symbolism x-xi,26,43

T

Toronto Dollars 149-150

U

undervaluation viii,45,57,69,95-96, 98-99,101-102,106,123-124,130, 132,136-137

unemployment 4,14-15,25,41,75,120,170

utopian xi,20-21,56,61,68,100,133, 147,169-171

V

valuation viii,xii,32,45-47,49-54,56- 57,59,61,67,69,95-96,98-99,101- 104,106,112,115,117,123-124,127, 130,132,136-137,171-172

volunteer work 89,93-95,120,129,136

volunteerism 80

W

wage gap 45,58

wages xii,42,51,58,67,98,102,104, 129,131,168

WomanShare 59-60

Z

Zelizer, Viviana 37-38

TRIUMPH OF THE MARKET

Essays on Economics, Politics, and the Media

Edward S. Herman

The unifying theme of the essays in this volume is the increasing national and global power and reach of the market and its growing impact on all aspects of human life.

Part One describes how market forces have extended their sway in the economy, culture, and within the economics profession itself. Part Two addresses the impact of the market on politics, along with reflections on contemporary political and historical issues and perspectives. Parts Three and Four deal with foreign policy and the media, respectively. In both parts the impact of the market forces and market-linked interests is front and center.

> *A non-fiction horror story, where what is good for private profit is hailed as good for the public. Where media conglomerates hail freedom of expression as the right of dissenters to be irrelevant and marginal on Hyde Park Soapboxes.*
> —Fairness and Accuracy in Reporting (FAIR)

> *Penetrating and brilliant analysis of the linkages between U.S. and global economics, politics, and media ever published in one volume.*
> —Robert W. McChesney, University of Wisconsin

> *A disturbingly blunt warning about the clear and present dangers to democracy, economic rationality, global economic stability, and international peace.*
> —Samori Marksman, WBAI-FM, Pacifica Radio

> *Demystifies the many ways that giant global corporations have worked to replace democratic and community values with market exchange.*
> —Elaine Bernard, Harvard University

EDWARD S. HERMAN is an economist and media analyst, Professor Emeritus of Finance at the Wharton School, University of Pennsylvania, author of *Beyond Hypocrisy: Decoding the News in an Age of Propaganda*, and with Noam Chomsky, co-author of the two volume *Political Economy of Human Rights*.

286 pages, index
Paperback ISBN: 1-55164-062-7 $19.99
Hardcover ISBN: 1-55164-063-5 $48.99

HUMANITY, SOCIETY AND COMMITMENT On Karl Polanyi
Kenneth McRobbie, editor

Based on some of Polanyi's lesser known works: his journalism, letters, articles, conversations, books long out of print, and translations of Hungarian poetry. The contributors include: Jordan Bishop, Michele Cangiani, Marguerite Mendell, Marco Eller Vainscher, Endre Nagy, Kari Polanyi-Levitt, Daniel Fusfeld, Abraham Rotstein, and Kenneth McRobbie.

KENNETH MCROBBIE is a poet and historian who teaches cultural studies and intellectual history at the University of British Columbia.

178 pages
Paperback ISBN: 1-895431-84-0 $19.99
Hardcover ISBN: 1-895431-85-9 $48.99

TOWARD A HUMANIST POLITICAL ECONOMY
Phillip Hansen, Harold Chorney

A collection of essays written between the late 70s and the present day that focus attention on the neglected cultural side of society in order to chart the progress of political change. As background some of the insights of writers as diverse as Hannah Arendt and John Maynard Keynes are examined.

...the themes are relevant for those trying to fathom the post-Reaganite political world of the 1990s.—Canadian Book Review Annual

HAROLD CHORNEY is a professor of public policy and social theory at Concordia University, Montreal, and PHILLIP HANSEN is a professor of social theory at the University of Regina in Saskatchewan.

224 pages, index
Paperback ISBN:1-895431-22-0 $19.99
Hardcover ISBN:1-895431-23-9 $48.99

THE PUBLIC PLACE Citizen Participation in the Neighbourhood and the City
Dimitrios I. Roussopoulos

Drawing on his experience in community journalism, Roussopoulos writes on a broad range of issues that affect the daily life of neighborhoods and cities.

Succeeds in making citizens conscious of their role in the community, and how they too can make significant change.—James Hörner, Canadian Content

DIMITRIOS I. ROUSSOPOULOS is an editor, writer, and ecologist who has written widely on international politics, democracy, and social change.

200 pages, bibliography, index
Paperback ISBN: 1-55164-156-9 $19.99
Hardcover ISBN: 1-55164-157-7 $48.99

CORPORATE RULE
Understanding and Challenging the New World Order

David Model

This hard-hitting book examines all aspects of corporate rule and the underlying ideology which serves corporate interests. In particular, it examines its main control mechanisms: trade agreements, the media, and the popular culture.

Though a searing indictment of an unjust international economic order, it is also a guide to the average person on how to understand and address the enormous challenges of our time.

A comprehensive and penetrating critique of how corporate power threatens our ecological survival, and undermines democracy and social well-being in North America.
—Michael Parenti, author of *Democracy for the Few* and *The Terrorism Trap: September 11 and Beyond*

Here's an insightful, easy-to-read and sensible guidebook for surviving and overcoming the corporate juggernaut sweeping the world.
—Linda McQuaig author of *All You Can Eat: Greed, Lust and the New Capitalism*

Offers an alternative vision of a society that supports the well-being of all of its members.
—Neil Brooks, Osgoode Hall Law School

A welcome addition to the growing volume of work critiquing neo-liberalism in its many forms.
—Thomas Walkom, *Toronto Star*, and author of *Rae Days: The Rise and Follies of the NDP*

Challenges us to move beyond debate to political activism.
—Basil 'Buzz' Hargrove, President, Canadian Automobile Workers

DAVID MODEL, Professor of Political Science and Economics, teaches at Seneca College, King City, Ontario. He is the author of People Before Profits.

216 pages, index
Paperback ISBN: 1-55164-208-5 $24.99
Hardcover ISBN: 1-55164-209-3 $53.99